ASAO Monograph Series

AGING AND ITS TRANSFORMATIONS

Moving Toward Death in Pacific Societies

Dorothy Ayers Counts and David R. Counts, Editors

University of Pittsburgh Press • Pittsburgh and London

ASAO Monograph #10
Published by the University of Pittsburgh Press, Pittsburgh, Pa. 15260,
by arrangement with the Association for Social Anthropology in Oceania
Copyright © 1985, Association for Social Anthropology in Oceania
All rights reserved
Eurospan, London
Manufactured in the United States of America

Library of Congress Cataloging-in-Publication Data
Aging and its transformations : moving toward death in Pacific societies / edited by
Dorothy Ayers Counts, David R. Counts.
    p.   cm.—(ASAO monograph ; no. 10)
    Originally published: Lanham, Md. : University Press of America, © 1985.
(ASAO monograph ; no. 10).
    Includes bibliographical references and index.
    ISBN 0-8229-5477-X
    1. Aged—Oceania.   2. Death—Social aspects—Oceania.   3. Oceania—
Social life and customs.   I. Counts, Dorothy Ayers.   II. Counts,   David R.
III. Series.
[GN663.A55 1992]
305.26'0995—dc20   91-38834
                                                                                         CIP

For Rebecca, Bruce,
David Riley and Stephen,
who were there

CONTENTS

Map 1. South Pacific

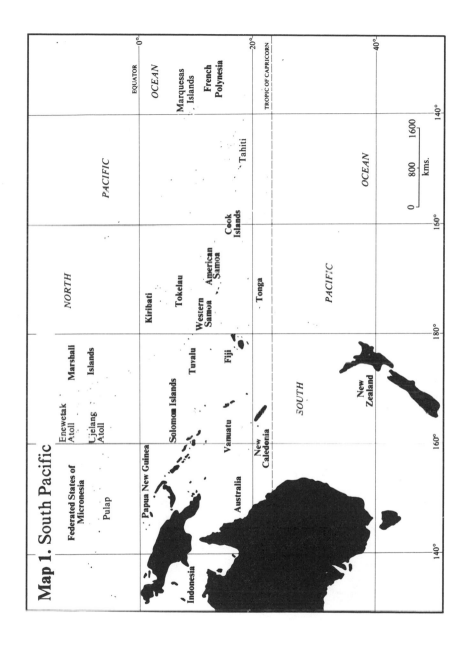

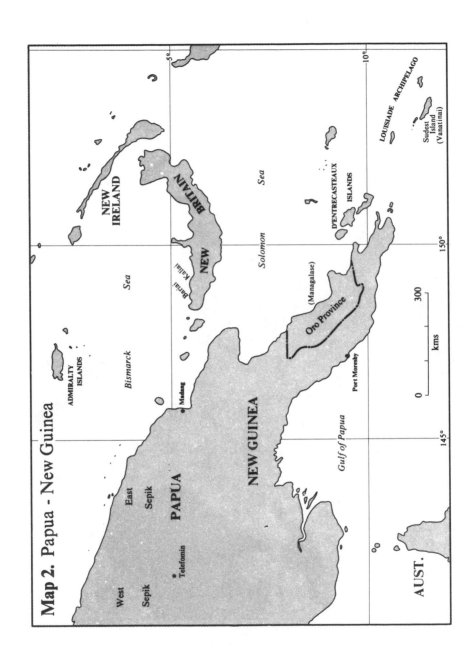

Map 2. Papua - New Guinea

PREFACE

This monograph is the product of what members of the Association for Social Anthropology in Oceania call the "ASAO process." The process began at the annual meeting of the association held in San Diego, California in March, 1981 when we invited those interested to join us for an Informal Session on relationships between aging, dying, and gender in the South Pacific. Most of the contributors to this volume were among the twenty-three who met for this initial informal discussion. The following year, 1982, fifteen of us met again with prepared papers in a Working Session at the ASAO meetings at Hilton Head, South Carolina. After presenting their papers, participants in the Working Session agreed on guidelines for revision that would focus the papers for discussion in a formal Symposium at the 1983 meetings to be held in New Harmony, Indiana. In New Harmony a day-long session was devoted to drawing out the themes running through the papers, which had been circulated in advance among the participants, and to agreeing on a schedule for final revision of the chapters and submission for publication.

Because our contributors have patiently borne with us through the numerous revisions, we are able to present in this volume case studies and analyses of the experiences of aging, dying, and gender role development from a wide range of Pacific societies. This wealth of variety gives the volume special strength, for it permits us to address a number of issues in the literature (issues such as those surrounding the question of disengagement, the possibility of gender transformation in old age, the negotiation of elderly status, and euthanasia) from a number of perspectives.

Inevitably, during this process a number of people have contributed who do not have chapters represented here. We are particularly indebted to Dr. Judith K. Brown who served as our discussant for the Working Session in 1982, but who was prevented by prior commitments from attending the Symposium session and from preparing a chapter for the volume. In New Harmony, the discussant's role was taken over by Dr. Martha Ward. All of the contributors to the volume are grateful to her, not only for the cogent and insightful comments that she contributed to the discussion, but also for the fact that she did so while under great personal stress and in grief. We are much in debt to her.

We have had generous and gracious institutional support for the preparation of this manuscript. In 1981-1982 both of us were recipients of Leave Fellowships from the Social Sciences and Humanities Research Council of Canada (SSHRCC) and of an SSHRCC Research Grant, and we were both granted sabbatical leaves by our respective universities. The Centre for Pacific and Oriental Studies at the University of Victoria, British Columbia, gave us a place to work and generously provided us with mailing privileges in 1981-1982 during the formative stage of this enterprise. Support for the preparation of the manuscript for submission to the ASAO Editorial Review Board was provided by the Faculty of Arts of the University of Waterloo and by a General Research Grant from the University of Waterloo SSHRCC Grant Subcommittee.

We also wish to express our appreciation to John Kirkpatrick and Naomi Scaletta for their extensive and helpful comments on the introductory chapter of this volume and to Carol Kieswetter who expertly entered most of the manuscript into the computer at the University of Waterloo.

Finally, we wish to express our appreciation to Dr. Margaret Rodman for her support and encouragement. She became Monograph Series Editor for the ASAO at the time when we were beginning to prepare this volume for submission to the Editorial Review Board. Her suggestions have invariably been helpful and have made the task a much easier one than it otherwise would have been.

Dorothy and David Counts
Dundas, Ontario
March, 1985

Aging and Its Transformations

INTRODUCTION:
LINKING CONCEPTS
AGING AND GENDER, AGING AND
DEATH

Dorothy Ayers Counts and David R. Counts

Aging and dying are processes experienced by all people in all socie-ties. With the advent of modern medical technology, we who live in industrialized countries have an increasing opportunity to experience the complete life cycle. Between 75 and 85 percent of us reach the age of 64 (Weiss 1981:55-56). We are closing the gap between average life expectancy, which is between 77 and 78 years for white North American women (Fries and Crapo 1981:74; Statistics Canada 1981: 124), and the human life span of 85 to 90 years (Cutler 1975; Fries 1980:130-135; Fries and Crapo 1981:3).

Although most of us can expect to achieve old age, in preindustrial-ized societies old age is still an experience limited to a relative few. In tribal societies, only about 10 percent of the population lives past the age of 60 (Weiss 1981: 55-56). We die of the degenerative diseases of old age and, consequently, we perceive death primarily as the inevi-table result of growing old and frequently treat the subject of aging with dread and avoidance: we suffer from 'gerontophobia' (Weiss 1981: 56; Pollock 1980:1419). In contrast, most people in tribal societies die of infectious disease, trauma, animal bites, childhood illness, and child-birth rather than of the degenerative diseases of old age. As Simmons noted almost forty years ago, people in preindustrialized societies more commonly associate death with youth and vitality than with old age and decrepitude (1945:217). In these societies "... life has been more often snuffed out suddenly than left to flicker out by degrees" (Simmons 1945: 217).

Advances in modern medical technology are responsible for differ-ences in life expectancy between industrialized and preindustrialized peoples and, it is argued, for dissimilar expectations and experiences regarding aging and death as well. Authorities in our own society have generally operated on the assumption that death is a non-reversible event and that life and death are opposed, non-reversible categories.

Before modern technological advances, the test of this event was simple: if there was no breath and no pulse, then death had occurred. The issue is clouded now. If attached to machines, bodies can be maintained without brain function or even heart function. Death, therefore, is not a single event affecting all organs simultaneously. Some vital parts of a person may be dead at a time when other parts still live. This has a number of implications. One is that the process of dying can be continued almost indefinitely. Another is that the technician has seeming control over the timing of death, control that may ignore the wishes of the dying person in favor of cost efficiency: the more "valuable" a life, the more effort is expended to ensure its continuation. As a result of the ethical complications arising from this state of affairs, the concept and definition of death is under reconsideration and some scientists and physicians argue that it must be recognized as a process.

> Clearly we are dealing here with a continuous process of death and decay. There is no magic moment at which "everything" disappears. Death is no more a single, clearly delimited momentary phenomenon than is infancy, adolescence, or middle age (Morison 1977:59).

The peoples of the South Pacific have long recognized that rather than being a single fixed event, death is a transforming, reversible process whose boundaries may lie to either side of the occurrence that we call clinical death. The essays in this monograph reflect the ideologies of the Pacific peoples with whom we and our countributors have lived and worked, for we all emphasize transformation and process in the life-death cycle. Some chapters focus on the changes that occur in gender roles as spheres of authority and support shift with advancing age, or explore the malleability of age and kin categories and the ability of people to negotiate their assignment to such categories as they age; others examine ideologies of aging and death with questions such as "Why do people age and die?"; "What part does death play in the broader scheme of things?"; "What is a good or a bad death?"

The topics that unite the chapters in this book are aging and dying. The themes that are examined include the ideologies of aging and death; aging and dying as processes; changes in gender roles as a result of aging; negotiation of status as people grow old or enter the category of the dying. The monograph's focus on the problems and processes of aging locate it squarely in a field of current anthropological debate. Anthropologists frequently rely on the elderly for information because they are most knowledgeable of the traditions, history, and esoterica of their society and it is they, past the demands of daily labor, who have the time to spend with the inquisitive researcher. Ironically, in spite of this dependence on the aged in their host societies, anthropologists have not considered aging and the elderly as a proper subject of their inquiry until recently. Perhaps, as Margaret Clark has suggested, this is partially due to a sort of "gerontophobia by association," in which the contemplation of old age is considered to be a morbid preoccupation akin to necrophilia (1967:56). At any rate, the first synthetic cross-cultural study of the subject, what Keith calls "the ancestral model for studies of old age" (1980:340), is Simmons' *The Aged in Primitive Society,* published in 1945. Not until the 1960s was any further interest shown. Then, with Kleemeir's collection of essays (1961), Clark and Anderson's (1967) study of aging Americans, and with chapters in individual monographs, a renewal followed. Finally, in the last decade there has been a host of studies of aging that are explicitly cross-cultural: for instance Cowgill and Holmes (1972), Watson and Maxwell (1977), Simic and Myerhoff (1978), Keith (1980a), Fry (1980a and 1981), Amoss and Harrell (1981b), Hendricks (1980), and Sokolovsky (1983).

Cross-cultural studies of aging have approached the topic from a number of perspectives. The analyses suggest that age is not a tightly bounded, precisely defined, unambiguous cultural domain, a point to which we will have occasion to return. Studies that treat aging as part of a psychological and cultural process to which individuals must adapt (Kerns 1980; Vatuk 1980) have tested the theory of disengagement offered by Cumming and Henry (1961). Disengagement theory postulates that as a person ages, he and his society mutually withdraw from each other. As will be clear from Marshall's discussion in the concluding chapter of this volume, the theory is a controversial one. In general, anthropologists seem to be in agreement with Cowgill and Holmes that "disengagement is chiefly a by-product of urban industrial society" (1972:13). Sinclair (chapter 2) accepts this view and argues that the expanded and vigorous activity of elderly Maori women offers a counter example to disengagement theory. Other case studies presented in this volume indicate, however, that a process of withdrawal, if not disengagement, does often occur in traditional Pacific societies when elderly persons become decrepit and senescent. As Amoss and Harrell have observed: "There seems to be little cultural variation in the plight of the incompetent aged; they are everywhere regarded as a burden" (1981b:3-4).

It is possible to formulate statements about aging that are nearly universally true: all societies have indices that mark an individual's progress through the life cycle; all recognize age categories, including one that may be glossed as 'old age'; almost all distinguish between the active and the totally dependent elderly.

There are several criteria that may be used to classify a person as old: chronological age, function, historical age, and social age. Chronological age is widely used, but there are problems with it as a definitive criterion. For one thing, preliterate people often do not have sophisticated ways of measuring time, and they may not keep records of its passage. Unless a person was born at the same time as some historically dated event, establishing his age is a matter of guesswork. Another problem is that chronological age gives limited information. We may know a person's age but know nothing about his physical or mental abilities or his social position. Consider what is meant by statements such as:

> In many such (primitive) societies a person is defined as old by the time he is 45 or 50 years of age. Such was the uniform response even among urbanized Africans in 1962. By contrast, in most modern societies old age is thought to begin only at 60, 65, or 70 years of age (Cowgill and Holmes 1972:8).

Are we to understand that a forty-five or fifty year-old African has functional abilities similar to those of a North American of sixty-five or seventy? Is he at the same place in his life cycle? Or does an African mean something much different by the words translated as "old age" than does a North American? Chronological statements do not clarify the issue, and they may actually confuse it.

Another criterion for defining old age is function. Keith reports that in a sample of sixty societies from the Human Relations Area Files, function was the most common basis for classifying people as aged (1980:341). Chronological age was second, followed by the stages of physical and mental decline. Use of this third criterion was rare, however, because most societies classify people as old before they become decrepit. It is not clear which aspects of function are used to classify people as aged, for there are at least four kinds of functional changes that may signal the approach of old age: change in facility, in appearance, in activity, and in bodily action. Change in facility involves reduced sensitivity to smell, taste, hearing, sight, pain, and vibration; loss of strength, muscle tone, teeth, and mental acuity; loss of functions that facilitate ease in moving, acting, or doing. Change in appearance includes greying and/or loss of hair, stooped carriage, toothlessness, and – especially in Oceania – wrinkled skin and a dessicated look (in this monograph see Counts and Counts chapter 7, Lepowsky chapter 8). Decrease in activity has two aspects. One involves a declining interest and participation in community affairs and ceremonies that preoccupy the energies of most of the younger, vigorous members of the community. Another aspect involves declining ability to meet one's own needs and increasing dependence on others to meet one's basic needs: loss of independence. Finally, changes in bodily action are usually experienced as loss. They are physiological and cognitive and result in the reduced functions noted above. Decrease in bodily action includes reduction in basal metabolic rate, oxygen intake in the brain, kidney function, cardiac output, and ability to readily digest food and eliminate waste. In addition to bodily deterioration, the aging person also sustains emotional losses – of parents, children, friends, spouse, and relatives – and these emotional assaults become more pervasive, contributing to a decreased level of activity, as an individual grows older. Indeed, the most common experience in old age is reported to be that of loss (Berezin 1978:542).

Pacific peoples respond to these losses in various ways. Some, for example the Marquesans (Kirkpatrick chapter 5) struggle against deterioration and the dependency and communicative impoverishment that accompany the movement from valued maturity to old age and senility. One strategy in the struggle is to recruit new dependents whose presence testifies to the continuing ability of an aging person to care for himself and for others as well. Others, such as the Marshallese (Carucci chapter 6) and the Managalase of Papua New Guinea (McKellin chapter 9), consider the signs of advancing age to be sources of pride, or the terms for the elderly to be terms of respect, as do the people of Sudest Island (see Lepowsky, chapter 8). To these peoples, the signs of physical decline are also marks of accomplishment, sexual experience, and learning. The maturity and spiritual strength that characterize advancing age are thought to counterbalance aging's disabilities. Carolinian men, on the other hand, can counter some of the losses of aging only by transforming kin categories ('sisters' become 'daughters') so as to provide themselves with supportive relatives on whom they can depend (Flinn chapter 4).

A person may also be classified as old because of his historical age: his birth during, or his ability to remember, events that are significant in the history of his society. In Oceania these events might include the first coming of the Europeans, the appearance of a plague, dramatic volcanic eruptions or seismic waves, or the battles of World War II.

Finally, a person may be categorized as old because of his social age. Social age, or what Neugarten and Datan call "social time" (1973:57), is not synchronous with chronological age or with maturational stage, but involves notions about appropriate timing of major events or rites of passage in the life cycle. The definitive unit of reference may be the individual: for instance a young woman experiences her first menstruation and is recognized as being a marriageable woman rather than a child. It may be the peer group who moves through the stages of the life cycle together; or the unit of reference may be another person or social unit against whom one is defined, for example the assumption of elder status upon the birth of a first grandchild. People may be classed in appropriate age categories according to a combination of function and social time, and the unit of reference may change as an individual moves through the life cycle. For example a girl may be classified as a woman with the onset of her first menstruation – an ego defined state based on functional changes – but she may be called "old woman" after the birth of her first grandchild, a characterization that is initiated by and focused on the movement of her own children through the life cycle.

The difficulty of assigning a content to the term "old age" is exacerbated by failure to specify the criteria used to define "old age," and by the shortcoming noted by Watson and Maxwell (1977:40): most ethnographers do not distinguish between the active elderly and the decrepit old. It is frequently unclear whether an old person is merely a senior member of his lineage or whether he is someone who is physically and mentally infirm. Another, perhaps more pernicious, basis for confusion arises when scholars neglect to distinguish between life span and life expectancy, and assume that because the average life expectancy of a group of people is in the mid-twenties due to a high infant mortality rate, the life span must be less than fifty years and old age must, therefore, begin at forty. This confusion leads to statements such as that by Cowgill and Holmes quoted above, and the following:

"The farther back we go in human society the earlier people become old" (Simmons 1959:6).

"Not many years ago old age began at forty. This age limit has now risen and sixty-five is accepted as the beginning of old age" (Berezin 1978:541).

Although life expectancy certainly differs from society to society, current research indicates that the human life span has been constant at between 85 and 90 years for the past 100,000 years (Weiss 1981; Fries and Crapo 1981). Reports of extraordinarily long life spans from the Karakoram mountains in Pakistan, Vilacabamba in Ecuador, and the Caucasus are now discredited by researchers (Mazess and Forman 1978; Fries and Crapo 1981). As Weiss observes, "There is no useful evidence for meaningful biological life span differences between any human races" (1981:31). Nor is there any reason to conclude that the normal forty to fifty-year-old member of a preliterate, non-industrialized society experiences the physiological disabilities of a sixty-five-year-old North American. Such a person is unlikely to be decrepit and senile, although he might well be a respected senior member of his community. Indeed, if we can generalize from our experience in Papua New Guinea, the average forty-five-year-old Melanesian villager could easily work, dance, or play many thirty-year-old North Americans into a state of exhaustion, and would give even the fabled sixty-year-old Swede a run for his money. The average life expectancy in an isolated Pacific community may be low, but that is not relevant to the physical and mental condition of the surviving individual member of the community. To the extent that estimates of chronological age are possible, all of the chapters in this volume reinforce this point: the processes and duration of physical aging are everywhere the same.

AGING AND GENDER

Another statement about aging that has widespread, if not universal, application, is that women and men experience old age differently. Beginning in the 1970s, scholars researching the processes and problems of aging began to explore the dynamic relationship that exists between universal phenomena previously treated as unrelated: the processes of aging and gender role behavior. It is, for instance, widely reported that women enjoy more authority, fewer restrictions, and more opportunity for achievement and recognition as they age past the childbearing years (Brown 1982). Both women and men undergo marked changes in their behavior and find that society's expectations of them change as they grow old, so that, as Keith comments, there is "... a universal shift among old men from more active to more passive orientations" (1980:350). At the same time:

A glass of beer with the boys, freedom to let out a four letter word, or let go in a public dance are the privileges of old age for many women in the world. Loosening up of previous constraint is the compensation available especially to old women in many cultures (Keith 1980:351).

Gutmann suggests that the neutralization of gender differences is part of the aging process (1969; 1975; Gutmann, Grunes and Griffin 1980). His cross-cultural research leads him to conclude that behavioral dimorphism of the sexes is associated with, and indeed may be a consequence of, parenthood. When parental responsibilities end, women and men move toward what he calls "the normal androgyny of later life" (Gutmann, Grunes and Griffin 1980:122). Not only sex roles, but the very qualities that lie at the heart of notions of gender are transformed by the process of aging.

Thus, neither sex is the final custodian of the qualities that we choose to call 'masculine' and 'feminine'. These qualities tend to be distributed not only by sex but by life period. Men are not forever 'masculine'; rather, they can be defined as the sex that shows the trait arrangement that we call 'masculine' *before* they show the arrangement that we call 'feminine'; and the reverse is true for women... (Gutmann 1975:181).

Gutmann goes on to suggest that gender pertains to parenthood rather than to biological sex, and that gender specificity is lost as the psychic structures that are predicated on parenthood are phased out.

Keith and Gutmann reached their conclusions without benefit of the graphic and dramatic examples of gender transformation that anthropologists report from Papua New Guinea. Indeed, most of this literature would not have been available to Gutmann in 1975, and it is not cited in Keith (1980). Our review here of Melanesian data is not exhaustive. It is, however, representative and demonstrates clearly that in many Pacific societies gender is a dynamic process rather than a static category, a process that occurs as one aspect of the process of aging.

Recent research in Papua New Guinea details the ways in which, in some Melanesian societies, categories of gender and age are interlocked in a transformational process that unfolds as the individual moves through the life cycle. For many Melanesians, aging is accompanied by altered gender roles but Weiner reports an inversion of this relationship in the Trobriands. There, sexually evocative dancing, skillfully applied body decoration, and magic reverse age and an old woman may briefly become young again. Weiner quotes a young man who says to his mother who is dressed for dancing: "To my eyes you always looked like an old woman, but today you have changed and now you look young and beautiful" (1976:132-133).

Other Papua New Guinea peoples, for example the Hua (Meigs 1976; 1983), the Etoro (Kelly 1976), the Bimin-Kuskusmin (Pool 1981), and the Sambia (Herdt 1981) view gender as transmittable and transmutable and expect transformations to occur as a normal accompaniment to the aging process. Review of the data from these societies enables us to generalize as follows:

(1) Gender categories may be defined by criteria other than – or in addition to – genital appearance and behavior. In discussing Hua notions of pollution and male pregnancy, Meigs notes that in addition to the criteria named above, gender classification may also be based on

...the fluids associated with sexuality, namely menstrual blood, vaginal secretions, parturitional fluids, and sperm. As these fluids are transferable between the two genitally different classes, this classification permits crossovers: where a genitally male person is classified as female through his contamination by female fluids, and a genitally female person as male by means of transfer of pollution out of her body. (Meigs 1976:405)

In contrast, the Etoro consider gender to be "an aspect of the soul" (Kelly 1976:46). Spirits determine the sex of a child by implanting a male or female immaterial spirit double in the fetus. Males and females are, therefore, differentiated spiritually as well as physiologically and behaviorally.

(2) Humans may be inherently androgynous or naturally female. The Sambia consider femaleness to be the natural state of birds and seem to fear that it may also be the inherent condition of humans (Herdt 1981). The Sambia assign birds to the female sex, first as immature "girls" and then as egg-laying, dull colored, old females. Birds are male for only a brief time, when they are youthful and brightly colored; maleness is a transitional stage between immature youth and reproductive maturity. Just as chicks are female, the bodies of all children contain female substances. It is usual for a Sambia father to worry that the substances may weaken the body of his son, and to express concern that an infant son may actually be a hermaphrodite (Herdt 1981:216, 208). Fathers fear that an uninitiated boy may change into a girl, and cite living hermaphrodites as proof that this sort of transformation actually does occur.

(3) A person's gender is not fixed and may change at any time

during the life cycle: it may happen in the womb; it may occur in childhood; or it may take place in old age. Strathern observes that Hagen men claim that women are incapable of the single-mindedness and reason that are required for political action, and say that a woman who shows exceptional ability obviously began life in the womb as a male, "... only happening to be born female" (1972:161). The Bimin-Kuskusmin claim that a fetus's genital sex changes repeatedly during the course of gestation, the sex at birth being determined by the last influence before delivery (Poole 1981:125). The arbitrariness of one's physiological sex is recognized when a man reminds his wife's brothers that they are behaving "like the women that they should have been," or when men comment, "We must treat our sisters well, for they might have been born our brothers" (Poole 1981:125).

Among the Bimin-Kuskusmin, too, a few women undergo a final transformation in old age. These women, who have during their lives embodied the ideals of virginal purity and maternal fertility, are chosen by men to be ritual leaders who preside during male initiations. Because the elderly woman is postmenopausal, she can neither bear children nor pollute. Her fertile fluids become as the semen from which they originated, and she can, therefore, promote fertility and growth without pollution. During the initiation ceremony, the ritual leader is dressed as a transvestite representing the hermaphroditic ancestors, and after death a hole is drilled in the soft spot at the front of her skull (considered by the Bimin-Kuskusmin to be the male navel) to allow knowledge to enter and to mark her skull as belonging to a woman. Then it is enshrined with other male sacrae (Poole 1981:150-154).

Gender change occurs for both old men and old women among the Hua (Meigs 1976:405-406). Old women become socially equivalent to younger males, for they may live in the men's house, they are privy to male secret knowledge, and they must observe rules that are normally limited to young men. Old men, on the other hand, take on some aspects of female social status. For example, at weddings they eat with women and children in a space that is segregated from the other men, they are placed in the category of polluting people that includes children, fertile women, and postmenopausal women with less than three children. Meigs demonstrates that, for the Hua, gender is experienced and transmitted along with the sexual fluids that define it. She says:

A person's gender does not lie locked in his or her genitals but can flow and change with contact as substances seep into or out of his or her body. Gender is not an immutable state but a dynamic flow. Such a view permits most persons to experience both genders before they die (1976:406).

When we began the research that has culminated in this monograph, we expected some of our contributors to report variations on the theme of gender transformation and reversal reported from the New Guinea Highlands. These expectations were, in fact, not realized; no reversals of gender identity appear in the chapters of this volume. For example, in our chapter 7 we note that those who stand to benefit from the social withdrawal of an elderly person may attempt to present that person as being defunct. One way of doing this is to invite the person, if a woman, to ignore ceremonial taboos that are imposed on younger women: by lifting gender-related restrictions on her, others can place her in the category of the defunct and socially incapacitated elderly. It is when people become dependent and begin the process of withdrawal that their gender-related behavior may begin to change or, as Flinn says (chapter 4), it is then that they are released from constraints on their sex role behavior. So it is that a Pulap woman is more free to express her opinion in public or play the clown (both prerogatives of young men) as she grows old, while an old man may give up fishing and become more sedentary – traits also associated with young women. So, while their behavior does change, the Pacific peoples discussed in this monograph do not undergo gender transformation.

The old woman in our study would not have become male if she had accepted the invitation to ignore taboos usually placed on women: she would have become an ineffectual old woman. The "natural androgyny of later life" (Gluckmann, Grunes and Griffin 1980:122) is not, for the peoples in this book, androgyny at all: rather it is the muting of gender differences and the generalization of many tasks and/or privileges ascribed by gender in younger people. Thus it is that old men may sweep the village plaza or baby-sit with their great grandchildren, and old women may witness sacred ceremonies that are usually reserved to men. Nevertheless, women remain women and men remain men: in these societies we find no creation of a third gender category that might be labeled "androgynous old."

Without calling into question the well-documented cases of gender reversal noted above, we suggest that the applicability of a category of "androgynous old" would disappear in many other societies, too, if they were given the close scrutiny that forms the basis of the chapters in this volume. Indeed, Lepowsky (chapter 8) even calls into question the regularity of stress on gender opposition during the parenting years. Her chapter directs our attention to the importance of differential access to power as a condition affecting both gender distinctions and more general changes that occur during the aging process.

The chapters in this monograph do question the broad application of concepts such as gender reversal or "androgyny" in old age, even in Melanesian societies. Instead our data, together with reports from other Melanesian societies, suggest the existence of a very complex relationship between social withdrawal, transition in gender roles, and change in the social spheres in which people hold authority.

As we observed above, most anthropologists seem to agree that disengagement theory does not apply to the elderly in preindustrial societies. Nevertheless, it is important to take into account the widespread practice, documented in this volume and elsewhere, of dividing the aged into two categories: one for those who are partially dependent but still able to meet their basic daily needs, and another for the totally dependent – a category that is defined by physical and mental decline and that is referred to as 'the already dead' or those 'in the sleeping period' (Keith 1980:341). The process of withdrawal may begin while people are still active (see Carucci's discussion of the behavior of elderly Marshallese men in chapter 6), but it is when they become decrepit and dependent – whether by mental incapacity, illness, or extreme age – that they become dependent or disaffiliated (see Scaletta chapter 11). As Leenhardt observes, it is common throughout Melanesia for the defunct to be classified with the dead, and for this classification to be embodied in both language and behavior. For example, the New Caledonian word *bao* refers to the corpse, the dead person, and the very old (Leenhardt 1979:30); the Gnau word *wola* is glossed 'ill', 'wretched', 'harmful', 'powerful', and when the completed action marker *bi* is added *biwola* also means 'old', 'ruined', or 'chronically ill' (Lewis 1975:130); the Umeda word for 'old man' is a compound of *nugwi* meaning 'rotten' or 'stinking' (Gell 1975:293). Barth observes that the Baktaman claim that living old men and ancestors have the same capricious, sometimes vindictive character, and that they are treated in the same way (1975:120). The Managalase say that the spirits of the very old, who spend increasingly more of their day sleeping, participate more and more in the society of the dead than in the society of the living. When an elderly person completes his transition from one society to the other, death is complete (McKellin chapter 9). The Gadsup recognize two categories of old person: the active old and the dependent elderly who contribute in no way but just sit in the sun waiting to be fed. "I got the impression," remarked Du Toit, "that clansmen and community members were simply waiting for them to die" (1975:276).

It is not uncommon for people to define the senescent old to be, in fact, dying, and to hasten death or conclude mourning ceremonies before physical death is complete (Van Baal 1966; Van Arsdale 1981; Counts and Counts chapter 7). Van Baal reports that the Marind Amin elderly are respected and well treated as long as they are in good health. When they become helpless and senescent they may be buried alive by their children (Van Baal 1966:171). Van Arsdale observes that the Asmat may conduct mourning ceremonies for a very old person before breathing and heartbeat have stopped, and that occasionally old, infirm people thought to be near death are left alone and untended in the corner of the hut until death takes place (1981:116). Counts and Counts (chapter 7) recount that the children of a decrepit, senile village leader completed final mortuary ceremonies for him while he still lived, thereby rendering him socially dead.

These data, together with the data in this volume (see especially Flinn chapter 4; Kirkpatrick chapter 5; Counts and Counts chapter 7; McKellin chapter 9), provide strong evidence that disaffiliation occurs in Pacific societies when old people are categorized as being decrepit, dependent or, in Leenhardt's term, defunct. Our data also indicate that in some cases categories of old age are negotiable. Marquesans, for example, display considerable ambivalence toward old age. The old are alienated, without public authority, and are said to be 'heathen'. Nonetheless, persons in their mid-forties often claim to be old. Kirkpatrick (chapter 5) asks why people behave in this seemingly contradictory way, and finds that old age carries connotations of maturity and support for the normative order as well as alienation and potential deviance. Old age, he observes, is a negotiated category as people reinterpret the culturally recognized signs of aging. Furthermore, the question of dependency – a condition that people try to avoid – is one of context, perspective, and negotiation. Does an old woman foster the young child who sleeps and eats with her, or do the child and her parents care for the old woman? How much labor may an old person contribute to the household and still be considered dependent? Who is, in fact, the the head of the household – the elderly parent or the married adult child with whom the elder lives? An elderly person would likely answer these questions in one way, his co-resident adult children in another. Also, the answers may be quite different if the aged person is female rather than male, for one's gender may significantly affect the nature and quality of the aging experience, a point that is made in many of the chapters of this volume, see especially Sinclair (chapter 2), Flinn (chapter 4), and Carucci (chapter 6).

When we discuss the activities and gender roles of the peoples with whom the contributors to this volume have worked, it is useful to draw on Rosaldo's distinction between the domestic and public spheres of influence and authority (1980). Although this distinction is an analytic one, and the spheres are neither recognized nor separated in all of the societies considered in this volume, we find that this distinction helps us to understand why there are changes in the amount and type of respect and authority that people enjoy as they grow old and why the experience of aging may be quite different for women and men. When we distinguish the domestic realm from the public realm we realize that:

(1) Men may lose their ability to exercise authority in the public realm as they grow old, while continuing to have considerable authority in the domestic realm. Although he has become marginal to public activities, an old man may continue to manage his house and land and have the right to evict recalcitrant adolescent and adult children, a right that empowers him with significant domestic authority (Kirkpatrick chapter 5).

(2) Elderly women who have established their authority in the domestic realm may seek to define questions of public policy as being within the domestic realm and being, therefore, questions over which they, by definition, have authority (see Dominy's discussion of the controversy over abortion legislation in chapter 3).

(3) Elderly women may act as bridges or middlewomen between the domestic realm, which they control, and the public domain controlled by men (see Dominy chapter 3), or between white and indigenous society (Sinclair chapter 2). While the social universe of old men becomes more circumscribed, the social universe of old women may expand and they may enter a new or redefined public arena to fill the vacuum left by the declining prowess of their male age-mates (Sinclair chapter 2).

(4) Women and men who have access to different sources and spheres of authority may exercise power at different stages in their life cycles. Myerhoff makes a similar point when she distinguishes between the expressive and nurturing "contingent" gender roles of women that derive from their activities in the market, household, and community and the instrumental roles of men emanating from their employment in the public sphere (1978:241-251). As men age they are replaced by younger men. They lose the instrumental dimension of their lives when they retire from active public employment, while the nurturing and expressive activities of women continue or expand with age as they acquire more experience and expertise.

Carucci (chapter 6) and Sinclair (chapter 2) do not use Myerhoff's terminology, but they do note that the prestige and authority of men in the public arena declines as they age, while women become more active and vital and enjoy increased authority in their elder years. Furthermore, Marshallese men begin to withdraw from active community life before women do (Carucci chapter 6). As their youngest children enter adolescence, men joke about getting old and increasingly assign more responsibility to men in the junior generations. Women, on the other hand, resist being categorized as elderly until they are great-grandmothers; a Marshallese woman waits until she is the respected head of a successful family before she talks of being old.

(5) Aging may be significantly more difficult for widowers than for widows. Flinn (chapter 4) and Carucci (chapter 6) observe that aging women experience continuity, security, and stability of roles and relationships. In contrast, an old man, especially a widowed old man, may find his status changed (in the Marshalls a widower is thrown back into the role of single adolescent), or be required to transform his kin relations (a dependent Pulap man must redefine his sisters as his daughters if he is to receive help without disrupting the social order), for there is no established social niche that an elderly widower can comfortably occupy. An elderly woman continues to operate in her accustomed sphere and set of relationships; her widowhood is not a time of upheaval. In contrast, a widower may face not only diminished public authority but the need to restructure his relationships to others as well. The lives of elderly widowers are not inevitably circumscribed, however. Compare the condition of the widowers described by Flinn (chapter 4) and Carucci (chapter 6) with that of Nathan, whose biography is sketched in chapter 7. Although an elder when he was widowed, Nathan continued to operate legitimately in the domestic as well as in the public domain, raising his young children and maintaining a household with the assitance of his female relatives.

AGING, DEATH, AND COSMOLOGY

Although aging leads inexorably to death, death is neither a simple event nor an experience that is confined to the aged. In their attempts to explain and find some order in the inevitable experiences of illness, aging and death, Pacific peoples have developed complex and exotic cosmologies that have long excited the interest of scholars. During the early 1900s, anthropologists approached the study of death from a number of viewpoints. One was represented by the cognitive emphasis of the English scholar W.H.R. Rivers. The other approach is exemplified by the work of two   French scholars, Robert Hertz and Arnold Van Gennep, who emphasized the sociological significance of death. Van Gennep (1960) argued that funeral rites are rites of transition that focus on the liminal status of the deceased, while Hertz concentrated on rituals of secondary burial and on the concept of death as process (Hertz 1960).   He noted that in Borneo death is not instantaneous: there is a period when a person is neither alive nor dead. During this period of transition, the state of the body provides a model for the condition of the soul, so that while the corpse is putrefying and formless the soul can neither enter the society of the dead nor re-enter human society (see also Metcalf 1982).

Although there is no reliable evidence that Rivers knew of Hertz's essay on death, there is – as Slobodin observes – "a good deal of congruence in the treatments, especially in the discussions of death seen as a kind of transition" (1978:167-168).   In his essay on the primitive conception of death published in 1926 (and reprinted in Slobodin 1978), Rivers used Melanesian beliefs about the relationship between life and death to demonstrate his point that people in other cultures order reality in a different way.   The widely used Melanesian terms *mate* and *toa,* although usually translated as 'dead' and 'living', embrace concepts that are not truly equivalent to our terms.   The boundaries are not the same.   The category *mate,* for example, includes the very sick and the very old (Leenhardt's defunct) in addition to the dead, while *toa* "excludes from the living those who are called *mate*" (Rivers 1926 in Slobodin 1978:211). What, then, is the nature of the condition that the Melanesians call *mate?*

First, it is a state that may last for years rather than being an event, as death is for us.   Second, life and after-life – the two states that lie on either side of *mate* – are more similar to each other in Melanesian cultures than we think of them as being.   To the Melanesian "...existence after death is just as real as the existence here which we call life....Further, life after death has the same general aspect as life before death" (in Slobodin 1978:216).

In 1947, twenty-one years after the publication of Rivers' essay on death, Maurice Leenhardt came to some of the same conclusions as had Rivers, Hertz, and Van Gennep.   In *Do Kamo,* his classic study of Melanesian thought, Leenhardt argues that the world view of the New Caledonians, with whom he worked as a missionary for twenty-five years, is uniquely different from our own.   He contrasts the Melanesian concept of death with our assumption that there is an opposition between life and death, a notion of final annihilation that covers every case of extinction that we witness. We view death as a rupturing of life, but not so the New Caledonian. In his mode of thought trees succumb but they do not die: only men and animals die. Trees "have a different mode of existence to which the word 'death' cannot be applied" (Leenhardt 1979:20). The Melanesian notion of death does not assume an annihilation of being: there is no fundamental separation between the dead and the living. The Melanesian emphasis is not on death, as such, but on social disaffiliation. The seriously ill, the aged, the insane, and the dead are defunct; they are disaffiliated from the society of the living.

Certainly not all Pacific peoples, nor even all Melanesians, have identical ideas about life and death. In contrast to Leenhardt's New Caledonians, Lewis found that the Gnau of New Guinea turn to plants rather than to animals for parallels with human experience. They suspect that while men and plants actually die, wild animals may not (Lewis 1980:137). There are, however, related concepts that run through Pacific cosmologies. Throughout the Pacific, people recognize boundaries between living and dead (or animate and inanimate) that are fluid and contextual (Malinowski 1916; Lawrence 1964; Lane 1965; Barth 1975; Du Toit 1975), and have the notion of a life force or animating spirit that may leave the body during illness or sleep (Buck 1934; Van Baal 1966; Heider 1970; Huber 1979; Counts and Counts chapter 7; McKellin chapter 9; Scaletta chapter 11). This force may have an existence that is independent of the host body, and it may be transformed – either before or after death – to appear in human, animal or bird form (Deacon 1934; Poole 1981; McKellin chapter 9; Scaletta chapter 11). The idea that the animating spirit may be temporarily alienated from the body shapes a people's understanding of the nature of death, for from this point of view sleep, illness, and death may be considered to be transformations of each other. Death is, therefore, neither a sharp break with life nor an absolute state of being. Instead it concludes a lengthy cyclical transfer of energies (Carucci chapter 6) or a reversible process with boundaries that are contextually defined (Wagner 1972:133; Barth 1975:124; Lewis 1975:137).

Behaviors that demonstrate the variety that exists in response to culturally defined death include the neglect of the critically ill (Heider 1970:229-230), premature burial (Van Baal 1966:171; Du Toit 1975:131), and the failure to bury a corpse (Panoff 1968). In these instances, the loss of the animating spirit, the soul, or the self occurs while the body is still vital. The person is, however, socially dead and, as Leenhardt suggests, no apparent significance is attached to the body once it ceases to be a container for the spirit. The living body may be treated as though it were a corpse, the husk may be buried while it is still breathing or, as in the Maenge case reported by Panoff, the body may be only a long-empty shell that is not worth the bother of interment.

One of humanity's universal concerns has been to explain the processes of aging and death. Why do people lose their physical and mental prowess as they age? Why do people have to die? For some Pacific peoples, for instance the Telefol (Jorgensen chapter 10), senescence and death may demonstrate the operation of a general cosmological principle. The Telefol view death as but one instance of the operation of the general process of entropy (Jorgensen chapter 10). According to them, the world and the place of humans in it is winding down, becoming nothing. Death, and other forms of loss such as wandering pigs and failing taro gardens, are but demonstrations of a single fact: the world is on the wane.

Others assume that the system of life and death is a closed one and that, in Kelly's terms, "accretion at one point in the system entails depletion elsewhere" (1976:45). The sexual acts that are necessary for the physical survival of society lead inevitably to the physical decline, aging, and death of the parents (see Counts and Counts chapter 7; Scaletta chapter 11). Some societies place emphasis on the polluting nature of sexually active females who may victimize men (see Meggitt 1964; Frankel 1980; Goodale 1980, 1981). Others stress that excessive sexual activity and/or contact with sexual effluvia may result in illness, general physical decline, premature aging, and death, and they emphasize that both women and men are vulnerable (Faithorn 1975; Counts and Counts chapter 7). Still others note that the male role in, and responsibility for, reproduction leads to aging and death. Some, such as the Etoro, think that there is a finite reservoir of life force, concentrated in human semen, that is depleted with each act of sexual intercourse (Kelly 1976). The sexual, reproductive, and nutritive acts and relationships that are the responsibility of each adult male and that are essential for the production of children result in the father's decline and death. As Gell notes, the father is consumed so that the child may thrive (1975:154). For these societies there is an inescapable "essential tragedy of human existence – that senescence and death are preconditions for the perpetuation of life through birth" (Kelly 1976:49).

Some Oceanic societies view death as a manifestation of a general process of entropy, while others assume that death and life are inexorably bound together and that aging and death are the inevitable by-products of the creation of life. However, because death comes to the young and vital more often than to the very old (or has done so until recent years) in most Pacific societies, people have been compelled to find reasons for the death of the young and, sometimes, to explain why it was that a few individuals did not die until they reached a very old age (see McKellin chapter 9). With the spread of modern medical treatment, this situation is almost certainly changing, but ideologies of death do not reflect this. In her essay on the Kabana of West New Britain, Scaletta (chapter 11) discusses indigenous explanations of death and describes the ethical dilemma of the family of a woman who is dying slowly and painfully and who begs them to hasten the process. Their predicament is one familiar to us: should they prolong her suffering while they search desperately for a cure, or should they give up and release her spirit to death? Is there no way they can spare her from a bad death?

The distinction between good and bad death is critical here. For many peoples (see Counts 1976-77; Counts and Counts 1983-84; Flinn chapter 4; Jorgensen chapter 10; Scaletta chapter 11), death of old age is a good death because old age is equated with a morally correct life. Most other death is bad death because it results from moral failure, either of behavior or of thought (Jorgensen chapter 10). In contrast, McKellin (chapter 9) argues that the Managalase assume that old age is, in itself, proof of control over magic power. People who die of old age are more powerful or more prudent than their contemporaries, not more moral. As Scaletta observes in chapter 11, the question of good or bad death is not merely a biological question of pain or its absence: it is a moral one. Being a moral issue, the manner of death often affects the nature and disposition of the ghost. Those who die a bad death – for example by suicide, in childbirth, or as a result of violence – may become malevolent ghosts (see Flinn chapter 4; Jorgensen chapter 10; Counts 1980b), while people who die of old age may, as with the Telefol, become guardian spirits who are responsible for the well-being of the community (Jorgensen chapter 10).

DISCUSSION

The aging process, grounded as it is in biological fact, is common to all groups of people and is, therefore, an experience with which people of all societies must come to terms. While the experience is subject to cultural interpretation, there are aspects of it that appear to occur in most, if not all, societies. The withdrawal of society from the decrepit elderly appears to be widespread, occurring in a number of the societies discussed in this volume, including those that are predominantly rural, preindustrialized communities. In some, the withdrawal of society is coupled with voluntary and mutual withdrawal from active life by elderly persons.

Another widespread aspect of the aging experience is a change in the content of gender roles with old women enjoying more freedom than young women and, perhaps, more of a public face than their elderly male counterparts (Brown 1982). The studies in this volume suggest that the phenomena of withdrawal and gender role change are interdependent and that they seem to operate in a context containing a complex of variables. These variables include:

(1) the way in which categorization takes place: whether persons occupy the status of active and partially self-sufficient elder or of totally dependent and defunct old person;

(2) the domain – public or domestic – in which the person is active and/or attempting to exert authority;

(3) the fact that old people are not passive recipients of the behavior of others. The elderly people in these chapters negotiate their status; they attempt to exploit the advantages and minimize the weaknesses of old age; and they employ strategies designed to maintain and extend their authority.

The following general statements seem to have validity in Oceanic societies and may be true in a broader cross-cultural context:

(1) As people grow older, related changes occur in the level of activity and amount of authority that they have and in the sphere where activity occurs and authority is held. Women and men often experience these changes differently. Men usually dominate the public sphere during their prime years, years that may extend well into active old age. During their prime years, women usually have authority in the domestic domain. As they approach dependent old age, men begin to withdraw; they are replaced by younger men or, in some cases, by old women who act as mediators or who redefine particular public issues as being within the domestic sphere, allowing them to extend their authority. The replacement process does not seem to work in reverse: old men, who have withdrawn from the public arena, do not replace elderly women and take over their authority in the domestic domain. It seems that old women are able to maintain their authoritative position much farther into the aging process than are men. Often they are able to do this, not because they *cease* to parent as Gutmann suggests, but precisely because they do continue their parenting role. By fosterage, by adoption, and by extending the responsibilities of motherhood into political life, women demonstrate their ability to

continue as active, responsible, contributing members of the domain where they have spent a lifetime building expertise and exercising authority.

(2) The factors that determine how an individual experiences the processes of aging and dying are not necessarily determined by the technological stage of his society. The data presented in this monograph demonstrate that it is the ability of a person to participate meaningfully in community life, not the level of technological complexity of his society, that determines how he will experience old age. Disaffiliation occurs when people are defunct, whether they live in a New Guinea village, on a Pacific island, or in the city of Auckland.

These data also provide compelling evidence that while the complexity of our society's medical technology may have had a profound effect on the dying experience, the assertion that simple medical technology means simple notions of death and dying is mistaken. Lofland, for example, argues that whereas death in modern society is often a prolonged affair, the duration of the dying period in premodern society is typically "mean, brutish and *short* (emphasis in the original)" (1978:22). Lofland offers several reasons for this brevity. First, early diagnosis of terminal illness that would permit people to interfere with the dying process is prevented by a low level of medical technology and a "simple definition of death" (1978:18, 24-25). Also, when a person in a premodern society is diagnosed as being terminally ill, it is common for him to commit suicide, for his kin to attempt to kill him, or for his relatives to respond with "fatalistic passivity" (1978:18).

These generalizations require modification, for they are based on overly simple assumptions about the ways that people in preindustrial societies diagnose illness, define death, and respond to the death of their members. The diagnosis of illness and the criteria by which people are assigned to the category of the dying are cultural constructs that have their referents in ideology rather than in medical technology. There are a number of classic anthropological studies that develop this point for peoples throughout the world: for example, the Philippines (Frake 1961), Africa (Evans-Pritchard 1937; Turner 1963; Edgerton 1966), Australia (Cannon 1942); Papua New Guinea (Lewis 1975; Lindenbaum 1979) to name only a few. The case study presented here by Scaletta (chapter 11) demonstrates clearly that the time a person spends in the dying process is not necessarily brief, that relatives do not always respond to a victim's plight with "fatalistic passivity," and that people in preindustrial societies face the same ethical dilemma as do we: whether to prolong the dying process and the suffering of a loved one while a cure is sought or to permit death to come.

Clearly the contrast between simple and complex definitions of death is a spurious one. Lofland argues that the issue is complex in modern societies because advanced technology has made the complex issue of brain function the basis for the diagnosis of death (1978:32). The arguments raised in the annals of the New York Academy of Science conference on brain death demonstrate that in our society the definition of death is, indeed, a complex matter (Korein 1978a). Various experts debate whether brain death includes cognitive death (Korein 1978b), and discuss death as being a religious (Hauerwas 1978), legal (Capron 1978; Keene 1978; Beresford 1978), and ethical issue (Veith 1978), and as being a matter of policy and concept (Veatch 1978). Death is a complex issue because, ultimately, it is a question of culture, ideology, and cosmology in modern industrialized societies and in traditional preindustrialized Pacific societies as well.

Finally, as Scaletta's detailed case study of Kabana death by sorcery illustrates, the response of people to the dying of a relative or friend is predicated on the perceived cause of death and the status of the dying person, not on the society's medical technology. As do North Americans, the people of the Pacific place a high value on prolonging active, meaningful life and desperately attempt to avoid being classified as decrepit and to avert premature death. As we have already discussed, premodern people passively accept some deaths, and they may even hurry their kin through the dying process by neglect or by the custom of premature burial. In this, Lofland is correct. However, these customs are not unique to pre-modern societies. Watson and Maxwell compare them to the North American practice of segregating the decrepit aged in institutions (1977:128-129). Both practices result in a situation in which the decrepit elderly are classified and treated as though they were already among the dead. We also share with pre-modern people the idea that some categories of seriously ill persons should be classified with the dead. One theme that ran through the New York Academy's conference on brain death was a concern with what we might call the Karen Ann Quinlan question: the question of when we should set aside our complex medical technology and permit the defunct to joint the truly dead.

If we are to learn anything about ourselves from the study of other peoples, we must focus on the similarities in our concepts of aging and dying as well as on our differences. But, differences do, indeed, exist and they may be profound. In order that we may not, inadvertently, nullify them we have in the chapters by Kirkpatrick, McKellin, Jorgensen, and Scaletta, abrogated the usual practice in this monograph series of avoiding the use of indigenous terms. These terms – for a particular age category, a concept of spiritual essence, a type of ghost or magical knowledge – cannot be translated into English without distorting the concepts for which they stand. These concepts derive from cosmologies that are exotic, that make assumptions about the nature of aging, life, and death that are unlike anything we know. It is, we think, useful to keep this fact before the reader by the use of these few native terms rather than to negate the differences by using inappropriate and inaccurate English glosses.

In conclusion, the thrust of this volume is twofold. One thrust is the process of aging and the changes that accompany it: changes in social status, in gender role, and in category as the old become defunct. The second thrust is the process of dying: the experience, the cosmology that structures it, and the attitudes of both the living and the dying toward it.

These two processes, however, are ones in which individuals are actors and not just objects. The elderly and dying persons portrayed in the chapters of this volume do not meekly and passively accept the labels applied to them by other members of their societies. Rather, they negotiate their status and the content of the status they occupy. They fight – often successfully – to control their lives and their departures from life.

The two processes, aging and dying, are related for, inexorably, humans age into death. The ordering and the focus of the chapters in this volume, too, follows this sequence, moving from aging and its attendant changes in gender role, to aging and dying, to death.

The focus of the concluding chapter by Marshall directs our attention to the relation between studies of social gerontology – largely centered on North American society – and the anthropological work on aging and dying. Marshall discusses the background and the implications of social gerontological theory – with special reference to modernization theory, disengagement theory, and the life course perspective – and explores the contributions that social gerontologists and anthropologists can each make to the other. The studies in this monograph have, he suggests, made implicit use of concepts of social gerontology as they explore the meanings that particular societies assign to aging and dying and the ways in which they organize the aging and dying processes. There is much of value to anthropology in the theories of social gerontology and, conversely, there is an opportunity in the study of aging and death for anthropology to move beyond merely providing an exotic foil to studies of North American society. We have the opportunity to enrich and refine social theory, for aging, gender and dying are culturally recognized and defined processes. If, in our search for social universals and theories with cross-cultural validity, we simply retain North American categories and highlight central tendencies in our data, we risk distorting it and overlooking much that other peoples have to teach us. We must attend to the seemingly exceptional cases and to the more commonplace ones alike, for both exemplify cultural constructions of human processes.

Part I: AGING AND GENDER

2

KORO AND KUIA:
AGING AND GENDER AMONG
THE MAORI OF NEW ZEALAND

Karen P. Sinclair

INTRODUCTION

The end of the life cycle often involves significant adjustments as men and women face new situations and are called upon to perform in a range of new contexts. Evidence from other cultures would seem to suggest that in many societies the elderly maintain an active involvement in the group, often expanding rather than limiting their behavioral repertoire (See for example Dougherty 1978; Keith 1980; Fry 1981a; Cool and McCabe 1983). For postmenopausal women this frequently means that their status and influence increase significantly (Myerhoff 1978; Dougherty 1978; Brown 1982). To some extent this is the natural culmination of increasing prestige and power achieved within their own homes as they grow older. But more importantly, and often quite contrary to traditional cultural prescriptions, older women may exercise a demonstrable authority that is no longer limited to domestic concerns (Myerhoff and Simic 1978:239). Indeed, such women fill roles not usually open to younger women of childbearing age (for example midwife or healer) and often perform in a public arena previously inhabited only by men (Poole 1982). In the Maori case, it is not merely that gender distinctions diminish; there does in fact appear to be a genuine reversal.[1] Men are certainly important, continuing to derive the benefits of a cultural ideology that favors masculinity. But as they age the social experience of Maori men and women follow very different paths. Women exist in an expanding social universe, while men find themselves in a rapidly diminishing, circumscribed social world. It is as though "women fill the vacuum left by more rapidly declining male prowess" (Myerhoff and Simic 1978: 240).

Aging successfully in any society requires preparation; in Maori culture, especially, aging implies changes in role and status that entail significant individual adjustment.   As Maori men and women age, they assume a pronounced and active interest in public affairs. There are formalized statuses – *kaumatua* 'male elder', *kuia,* 'female elder'– which carry with them ritual, social and political prerogatives and obligations.[2] These obligations frequently center around crucial aspects of Maori social life; the elderly are preeminent at feasts, funerals, and on all occasions that distinguish the contemporary Maori situation. Such events are especially significant because it is at these times that the values implicit in Maoriness can be expressed and affirmed.

The postcolonial situation in New Zealand is ambiguous in many ways. While there is clearly a resurgent interest in Maoriness on the parts of both Maoris and Europeans, the contexts in which this is important have altered in the last fifty years. Hence cultural prescriptions mandating the ascendancy of the elderly are somewhat confusing to the young who can look only to their elders as a source of tradition, but who must also come to terms with a European dominated social world. For the elders, who have witnessed the dramatic transformation of New Zealand society, the new dispensation confronts them with novel, often unanticipated, responsibilities. For them the consequences of aging are increased ethnic awareness and public participation in distinctly ethnic contexts.   Moreover, the expanded and vigorous activity of elderly men and women would seem to be an important counter example to disengagement theories propounded by sociologists and psychologists in their description of the elderly in Western society (Neugarten 1968). Such a study also prompts us to realize that individuals continue to learn and to adapt throughout their lifetimes.

The elderly women who are the subjects of this chapter are also members of a religious movement called Maramatanga.   The term *maramatanga* may be glossed as 'knowledge' or 'enlightenment'. Involvement in this movement accelerates and reinforces the growing importance and influence of aging Maori women; for to participate in such a movement is to participate actively in the definition and formation of a Maori identity. The adherents of Maramatanga are members of an extended kin group, whose participation goes back fifty years to the origin of the movement.   While younger urban members attend feasts and celebrations and even express more than passing interest, the adherents today are predominantly rural and elderly (the reasons for this are discussed below). Women who participate in this movement handle the stresses and strains of being elderly members of a minority culture far better than do men. They dispose of their commitments to Maoris and to Europeans with a degree of social deftness that men simply do not possess. In postcolonial New Zealand, characterized as it is by ill defined and shifting circumstances, women have been more successful than men in negotiating their roles and positions in the social world.   As they age, women manipulate their social and cultural worlds, often providing a bridge between Maori and Pakeha domains. It is significant that in New Zealand such roles fall to older women (see Dominy, chapter 3). This chapter, then, is concerned with gender differences in aging, which in turn are related to the different roles men and women assume in the course of the life cycle.   The questions I am concerned with are: what are the differences in developmental history that lead to this situation in old age? In other words, what prepares women for their ascendancy as they reach this point in the life cycle? In what arenas do men and women perform? And finally, how are women's performances enhanced by their participation in a religious movement?

MAORIS AND NEW ZEALAND SOCIETY

In slightly over two centuries Maoris have ceased to be members of locally organized chieftainships, becoming instead members of a complex western democracy.   The burden of accommodation has fallen on Maoris, whose relationship with Europeans has been characterized by frequent mutual misunderstandings and antagonisms.   As Europeans inexorably took over New Zealand land and imposed their own institutions, Maoris responded with armed combat, religious iconoclasm, appeals to the judiciary and to the Crown, and recently with organized political protest. Two hundred years after the arrival of Captain Cook, a legacy of suspicion and distrust inheres in relations between Maori and European.

In the twentieth century, Maoris are a minority whose place in the larger New Zealand social context has been subject to almost constant redefinition.   As in many other aspects of Maori experience, compromise has proved to be an effective tool.   Resisting assimilation, Maoris have instead adapted many of their traditional institutions to accommodate the European presence and their own minority status.   The changing role of women can be understood only in terms of the more encompassonly ing alterations only in the Maori social world.   To a significant degree, the power that older women wield today is the consequence of a cultural hiatus that has granted formal recognition to the informal influence that women have always exercised.

Many traditional customs and ideals have gained a new purpose as they now serve to differentiate Maori from Pakeha, (the widely used

New Zealand term for 'European'). The contemporary importance of
Maori language, the enduring attachment to the land of one's ancestors, the retention of the *marae* 'ceremonial courtyard', the *hui* 'gathering', the *tangi* 'funeral and wake' are important for more than their
assertion of continuity with Maori traditions (Metge 1976:49). Such
cultural features maintain Maori distinctiveness in the face of strong,
often overwhelming forces towards assimilation.[3] Moreover, many
religious ideas have persisted, modified sufficiently to continue to lend
meaning to the contemporary situation. Underlying many superficial
changes, an enduring commitment to traditional ideology has prevailed
despite almost two centuries of mission activity.

Maoris are today slightly more than 10 percent of the New Zealand
population. However, they comprise a young and rapidly growing
ethnic group.[4] These two factors are certain to lead to major changes
in Maori-European relations and are likely to promote dramatic transformations within Maori culture. Several writers (Walsh 1973; Metge
1976; Macpherson 1977; King 1984) have voiced concern over the
probable racial tensions that will erupt as Maoris become more
numerous. While ethnic relations are not manifestly strained at
present, most Maoris, and recently some Pakehas, recognize that
discrimination and inequality permeate many New Zealand institutions.

No one can be sanguine about race relations in contemporary New
Zealand (Mol 1964; St. George 1972). There is a tendency not only
to segregate Maoris but to view their life style as inferior to that of
their lighter skinned compatriots. A. Joan Metge (1976:294) has noted
that the situation is aggravated by the use of stereotypes on both sides:
Pakehas consider Maoris to be childlike, happy-go-lucky and innately
musical; Maoris view Europeans as selfish, individualistic, and overly
preoccupied with material status. Although the expressed goal of the
government, and indeed of concerned citizens, is intergroup harmony,
the realization of such an ideal is, at present, elusive.

Maori and European segments of society are far from integrated,
although some areas reflect this more than others. Occupationally,
Maoris are in less skilled, less secure and lower paying jobs. There is a
consistently lower standard of living for Maoris: they suffer from a
greater susceptibility to disease, a lower life expectancy, and a higher
rate of infant mortality when compared to the European population.[5]

Furthermore, Maoris are by no means insulated from the problems
of European life or from the difficulties posed by the need to adapt to
two worlds. Mental hospital admissions for Maoris are on the rise,
prompting this comment from A.C. Walsh, a New Zealand demogra-
pher:

...showing a more significant proportion of Maoris being admitted to mental hospitals suffering from schizophrenia suggests increasing tensions in the Maori population. The cause is not known, but one is tempted to suppose that it could have something to do with difficulties in maintaining dual cultural identity or in choosing between different sets of cultural values (1973:30).

Unfortunately, such choices have become an essential part of Maori experience.[6]

The most radical change has occurred since World War II as Maoris, especially the young, have increasingly become urban dwellers. Michael King has written (1984:250):

And the combination of rural population displacement, urbanization, and a relative lack of educational qualification among Maori workers produced a brown proletariat in New Zealand cities, a situation that some commentators viewed as a dangerous ingredient in urban race relations.

Both Forster and Ramsey (1970:202) and King (1984) have noted the self-reinforcing and self-perpetuating aspects of urban poverty. Lower standards of education, lower income and underemployment, poor housing and health, and high crime rates all interact with and reinforce one another, making it unlikely that the situation will improve much in the next generation.

Inevitably there has been a rupture between those who have turned to the city and those left behind in the relatively underdeveloped rural hinterlands. The experiences of the rural elders do not really touch on the concerns of their urban grandchildren. However the connections between urban youths and rural elders are far from tenuous. Significantly, it is women who initiate and maintain such ties. Nevertheless there are conflicting tensions in Maori culture: on the one hand there is respect, if not longing, for a heritage that some feel is on the wane. On the other hand, the traditional basis of leadership, elder status, must be redefined and adapted to a changing world.

GENDER IDEOLOGY AND AGING

Cultural ideology among Maoris emphasizes the importance of men over women.   While in fact many activities are cooperative in nature, most tasks are accomplished in complementary, if separate, spheres. Gender relations are discussed in terms of complementarity, but in the Maori case, complementarity does not suggest equality.[7] This is because there are public and symbolic dimensions accorded to the performances of men that are absent in the case of women. In all ceremonial gatherings, whether they be festive celebrations or solemn occasions of mourning, men and women work side by side, but in essentially separate domains. Nevertheless, such separation does permit the ready establishment of solidarity with members of one's own sex and thus produces important allies in the later years (see Dominy, chapter 3 and Sinclair 1984).

In most areas of Maori life men retain preeminence, especially in public oratory and genealogical expertise.   This is a view shared by women who, although aware of their own considerable abilities, nevertheless defer to men. This gender inequality has its source in a cultural ideology that affirms both male ritual purity and female pollution.[8] Men, therefore, have access to activities from which most women are excluded.

Traditionally, rules that limited women because of their inherent uncleanness and contamination essentially kept women from activities deemed critical to the continued well-being of the society (Heuer 1969).   Such proscriptions made a clear public statement for "to express female uncleanliness is to express female inferiority" (Douglas 1975:62). Pollution beliefs attest not only to the difference between men and women but express as well the cultural conviction that legitimacy is a male preserve.

Notions of female pollution worked to maintain a strict division of labor by separating male and female domains.   Thus women were excluded from all canoes under construction, from all house sites and from all ritual activities. Heuer contends that

> ...the presence of women or more precisely of the female organs, was deemed destructive to sacredness, as was the presence of cooked food. For this reason, there were no women priests; women were however, not infrequently seers or mediums for lesser gods (1969:477-478).

Women's life giving powers were handled with suitable gravity; strict proscriptions limited the activities of menstruating or pregnant women. Entire areas of the social and physical landscape were declared off limits. Violations of these rules were believed to produce striking consequences: shellfish would leave a beach that was tainted by the presence of a menstruating woman, muttonbirds would similarly flee their traps, and crops would fail (Best 1905:215; Heuer 1969:466-7).

For many aspects of contemporary Maori life, such beliefs are no longer relevant. Nevertheless there is a consistent core of notions surrounding female pollution, a core that concentrates on female genitals and/or female processes such as menstruation and childbirth. Young girls are instructed never to walk over a male and to refrain from sitting on a table where food is to be served. In a society where scarcity of water means shared baths, men always bathe first. The message is unequivocal, despite two centuries of social change: women are polluted and polluting, in many ways inimical to ordered social life.

Many women work outside the home today. They are not only more involved in the larger New Zealand economy, but their role in community Maori affairs is increasingly active and public. In the two rural communities in which I have worked there were numerous tribal committees, with important decision making powers, that were comprised of both sexes. However, one of the most important of modern phenomena is the single sex committee, such as the Maori Women's Welfare League, in which women attain local and, not infrequently, national recognition.[9] Inevitably then, as other observers have pointed out, the "role of women has changed with changing family and community structure, the possibility of wage earning, and the creation of powerful groups such as the Maori Women's Welfare League" (Salmond 1979:49).

As men and women mature, they move formally into the position of *kaumatua* 'elder'. Men are now called *koro* 'male elder', women *kuia* 'female elder'. The prominence of both men and women is especially notable at major ceremonial events. At such times, Maori identity and the creation of a uniquely Maori context constitute a major focus.

Men should be able to demonstrate competence in oratory, genealogical knowledge, and traditional history and lore. While in the past young men of high rank were specifically instructed so that they could assume their positions in the community upon their fathers' deaths, today young men are prepared for these responsibilities only through observation. No longer is systematic instruction available (Winiata 1967:87).

The *kuia* 'female elder' is defined as the complement of the *kaumatua* 'elder'. Winiata writes:

> Her duties are primarily of a domestic nature; while the
> *kaumatua* delivers his oratorical efforts in welcome to distin-
> guished visitors, it is the *kuia* who is responsible for arranging the
> catering and the accommodation for the visitors (Ibid:90).

Many of the responsibilities assigned to women (especially the more
tedious) can be undertaken by younger females. Thus their tutelage
begins early and is characterized by considerable continuity. Winiata
tells us that the status and duties of the 'female elder' "are more clear
today than they were in traditional society, where she seems to have
been overshadowed" *(Ibid.)*. Moreover, in general women outlive men,
and as traditions become attenuated it is women who know tribal lore
and who become the major arbiters of community morality. The
increased activity of older women is also indicated by their proficiency
in and understanding of Maori culture, a proficiency that allows them
to be mediators between the two cultural traditions of New Zealand.
Unlike men, whose expertise is directed into the community, the
knowledge these women control is often used to tutor the uninformed.
The role of such older women illustrates the complexity of the current
situation; their position is indebted to tradition but they are by no
means tradition bound. On the contrary, they bring to the problems
confronting the Maori a very modern sensibility.[10]

A woman's nurturant role does not end with the cessation of
fertility. The relative poverty of most Maoris makes the autonomous
self-supporting nuclear family an ideal that most Maoris could not
reach and which, in any case, does not appeal in the way that the
extended family does. Grandmothers babysit or take over the long-term
care of their grandchildren. For most, domestic life is incomplete
without at least one young child at home. Older women persist in
mediating and adjudicating the difficulties of culture change faced by
their adult children. Their continued closeness to their offspring and
their awareness of the difficulties they face have provided such women
both with allies and with a precise knowledge of the contemporary
social situation. By contrast, few men are knowledgeable about the
specific problems that confront their children.

In groups, or individually, these women also instruct the community
in traditional arts and crafts. They teach weaving and basketry, mat
making and flax dying, Maori songs and language to school children,
church groups, their own youth, and to curious Europeans. Their
continued intimacy with their grown children and their awareness of

the complexities of the contemporary situation draw the younger generation to them.

Traditional gender ideology, therefore, no longer constrains elderly women, but it frames the nature of their experience. These women have learned to operate in an essentially female universe and have grown adept at executing the responsibilities defined as suitable for such individuals. As women age, the restrictions of gender diminish, often permitting them to wield a reasonable amount of political authority. This is not a novel turn of events. Rather the contingencies of the colonial situation have enhanced the authority and influence that Maori women were traditionally permitted to claim.

Ideally, even in ceremonial affairs, women should have a supportive rather than an active role. Oratory and public speechmaking remain essentially masculine enterprises; women lend support by calling, wailing, and chanting.[11] But old women present a truly formidable interest group and through a variety of informal means see that the canons of etiquette are not breached. Salmond writes:

> This does not mean however that women are lacking in influence on the *marae* or elsewhere. It is notable that whenever a man oversteps the bounds of *marae* protocol, it is nearly always the women who carry out corrective action. If he speaks too long and fails to hold the attention of his audience, the old women become restless, whisper to each other, then make quite audible comments of *hoha* (boring). If these tactics fail, an elderly female relative of the speaker may stand and announce 'here is your song,' then start to sing, effectively cutting him off (1975:127).

The major insult, however, is *whakapohane* (this word has no English gloss) in which women express their disdain by bending over and lifting their skirts in contempt at the speaker.[12] In light of the discussion above, it is no accident that the display of a woman's genitals brings a sudden and abrupt halt to social interchange.

While in general women's exercise of authority is informal, consisting mainly of support functions, the role that these women regularly assume as social facilitators must not be overlooked. Elderly women are the chief mourners, sounding out the early cry for the dead, weeping with those closest to the deceased, and engineering many of the intricate details that demand attention at times of community crisis.[13] Although men participate, it is women who organize 'tramping', the ritual cleansing to make a house safe and liveable again after death. In a fundamental way, it is women who make living possible:

they stand at the ritual entrances and exits of social life and superintend most social events by facilitating social relations.[14]

MARAMATANGA

Over the course of two hundred years of culture contact, many Maori prophets have arisen. These men (and to a lesser extent women) possess gifts that include the ability to communicate with spirits of the dead and to imbue the world of their beleaguered followers with meaning and purpose. The means have varied; some religious leaders have urged separation, others passive resistance, while still others sought to demonstrate Maori spiritual ascendancy over European materialism. Whatever their means, each has attempted to create a social order in which to be a Maori is to be a valued social participant. All have blended mission Christianity with indigenous Maori religion. In this manner, critical Maori ways of looking at the world have been perpetuated. Moreover, for many contemporary individuals, the past has become a renewed source of interest; it is reexamined, reevaluated and ultimately reclaimed.

The deteriorating social position of Maoris in the twentieth century has strengthened the appeal of such prophetic movements. The men and women discussed in this chapter belong to one such movement, Maramatanga. The ideology and ritual of the movement reinforce the advantages conferred by old age, while counterbalancing the liabilities of gender. As is the case in many similar movements, Maramatanga sustains notions of value and merit among members of an essentially dispossessed group.

The various rituals of the movement indicate a concern for a knowledge of Maori language, of Maori art forms such as action songs, and for the complexities of Maori oratory which is frequently rich in metaphor and allusion. Moreover, the ideology and ritual of the movement evoke a comprehensible universe that permits the adherents to establish a sacred domain, a domain in which their Maoriness has come to have a positive value.

While the movement is affiliated with the Catholic Church, its ideology draws heavily upon both traditional Maori religion and the Maori prophetic tradition. The members of Maramatanga are all aware of the prophetic heritage and consciously view their movement as its culmination. They refer to themselves as the *kaimahi* 'the workers', the *hungaruarua* 'the chosen few', and to their beliefs as the *tikanga* 'the correct way'.

The movement is comprised of some three hundred people who, although geographically dispersed, are related through a complex weave of overlapping consanguineal and affinal ties. All are descendants of the original prophet, Te Mareikura. From descriptions, he emerges as a humble and gentle individual with considerable personal appeal. But it is his legacy and the work done by the women who succeeded him that make his followers unique. When his granddaughter died in the 1930s her grief-stricken mother made contact with her spirit before the girl was buried. At first, communication with a deceased individual was a terrifying prospect and the mother, though grieving, was reluctant to persist. An old woman (the mother of Mihi described below), forcefully insisted that the child be allowed to speak and the followers of Mareikura be permitted to hear what she had to say. From that time on, members maintain, 'the channels were opened' and successive generations of followers have communicated with the *wairua* 'spirits of the dead'. Mareikura is referred to as the 'last of the prophets'. In subsequent years, no leader has been necessary, for members hold that they now all have access to the spiritual world.

Thus the history of the movement is dominated by women. The girl described above became known as 'the messenger of love', her mother – the prophet's daughter – took over his work and formally renounced the necessity of future leaders, while the channels were opened by the obstinacy of yet another woman. Today, the importance of women continues. Although men participate, it is women who tend to receive messages, who return as 'spirits of the dead', and who maintain a close monitoring of human/spiritual relations. This is not surprising, for women's participation in Maramatanga gives them a voice equal to that of men. Women can and do engage in public speechmaking and have moved into many domains previously reserved only for men. When traveling or receiving visitors, however, the behavior of women is frequently modified to accord with prevailing Maori tradition. Middle aged and elderly women, who are free from domestic pressures, participate more vigorously that does any other segment of Maramatanga's membership.

Equality has replaced hierarchy. Indeed, the ideology of the movement is unequivocally equalitarian, stressing the equality of Maori and European, old and young, male and female. This suggests a dispensation that will eradicate status distinctions typical of contemporary New Zealand society.

Deceased friends and relatives commune with their descendants, warning of coming adversity, counselling in times of trouble, and supplying the living with a continuing source of songs that win them acclaim in major cultural competitions. While on occasion the spirits may divulge information of cosmic significance, they are just as likely to comment on the domestic affairs of the present membership. In life they were fairly intimate with the present participants in the movement and would, therefore, be expected to approach the world in much the same manner. Consequently, their motives are seldom suspect and their messages generally have a reasonable amount of credibility and authority.

The rituals of the movement depend largely on a knowledge and understanding of traditional art forms; oratory, singing, and chanting must be performed with skill and facility. The extent to which women participate competer.tly indicates their capacity to master and to retain traditional cultural forms. Such activities clearly preserve the past but, far more importantly, they sustain the value of the present. By defining the work of the ancestors as worthwhile, as worthy of preservation, they have legitimated their position as Maoris in contemporary New Zealand. Moreover, the triumphs that accompany participation (the successful pilgrimages, the admired songs, the victories in cultural competitions), all enhance women's status and prestige in the eyes of the membership.

On several occasions throughout the year, kinship ties and individual commitments are activated in a series of celebrations known as *ras* that commemorate important events in the spiritual history of the movement. At such times, those members who are able gather to discuss spiritual matters and to avail themselves of Maori hospitality. Commensality and solidarity are often explicit themes; traditional inequalities based on rank, geneology, and gender are deemed insignificant.

That the membership of Maramatanga is elderly is not surprising. Most middle aged and elderly individuals were present in the early days of the movement's history and share intimate knowledge of the individuals and circumstances involved in the movement's founding. Moreover, discussions of messages and analyses of dreams are conducted almost solely in Maori. Lacking both the nostalgia for early days and the necessary proficiency in Maori language, young people are tempted to see much of what goes on as irrelevant to their immediate interests. But, on the other hand, they have witnessed the successes of their elders and the attribution of these to participation in Maramatanga. Furthermore, their urban experiences have taught them that success in a Pakeha world, on Pakeha terms, is a formidable undertaking, one very likely beyond their grasp. An organized kin group, with a structured belief system does, therefore, exert some appeal. Many young people are struggling to learn the language and to acquaint themselves with a basic understanding of the movement's tenets. In turn, their experience is characterized by more stability than is common for urban migrants from other groups. Their contacts and ties with their home *marae* 'ceremonial courtyard' tend to be maintained through women: their mothers, aunts, and grandmothers.

Finally, it is only those women past childbearing age who are capable of full participation in a movement such as Maramatanga. Tied neither to jobs nor to persistent domestic responsibilities, members are free to travel to *ras* 'celebrations', to go on pilgrimages (see Sinclair n.d.), and to represent the movement and its interests at gatherings sponsored by the church and by other Maori organizations.

Many women attribute the ease with which they are able to assume their increased ritual obligations to spiritual assistance. But the 'spirits of the dead' have done more than assist them in the execution of their anticipated duties. Under their auspices, several women have become healers. Others have less spectacular gifts. But it is assumed that each woman has something to contribute and should, therefore, be accorded the respect due to an important, productive member of the community. Many of the women who now assume prominent community roles as 'female elders' credit their accomplishments to spiritual tutelage. Certainly, several life histories reveal a coincident pattern of commitment to Maramatanga and ceremonial and ritual expertise.

To a much greater degree than men, women use what they have learned from Maramatanga to take an active role in the affairs of the wider society. Several women participate at all levels of church organization. Far from being alienated from Catholicism, members of Maramatanga have assumed an elite role in the administration of the Maori Mission. It is women, and not men, who serve on district and parish committees for the Catholic Church. Maintaining ties with the church in this manner involves women in concerns that transcend those of the local community. For it is in such tribunals, which are often overwhelmingly European in membership, that the tricky area of interethnic relations is an explicit item for discussion. The church has also come to depend on women to do most of its community public relations work. Indeed, institutions outside the community, such as the church and the schools, generally gain access to Maoris through women. By their continued involvement in these institutions and by their enduring commitment to their children and grandchildren, women have come to understand a European dominated social world (see Dominy, chapter 3, for a discussion of this from a Pakeha perspective).

Membership in Maramatanga allows women to confront and overcome their marginality. As Maoris and as women, they are at a serious social disadvantage. However, these liabilities become somewhat less significant in the face of women's demonstrated spiritual ascendancy. Religious activity thus encourages women to redefine their roles and to be more than mere complements of men.

Men who are active in the movement will also frequently preside over their home *marae* 'ceremonial courtyards', a prerogative they hold as 'elders'. But their participation tends to be limited to a Maori context. By contrast, women reach out far more extensively and are involved in far more community activities. In their communities women's influence may be seen in their organization of various committees and in the long hours they contribute to the instruction of willing novices in the intricacies of traditional Maori arts and crafts. Many of the women were active in organizing several gatherings in which young members of the kin group were called home from the city to learn of their spiritual heritage. Here the equality of men and women was especially obvious for it was women who organized and then dominated the proceedings.

For Europeans, these women often provide examples of a noble past heritage distilled for contemporary New Zealand consumption.[15] For Maoris, they represent a capacity to use traditions to define, but not to limit, a behavioral and symbolic repertoire that is exclusively Maori. Moreover, the kinds of skills women possess make them focal points for the younger generation who are searching for a way to apply their Maoriness to their present circumstances. Women rather than men have become effective culture brokers. These women, elderly and involved in a religious movement, are witnessing the transformation of Maori culture. But women who are comfortable with tradition and yet who can simultaneously accommodate themselves to modern directions have a considerable contribution to make.

Mihi

Mihi provides us with an example of a woman whose position expanded as she aged. Because her influence and stature grew as her familiarity with Maoriness increased in her later years, she attributed much of her success to her involvement in Maramatanga.

The last child in a very large family, she spent her youth being spoiled and petted. Unlike her older siblings, especially females, she was given no responsibilities. Although her mother was one of the principal founders of Maramatanga (perhaps the most influential of all the older women in the 1930s) Mihi seldom felt it necessary to participate in any of the rituals that she witnessed as she grew up. In large part this is due to particular historical conditions. Maori leaders, such as Sir Peter Buck and Sir Apirana Ngata, urged the assimilation of Maoris. Her earliest experiences with the movement occurred in adolescence, when her mother took her to the settlement of one of the most notable of Maori female prophets, Mere Rikiriki. There, Mihi was cured of the illness that had prompted her mother to seek help. However, although she was far from a nonbeliever, Mihi was certainly not motivated by a strong commitment to the belief system of Maramatanga, although she had strong affection for its members. At eighteen she married and almost immediately had her first of thirteen children. Despite the fact that she and her husband spoke Maori, they taught their children only English, again a concession to the prevailing sentiments of Maori leaders. As a result, her children participated only minimally in Maori rituals, while she and her husband turned their attention to predominantly domestic concerns. She kept abreast of what was happening in the movement because of the continued involvement of her kinspeople, most notably her mother, brother, and several of her nieces, who had married prominent movement men. In general however, she demonstrated little concern with traditional Maori ways – relegating such interest to feast days and funerals. She was therefore on the fringes of Maramatanga until, in her fifties, she was widowed, with few children remaining at home.

Increasingly after the death of her husband, Mihi reinvolved herself with her kinspeople and with Maori tradition. She, too, received messages from the spirits. One message facilitated her acquisition of a house from the Department of Maori Affairs. As she approached her sixties, she became the senior woman of her community, relying on spiritual assistance to learn the chants and prayers that mark the performance of a female elder.

Soon after her husband's death, she was inspired with the design for one of the movement's flags and started to attend the ritual occasions of the movement more regularly. It was at this time, too, that her arena expanded considerably; she was asked to speak before Parliament (an event that she prepared for by studying in the meeting house and brushing up on her genealogies), she became active in community committees, and initiated a local chapter of the Maori Women's Welfare League. As a middle aged widow, she travelled all over the country, attending the opening of meeting houses and commemorating the celebrations and funerals of friends and kin.

In general, she was held up by the European community as the ideal Maori *kuia* 'female elder', dignified and knowledgeable. More effectively than almost any other Maori in her community, she explained

Maori ways to the European. Similarly, she had a profound understanding, culled from years of experience, of the Pakeha point of view.
As a public figure within Maramatanga, she became one of the
strongest proponents of the belief system. In matters of Maori tradition, her children, nieces and nephews consistently turned to her for
guidance and interpretation. Publicly she organized gatherings and
officiated at the more solemn occasions.

Her activities in and commitment to Maramatanga increased. She
figured prominently both as an elder in the movement and as a 'female
elder' to those outside. Her coincident activity in the movement, and
her ability to command the repertoire attendant upon old Maori women
were, in her mind, interwoven. Indeed, her heritage and her participation in the movement prepared her for the crucial public role that she
was to occupy. The movement's ties to past Maori achievement and
her mother's forceful personality provided the background necessary for
her later preeminent position. Her increased political and social activities derived from her status as an old woman and were reinforced by
her involvement in a religious movement that provided her both with a
forum and an ideology to make a significant contribution.

GENDER, AGING, AND RELIGION

Maramatanga illustrates that social and cultural change need not,
inevitably, contribute to a decline in the status of women (Boserup
1970). On the contrary, participation in this religious movement would
seem to confer prestige upon women within the movement and within a
wider social context. In colonial situations, such religious innovations
are especially effective because they can address themselves to the
crucial question of equality. The entire Maori prophetic tradition,
spanning almost two hundred years, has confronted the issue of Maori
subordination and Pakeha domination. While the initial intention might
have been only the suggestion of equality between conquered and
conqueror, it is not difficult to extend its scope to include relations
between men and women. In the case of Maramatanga, equality
explicitly has this dimension. Thus women have gained prestige not
only as a result of their spiritual ascendancy, nor solely as a consequence of aging, but because for both reasons they are held up as
models of Maori society for both Maori and European audiences. The
informal power that Maori women have always held has been transformed as these women have become instruments, not victims, of social
change. What has happened to Maori men? As they age, Maori men

certainly acquire ceremonial expertise and prestige, but the context in which they perform becomes more limited and circumscribed. Unlike women, their focus in old age is the Maori community. Why is this the case?

The answer may be found in the continuity of roles begun much earlier in the life cycle. These women grew up in a world in which the prevailing cultural ideology maintained a strict separation and inequality between the sexes. Despite the existence and prominence of the female founders of the movement, who would surely serve as models at a later time, many women framed their social contributions in terms of a supportive role: they socialized children, maintained a home, and assisted with the tedious details of community organization. Men had jobs and were involved in ceremonial activities. The consequence of this division of labor is the apparent attention of women to mundane details and the ostensible preoccupation of men with more esoteric and, implicitly, more important matters. But "ultimately everyday decisions shape everyday life" (Myerhoff 1978:245) and few Maori women hesitated to exercise authority in that sphere.[16] In the final analysis it is Maori men who operate in a much more circumscribed arena, while it has been Maori women who have confronted European society – in the form of European shopkeepers, school administrators, community leaders – and learned to communicate with it.

Indeed, although the 'female elders' in Maramatanga now stand beside the men on ceremonial occasions, they continue many of the activities that are defined as suitable for women. They shop, sew, prepare for gatherings, minister to the sick, and maintain a high level of participation in community and civic activities. By contrast, Maori men are insulated by Maori 'mates' on the job and by kinsmen in other aspects of their lives. They invest little of their identity in commerce with the world of European affairs. While the social universe of women expands, that of men contracts. For elderly men, who were clearly highly esteemed within the boundaries of Maramatanga, there was a much bigger gap between their status in the movement and their position in the community. This was not true for old women, who enjoyed high status in both arenas. Moreover, as "custodians of the mundane world" (Myerhoff 1978) women, especially widows, are often raising one or two grandchildren. While men may playfully fondle a young child, women continue to be active socializers well into old age. They are especially effective because they have stayed in touch with a changing world. Thus, the lives of women are not marred by the dichotomies that characterize the social lives of men (see Flinn chapter

4, Carucci chapter 6, and for a contrasting case Counts and Counts chapter 7). By contrast, women's lives demonstrate far more continuity and integration.

Participation in a religious movement such as Maramatanga is an effective strategy in a colonial situation, for it provides an arena where a dispossessed marginal group may define its worth and dignity. For Maori women, traditionally defined as even more marginal than men, religious activities grant a fuller measure of social participation. These old women have a twofold advantage: they have the authority that age grants them and knowledge that is rare and valuable in a colonial situation.[17] Women, not men, are *bricoleurs* in this situation, both because they have always been and continue to be more accessible to the young and because they have created ties to the European community. Over their lifetimes they have come to terms with, and they have raised their children to adjust to, the Pakeha world. Then, in old age, armed with the status of 'female elder' and the assistance of the 'spirits of the dead', they have forged a distinctly Maori identity. Such accommodations require an intricate knowledge of human beings and of social relations. Perhaps the perpetuation of Maoriness depends not so much on the maintenance of oratory or arts and crafts – although certainly these are visible symbols of ethnic identity – but upon the inculcation of certain values, certain ways of looking at the world. This is the province of women, who teach and display, reinforce and sanction what lies at the heart of Maoriness.

NOTES

The research for this paper is based on two years of fieldwork in 1971-1973 financed by a National Science Foundation Research Traineeship and a Fulbright fellowship, and in the summer of 1982 assisted by a sabbatical and faculty research grant provided by Eastern Michigan University.

1.   Several writers (notably Gutmann 1975; 1980) and Neugarten (1982) have stressed the androgyny of later life.

2.   While *kaumatua* means elder with all the attendant connotations of prestige and ritual responsibility, *kuia* and *koro* may be glossed as 'female and male grandparent' respectively. While this gives some indication of the markers of old age, by itself it is insufficient. Many women in their forties with grandchildren eschewed the title *kuia.* I was told that while everybody ages, not everyone can qualify for this status, which accords prestige and honor.

3.   Rangi Walker (1972: 61) has written:

> While the primary purpose of Maori institutions is to
> perpetuate Maori identity with the social mainstream of
> New Zealand Society, they can also be construed to be

> an adaptive mechanism. In addition to providing an
> alternative value system from that derived from
> Euro-American culture, they give training in social skills
> that enable the individual to adjust more readily to the
> major social system.... The destruction of what remains
> of traditional Maori society by the pressures of urbanism
> and the continued application of assimilative policies of
> the decision makers in the interest of social equality
> (meaning social uniformity) will create more problems
> than it will solve.

4. According to Walsh (1973:4) the Maori population doubled between 1945 and 1966
    and should double again between 1966 and 1985. More importantly, in this time
    period the number of women of reproductive age should also double. Furthermore,
    half the population was under 15 in the 1971 census.

5. In a preliminary report of the 1981 census, 10 percent of Pakeha men were classed
    as professional/administrative while just over 2 percent of Maori males fell into that
    category. Similarly, less than a third of European males were laborers while almost
    half the Maori men were so labelled. In 1969 (the 1981 statistics were not available
    at this time) Maori infant mortality was 29.8/1000 compared to 18/1000 for
    Pakehas. Similarly, while a European man can expect to live 69.2 years, the life
    expectancy for Maori males is 59. In education, 47.3 percent of the European
    population had school certificate or more while only 13.1 percent of Maoris had
    reached this level of educational attainment (cited by Walsh 1973).

6. Maori women are by no means exempt from these tensions. While one of the major
    points in this chapter is the contention that women flourish in old age, it should be
    clear that the current situation is far from stress free. Maori women have the
    highest death rate from lung cancer in the world, while hypertension represents a
    significant problem. Blank (1980) maintains that these figures suggest that Maoris
    are subject to strains for which they have inadequate coping mechanisms and for
    which they have inadequate health care available.

7. Jane and James Ritchie make a similar point (1979:95). They write: "The roles are
    certainly complementary, but they are not equal."

8. Hanson (1982) has recently argued against the existence of female pollution in
    Polynesia generally and for Maoris specifically.

9. Kernot has written that the League is essentially conservative, emphasizing tradi-
    tional Maori values (1975:232).

10. Winiata (1967:170) writes:

> Here we see one of the important, though rather
> contradictory roles of the women leaders – and for that
> matter of all Maori European sponsored leaders. They
> frequently provide a focus for protest. They embody
> Maori values, they support efforts towards Maori self
> determination, while at the same time attempting to
> refashion Maori society to conform more and more with
> the standards of the wider New Zealand society. They
> are nevertheless, behaving consistently with the circum-
> stances of their living in both a Maori and a European
> world.

11. Salmond (1975:43) notes that women of high rank on the East Coast may on occa-
    sion speak on the *marae* 'ceremonial courtyard'. She writes:

> ...but they do so because their descent entitles them to

act as honorary 'men'. A woman taking this role will often begin by declaring 'kia whakatane au i ahau.' (Let me make myself a man)... Even then her rank must be impeccable if she is not to be challenged and if she should stand on a *marae* outside her home territory, the reaction is likely to be immediate and furious.

12. Kernot (personal communication) has pointed out the consistency of *whakapohane* with notions of female pollution.

13. The ambiguous position of women, their polluting characteristics, link them ideologically with death. In mythology, Death is conceptualized as a woman who kills the culture hero by entrapping him in her genitals. It is not surprising, then, that death work in the Maori community is undertaken by women. This point is elaborated elsewhere (see Sinclair 1985).

14. The interrelationship is expressed in a Maori proverb, quoted by Winiata *"Kia tika mai o muri, ka tika atu a mua."* ("It is when the back – i.e. the catering – is working well, that success comes to the front – i.e. to the public part played by the *kaumatua"* 'male elder' [1967:91]).

15. Because it is expressed in so different a mode from that used in Western society, women's power and authority is seldom recognized by Europeans.

16. Michèle Dominy (chapter 3) writes of the same continuity for Pakeha women and notes that, for them, the role of mother continues to lend meaning to their existence as they age.

17. Pamela Amoss (1981) points out that for the Coast Salish, the status of the elders is enhanced by their importance in maintaining Salish ethnic identity. Similarly, Schweitzer (1983) notes that Indians have social supports within their community that buttress them in old age. On the other hand, Maxwell and Watson (1977) indicate that social change has contributed to the decline in the importance of Samoan elders.

3

GENDER COMPLEMENTARITY, AGING AND REPRODUCTION AMONG NEW ZEALAND PAKEHA WOMEN

Michèle D. Dominy

INTRODUCTION

In this chapter, I argue that the actions of older New Zealand (Pakeha) women are motivated by an ideology of motherhood.[1] These actions reflect the primacy of the domestic sphere through the life cycle. In addition, the actions suggest a redefinition of the boundaries of the domestic sphere and an extension of its influence into the public domain. These older women, whom I call traditionalists, use a biological model to explain female uniqueness as resting in the power of, and control of, reproduction and sexuality. Women control maleness through ideas of social purity and socially transform biology through motherhood.

Both age and gender provide women with certain resources and constraints within which they must maneuver to achieve their goals and to generate meaning in their lives. Cool and McCabe (1983), for example, destroy the myth of women as "scheming hags" or "dear old things" and illustrate instead the paths by which women gain power and satisfaction in later life, increasing their status most significantly through female solidarity groups. Menopausal and postmenopausal Pakeha women negotiate their status in the extra-domestic world of voluntary activity by employing an ideology of motherhood as a strategy for preserving the primacy of their domestic roles. While grandmothers often perpetuate their role as nurturers in a domestic sphere by caring for grandchildren (Kerns 1983; Moore 1978), they often work, as do these Pakeha women, through an extended sphere of voluntary activity to control the reproductive lives of their children. Increasingly, the role of female solidarity groups in women's experience of aging is stressed by researchers (Barnett and Baruch 1978; Davis

1983; Fennell 1981; Keith 1983).

Involvement in common-interest associations is a key strategy for traditionalists in establishing and maintaining their power. As studies of women-centered kin networks in complex societies (Bott 1971; Smith 1976; Stack 1974; Yanagisako 1977; Young and Willmott 1957) and of female solidarity groups in general (Cassell 1977; Fallers and Fallers 1976; Freedman 1979; Okonjo 1976; Van Allen 1976) have shown, female bonding gives women control of important information and influence. Women are recognized as information brokers who can mediate social relations within the family and between the family and larger society by seeking alliance and social support from other women (Nelson 1974; Riegelhaupt 1967; Smith 1976). Boundaries between domestic and public categories are blurred as women create a public world of their own. Here my primary concern is the increasing political significance and meaning of extra-domestic ties and friendships between women over the course of the life cycle (Hoffer 1974; Leis 1974; Myerhoff 1978; Wolf 1972). Cross-cultural accounts of women's status must compare the social lives of young and post-reproductive women (Kerns 1983:193).[2] While younger women may also ascribe to an ideology of motherhood and belong to the traditionalist analytic category, older women dominate and predominate in associations. In particular, this ideology in which biology provides a model for femaleness remains constant for traditionalists regardless of age and yet is problematic for older women as they lose their reproductive powers.

Similarly, Kerns argues for Black Carib women that social identity derives from motherhood and reflects a constant concern for children throughout the life cycle despite the loss of reproductive capacity. Elsewhere, Kerns (1984:1) writes of the control post-reproductive Black Carib women maintain over the sexual activity of their children. She especially has noted the importance of focussing on the links between the loss of women's reproductive capacity and the "public and collective aspects" of their actions (Kerns 1983:191). Sinclair (chapter 2) points to the "expanding social universe" and increased involvement in female solidarity groups of postmenopausal women as their concerns extend beyond the domestic sphere. Maori women, like Pakeha women, seem to develop extensive ties as they become involved in community activities.[3]

Data are drawn from research conducted with the National Council of Women (NCW) in Christchurch, New Zealand. The organization has 109 delegates who represent 53 organizations and who attend meetings monthly. Despite the diverse range of women in attendance at the meetings, the leadership group is self-selecting in that young women and radical women tire of being in a minority and frequently step down after one or two terms. Because of its heavy time demands, NCW draws on the older, non-working woman whose family is grown.[4] Few of these women are single and most are mothers. As a result, I focus upon the nature of power of traditionalist older women who are in the process of dispersion or fission in the developmental cycle of the household (Fortes 1958). This process begins with the departure of the oldest child from the household. The implicit basis of comparison is the phase of expansion from marriage until completion of the family of procreation.

Age differentiation, like gender, creates conceptual categories based on the perception of natural differences (La Fontaine 1978:2). Such a perspective recognizes the significance of the sociocultural context. Elsewhere I have examined variations in gender conceptions between women in shared sociocultural contexts to illustrate the multiplicity and complexity of roles for women.[5] Such roles have often been simplified in the literature by the tendency to search for universal explanations of sexual asymmetry. Often such explanations rely on biological differences. A more useful approach is to interpret the logical and cultural meaning of such categories from a symbolic perspective. Aging, like gender, as Counts and Counts (chapter 7) have argued, is explained less by biological factors than by social factors and demands a similar focus on sociocultural context and on indigenous concepts. Following MacCormack's lead (1980:18), I argue that the meanings attributed to the domestic/public spheres of activity, like those she attributes to the nature/culture concept, are as socially defined as are the meanings attributed to female and male.[6] My recent research has evaluated the use and application in a western context, of the domestic/public model developed by Michelle Rosaldo (1974, 1980) by looking at how women use the model as an emic category to make sense of their position and role in society and to provide them with a model for change. The categories, content and evaluation of gender may change at any time during the life cycle if such categories are defined by criteria other than sexual appearance and behavior. My analysis does not root femaleness in biology and maleness in the social domain, but rather suggests that biology serves as a model for traditionalist women's gender concepts. Reproduction as a biological function is socially transformed, and as Weiner (1979) has argued for the Trobriands, is significant for the regeneration of social relations. An increasing emphasis placed on the social transformation of reproduction accompanies the aging process for Pakeha women in New Zealand society.

Why should older women promote an ideology of motherhood and conceptualize femaleness in terms of reproduction? The answer lies in the changing interpretation and significance of reproduction, in the control of children's reproduction, and in an expansion of the domestic world of familial relations.

My data contribute to a central concern of some of the articles in this volume – an examination of the articulation of gender differentiation and age differentiation, and of aging as strategic social interaction in which the elderly manipulate their social and cultural worlds and negotiate status to gain power and satisfaction in later life. I do not argue, as Sinclair (chapter 2) does for the Maori, that strongly polarised gender distinctions in early life are balanced by gender muting or reversal for the aged; nor do I argue, as Lepowsky (chapter 8) does for sexually egalitarian Vanatinai, that there is no discontinuity between the status and influence of premenopausal and postmenopausal women. Instead I suggest that gender differentiation is continuously elaborated throughout the life cycle even though the specific role content associated with gender may change, especially as women lose their reproductive potential and extend the boundaries of the domestic into the public sphere (see also Flinn, chapter 4, and Kirkpatrick, chapter 5). Pakeha traditionalist women negotiate their status in the extra-domestic world of voluntary activity by employing the strategy of an ideology of motherhood to preserve the primacy of their domestic roles.

TRADITIONALISM

Traditionalist conceptions of social activity imply acceptance of the domestic/public model as formulated by Rosaldo: "...the domestic sphere built around reproduction, affective and familial bonds; [and the public]...providing for collectivity, jural order and social cooperation..." (1980:397). While traditionalist Pakeha women believe that their activities in the domestic sphere should be valued equally with those of men in the public sphere, they also believe that these activities should be maintained as separate and female. One important aspect of domestic activity is public voluntary activity which traditionalists subsume under the rubric of homemaking. In extending the meaning of the term domestic, elderly traditionalists are attempting to preserve the status quo while simultaneously extending the dimensions of influence from the home to the community.

We can begin to see how older traditionalists' conception of themselves as women is linked to an acceptance of the status quo by examining their use of Christchurch's founding myths. These origin myths portray a pioneering image and strong family role for women and, therefore, provide a blueprint from the past for the power these New Zealand women perceive themselves to wield in the present. New Zealand mothers have a sense of total control over the family and a "sort of self-imposed yoke of responsibility to an abstract concept of society that can neither be avoided, fulfilled nor be validated..." (Ritchie and Ritchie 1973:83).

Historically, two conceptions of Christchurch's past prevail. One argues for a massive settlement by commoner colonists who sought to escape the pressures of industrialization; the other argues for settlement by an elite, cultured segment of the English gentry. Both versions of the past say that class distinctions were impossible to maintain in the new colony; both portray the New Zealand settler as hardworking and pioneering, with drive and initiative. The former conception attributes these characteristics to the conviction of those wishing to establish a classless society different from Britain; the latter to the conviction of religious belief.

Both commoner and gentry myths are especially significant in providing for traditionalist female images, either of the strong pioneering woman who had to work beside her husband or of the iconoclastic woman whose ideals were born of religious conviction and pioneering spirit. One prominent Christchurch woman suggested that this heritage was not one of conservatism but rather of strength born of religious conviction to fight for what was right; thus, Christchurch has always been in the forefront both as the birthplace of suffrage in New Zealand (1893) and as the home of National Council of Women (NCW), founded in 1896.

Elderly traditionalists negotiate status and perpetuate the status quo through their willingness to adopt a strict parliamentary model of procedure in the workings of NCW.[7] Consensus on rules of order and the use of formal titles and dress, polite speech, and a commitment to the consequences of such rules which function to distance women from each other as individuals, serve to stress their roles in NCW as delegates, that is, as representatives of constituencies who work through the organization.[8] Procedure, like politeness as a communicative form, is "rational, strategic, face-oriented behavior" (Brown 1980:114). Procedure and politeness as strategies share a set of connections with social categories such that strategy reflects social motivations. Their use as strategies to perpetuate status varies between women and implies choice which, Penelope Brown (1980) has argued, both saves and promotes face. Older NCW women favor decorum, propriety and formality, which reflect uniquely female values of respectability. As I shall discuss later, in defining female reproductive biology as central, post-reproductive traditionalists are concerned with the social transformation of biology through forms of social control such as politeness, formal procedure and motherhood. Such forms of control permeate NCW activity. In other words, social conduct and procedure result in social forms which are both based on conservative ideology and function to sustain it.

As an ideology, traditionalism must preserve elements of the status quo while simultaneously transforming other elements to protect it against threats of change from competing ideologies. Eisenstadt (1974:19) describes traditionalism as "...an ideological mode and stance, a mode oriented against...new symbols, making some parts of the older tradition into the only legitimate symbols of the traditional order and upholding them to counter 'new' trends." The women, therefore, maintain the categories of female and male, domestic and public, while at the same time altering the connotation of those categories by changing their content and evaluation. Thus, they argue that the structural category of domestic should be complementary, but not subordinate, to the public and be rooted in women's reproductive biological capacities while also expanding to encompass aspects of the public domain by fostering extra-domestic ties.

THE IDEOLOGY OF MOTHERHOOD

The National Council of Women unites women for mutual counsel and cooperation, promotes the spiritual, moral, civil and social welfare of the community, and works for the legal, economic and social advancement of women. These women's roles flourish at the community level through their voluntary activity. Voluntary organizations are particularly concerned with promoting community health centers and services for the elderly that are family oriented. They enable post-reproductive traditionalist women to protect the primacy of the domestic sphere by extending its boundaries into the public domain and into the activities of the nation as a whole. Thus, the domestic sphere is not merely the domain of home and family.

The following case study focuses on the establishment of a subcommittee of the Christchurch NCW branch, composed primarily of members of two groups – the Society for the Protection of the Unborn Child (SPUC) and the Abortion Law Reform Association of New Zealand (ALRANZ) – with a brief to "study the working of the Contraception, Sterilisation and Abortion Act (CSA) to ensure the welfare of women seeking abortions." An analysis of the subcommittee's study shows how older post-reproductive women (and the occasional non-reproductive and younger reproductive woman) attempt to control the reproductive activities of other people through their participation in SPUC and their adoption of a traditionalist stance. The analysis also shows how these women use a biological model of femaleness in which motherhood is central to conceptualize their gender.

The Society for the Protection of the Unborn Child (SPUC) and the Abortion Law Reform Association (ALRANZ) belong to the NCW in order to ensure that their respective stances are heard and to use the organization for their aims. SPUC's aim is to protect the life of the unborn child by supporting and protecting the CSA Act, passed in 1977 to control abortion in New Zealand and to require that any woman needing an abortion for reasons of health or because of rape must petition and receive approval from "certifying consultants." ALRANZ asserts the primacy of a "woman's right to choose" and is committed to repealing the current law and promoting social reforms to reduce unwanted pregnancies. Certainly, a spectrum of opinions ranged through SPUC and ALRANZ, but the opposition outlined above reflects the essential elements of their stances. Reproductive, non-reproductive and post-reproductive women, women who represent all stages in the adult life cycle, belonged to both groups although, on the whole, SPUC women were older. SPUC women, however, typify the traditionalist stance characterizing NCW and involve themselves in extensive voluntary activity throughout the organization. ALRANZ women participate in NCW only to challenge the conservative position and to use the mechanism of the organization to present their views about abortion to other women.

In April 1979, SPUC had brought to NCW a notice of motion for an amendment to the Guardianship Act which reads as follows:[9]

That because of the widespread public concern that the Guardianship Act does not require the consent or notification to Parents or Guardians, of girls under the age of sixteen having abortions, this branch discuss and forward recommendations to amend the Act so that notification must be given to Parents and Guardians. (NCW Christchurch Branch Agenda, April 17, 1979a).

SPUC's actions reflect a tendency to fight abortion on two levels: (1) to prohibit it entirely; and (2) to make it more difficult to attain by exercising and modifying current laws. The issue in this motion, while ultimately abortion rights, was stated to be the rights of parents versus the rights of children. Ironically, the consequence of SPUC's aim is to protect the right of the unborn child above those of the mother of that child, while the issue for these women is the right of parents to control the lives and reproductive rights of their children. Thus, for many women, control over reproductive issues persists beyond their own childbearing years.

Explicitly, those members of SPUC who argued for the motion reasoned that it would (1) affirm a woman's right to know what is happening to her daughter especially in light of laws which hold her responsible for criminal activities of children under the age of sixteen; (2) enable parents to discuss alternatives with their daughters prior to an abortion and to strengthen and support their daughters; (3) strengthen parent/child relationships, noting that in cases where they are already weak the Act can surely do no further harm; (4) prevent the diminution of family responsibility. Those members of ALRANZ who opposed the motion argued (1) that if children do not tell their parents they must have good reason and, (2) that in disturbed homes (i.e., those where child abuse or pregnancy from incest occurs) a child who cannot consult her parents should not be forced to tell them.

The SPUC stance implies that "a woman's right to know" is based on her identity as a mother and that decisions about matters such as abortion should be made within the domestic unit – an ideal unit characterized by love and support – rather than in the public sphere, i.e., a doctor's office or a feminist-oriented agency such as the Family Planning Association. SPUC is also opposed to abortion. This opposition, I contend, is rooted not only in a desire to protect the unborn child, but in the belief that sexuality should be controlled by mothers and occur only as an aspect of the reproductive function. Women are understood to be sexual beings only in so far as they are potential mothers. Control of sexuality must rest within the domestic sphere of women and not the public sphere of men. In this way, women maintain real power through their participation in the domestic sphere.

The ALRANZ stance, in contrast, stresses the importance of a woman's identity as a sexual woman and not as a mother who has a relationship to an unborn child. An individual's autonomy transcends the sanctity of the family as a unit where decisions and reproduction can take place. Women are women first, mothers second. Similarly, children in an unstable family unit have rights as individuals which transcend those duties they have as children, i.e., as members of a family unit.[10] Sexuality, in this view, is not merely a reproductive function; thus, the right to abortion arises from the fact that pregnancy may be the unintended consequence of sexual activity.

Responding to SPUC's motion to amend the Guardianship Act, ALRANZ also decided to use NCW to further its aims. In June 1979, it brought to the branch this motion:[11]

> That NCW set up a group to study the working of the Contraception, Sterilisation and Abortion Act to ensure the welfare of women seeking abortions. (NCW Christchurch Branch Agenda, June 19, 1979b).

Meeting four times during the year, the subcommittee unsuccessfully forwarded resolutions to the branch in April 1980 and, subsequently, disbanded. In July 1980, the subcommittee's convener, in her yearly report, summarized the activities of the group as including discussions of the following: data from the Abortion Advisory Committee, questionnaires and answers from the abortion surveys conducted by the major hospitals, contraceptive education, reading materials for the young, letters from consulting psychiatrists and a member of parliament. The group viewed health films for high school pupils distributed by the Family Planning Association and formulated two resolutions to the branch. Both resolutions urged amendments to the Act which would make contraceptive information easier to attain. Neither resolution was accepted by the branch or voted on. Some branch members maintained that it was beyond the original brief of the subcommittee to make recommendations; their task was merely to study and report back. On the subcommittee, those opposing abortion and favoring the CSA Act tried to thwart others' public claim that the Act was not working. Despite disagreement, their discussions clarified the ideas of both groups, ideas reflecting their notions of female gender identity.

Two positions were taken with regard to the CSA Act: older women who supported the Act frequently referred to the "good old days" when women were not sexually active until marriage, and chastity was valued. They argued that self restraint is desirable as an alternative to non-reproductive sexual activity. Contraceptive information and abortion encouraged "moral slip ups." In their roles as "mothers," "grandmothers," and "aunts" they had the duty, and more importantly, the influence to change the behavior of future generations. The stance of these women was that the Act sought to protect the unity of the family.[12] Their statements suggest they act with a conviction that is based on their understanding of their roles in society. Reproduction, in their view, should be controlled by women who also should influence and control male participation. Catholic women who supported SPUC told me that the family is the fundamental unit of society and is sacred; if the family is society's basic component, clearly their role is powerful and potentially significant.

Those in opposition suggested that supporters of the Act were avoiding current problems and couching beliefs in terms of the past, be it imagined, real, or naive; in the present world, different solutions are imperative. If children are sexually active and women have abortions, the solution is to make the activity safer rather than to change behavior. The problem is "that these women have no conception of others' lives;" ALRANZ supporters have a notion of traditionalist women as ignorant, isolated, and constrained by their roles as mothers and wives and by their spatial worlds (the home and the suburbs). As one ALRANZ speaker suggested, the family is not the cocoon SPUC would like to think, because the influence of peers is strong. Thus, individuals must reject the fear of sexuality and learn early to value themselves apart from their relationships to others.

Elderly traditionalists simultaneously stress the primacy of their domestic roles as mothers and the importance of their roles in a female extra-domestic sphere of voluntary activity. For women who believe the family is society's foundation, power resides in their claim to the roles encompassed by it and in the broad extension and definition of those roles. They see the domestic sphere encompassing voluntary activity such as NCW and more particularly SPUC which give them access to government and brings into the public arena such issues of concern to women as the protection of their domestic rights.

Mrs. Smythe

Mrs. Smythe, a mother of four children, wife, and homemaker in her sixties is an advocate of traditional motherhood and wifehood and sees feminism as a threat to women's position. She sees the role of women as distinct from that of men, as complementary to men, but neither subordinate nor identical. Such differences are inherent. She argues for the preservation of difference by expanding the dimensions of the domestic domain to incorporate community politics. A SPUC sympathizer, an NCW official, and a local district representative, she is archetypal of the traditionalist stance in her gender concepts, concepts which define her role in the domestic sphere and affect her commitments to the community.

I begin with an analysis of her two primary voluntary involvements: (1) work through NCW, and (2) work through the local district assembly. She defines herself as primarily a homemaker whose voluntary activity is one facet of that role. She sees roles as an officer of NCW and as a district representative as vital and potentially effective political strategies for women. She believes that the former is effective on a national level; the latter, as a direct way of making and implementing decisions and being observed, is effective on a local level.

As a young mother, she was first involved with NCW as a delegate from an educational organization to a local rural branch of sixteen delegates. The small size of the branch offered her a good learning situation, but while acknowledging that the function of NCW is to expose women to each other's ideas and provide a training ground, she assured me that an even more important function was to pass and promote remits to the government.[13] Larger branches prepare remits by delegating research responsibilities and recommendations to small subcommittees. In the small branch of which Mrs. Smythe soon became president, the executive committee did all of the research. She feels much of their work "reflected opinion more than research." After her family moved to Christchurch, she joined that branch as a delegate.

Participation in local level politics as district representative is the second major area of Mrs. Smythe's voluntary activity.[14] She felt qualified to run for the position because of her six years experience on the school board of governors and her experience in NCW; other factors included her active role in the church as an elder and as a member of an Anglo-Christian women's fellowship group. Mrs. Smythe feels that women have different perspectives from men because of their experience and different concerns about the community that should be represented on the assembly. While women are both inherently and experientially different from men, changing work patterns will change the distribution of the sexes in homemaking, career and leisure. Even so women's roles in these spheres, especially the political sphere, should complement those of men and reinforce gender differences.

NCW and the district assembly are both arenas where political action is effective. NCW is a highly structured female sphere in which informal power is wielded in an attempt to levy pressure on government; the assembly is a mixed-sex sphere in which public formal power, defined by Mrs. Smythe as "a direct way of making and implementing decisions and being observed," is available. Despite these differences in composition and strategy, both arenas enabled Mrs. Smythe to play an active and responsible role in her community.

She considers community concern to be an extension of one's domestic role as a homemaker. Her determination to protect the role of homemaker for women is apparent in Mrs. Smythe's stance and motivates her actions. One way to enable women to stay home and fill this important role is by institutionalizing an allowance to do so; only then, she maintains, "will the notion of equal pay not be meaningless." Her determination to protect the roles of homemaker and mother is also seen in her strong stand on the position of the Johnson Report which concerns sex education in the schools. She believes that material on sex education should not be taught in schools on the primary level but should rather be distributed to parents when children enroll so that they can receive training in the home "where it should be done" in private. Parents, not teachers, should be entrusted with children's morals.

In both arenas Mrs. Smythe adopted an indirect political strategy. She performs those activities shared with her male colleagues differently from men. In dealing with a colleague in the assembly whose office enables him to control information she attempts to "be on the right side of him, feed ideas to him, and maintain contact with him." Her strategy is to plant ideas in his head and let him take the credit for them. It does not matter to her whose idea it is as long as desirable action is taken. Similar kinds of indirect politically motivated actions occur in NCW itself, in particular an action I call "procedural maneuvering." For example, Mrs. Smythe attempts to sustain traditionalist ideology by manipulating the rules when "the majority opinion...is not right." Sometimes she works with the Executive Committee to prevent undesirable remits from coming to the floor for discussion and voting.

I contend that Mrs. Smythe's participation in community politics and in NCW enable her to wield power without conflicting with the primacy she places on the domestic sphere for women precisely because she defines voluntarism and participation in local level politics as part of the role of the homemaker. Her participation is a strategy designed to protect the domestic primacy of women. But, as I have suggested, her actions are motivated not just by her gender concepts, but also by a broader belief system shared with men which acknowledges the complementarity and interdependence between the sexes.

CONCLUSION

Although elderly traditionalists do not consciously articulate an ideology or speak of their activities as political, I have suggested that an ideology of motherhood motivates their actions. This ideology suggests that the family is the basic unit of society and defines women as mothers and wives whose role within the family is powerful. These women's conceptions of femaleness are rooted in their domestic roles in the home. Activities within the domestic sphere are constrained socially within the roles of mother and wife and, spatially, by the home; "domestic" refers to "nitty-gritty of daily life and interaction that really matters." Such women think of the public sphere as the world beyond the home and the community; it is the domain of government activity, of men, of formal power. Traditionalists believe that their activities in the domestic sphere should be equally valued with those of men in the public sphere; they also believe that these activities should be marked as separate and female. Thus, I argue that their actions contribute to an evaluation of the domestic sphere as being of primary importance. In addition, their actions suggest that they are redefining the boundaries of the domestic sphere and extending its influence into the public domain by treating voluntary activity as an aspect of homemaking in which informal power, as opposed to the formal, legitimized power of the public domain, is wielded. Women form extra-domestic ties with each other, develop leadership skills, and define a role for themselves within the community as social actors by moving the domestic sphere into the public realm.

Examining the informal dimensions of elderly women's power highlights the significance of female solidarity groups as arenas in which women negotiate their status through an ideology of motherhood and reinforce their roles in society as social actors with an interest in controlling the reproductive lives of their children. As they age, women adopt strategies for shaping their daily lives and worlds in significant ways, often bridging familial and public worlds, or white and indigenous worlds, (see Sinclair, chapter 2) and expanding their authority by redefining the boundaries of the domestic realm.[15]

I maintain that traditionalists share a desire to exert their power at the community level and by extension at the national (through NCW) and global (through church and mission work) levels. The essence of traditionalism rests in acting to preserve the status quo.[16] For this reason, the primacy of the domestic sphere is reiterated and the allocation of women to this sphere is maintained. This is rooted in an acceptance of the myth of origins in which New Zealand women were strong, driven pioneers with initiative who helped to create a classless society.

The power of biological reproduction and its social manifestation in motherhood is intrinsic to the power of women. Aspects of women's sexuality provide a model for conceptualizing femaleness, hence traditionalists stress the centrality of their roles as mothers and argue that women's power lies in their control of reproduction.[17] In her article

"The Origins of the Women's Movement in New Zealand: The Women's Christian Temperance Union, 1885-1895," Phillida Bunkle (1980) argues that early suffragists (whom these women use as a model), rather than seeking equality between the sexes through restructuring institutions, were seeking instead an elevation of separate roles and the expression of specifically female values through the transformation of individuals. In particular, women crusaded for social purity by arguing that sex should be limited to reproduction within marriage; thus, they rejected definitions of women exclusively in terms of sex and attempted also to undermine a male double standard which they believed to underlie the sexual exploitation of women.[18]

> It was through reproduction that woman made her claim to power. Interior purity transformed male sexual energy into reproduction and the construction of family life. It was her purity that conferred this transforming power....Organised motherhood was to redeem humanity (Bunkle 1980:73).

The Women's Christian Temperance Union (WCTU) was successful since it was based, as DuBois (1977) has suggested was also true in the United States, on the significance of the private sphere and of familial concerns. Ryan (1979:73) writes:

> Female moral reform, then, constituted a concrete, specific attempt to exert woman's power. Led and initiated by women, it was a direct, collective, organized effort, which aimed to control behavior and change values in the community at large. Because female moral reform entailed explicit social action it is possible to examine its origins, impact and limitations as an exercise of woman's power.

The adoption of the same term "domestic" and the redefinition of the dimensions of the term to include activities which historically have been "public" lets Pakeha traditionalists remain seemingly conservative. Thus, they consider themselves to be representative, ordinary and middle-class. Because they stand for a normative New Zealand belief system they see themselves not as political actors with an ideology but as social actors with a belief. The belief they espouse is Christian in the sense of reflecting the values of the church settlers who founded Christchurch.

Traditionalists reject male behavior patterns and stress the value of female behavior patterns. Separation between the sexes is valued, although there is appreciation of the value of women and men learning to cooperate and complement each other in the same spheres. Women should do the same activities as men, but do them separately. Women involve themselves in voluntary activity outside of the home to protect their role within it; thus, for example, they argue that reproduction falls within the control of women who also should influence and control male participation in this process. Accordingly, reproduction is a family, therefore a private, domestic issue, rather than an issue for governmental (male) control. Furthermore, fatherhood is not a model for conceptualizing male behavior; this implies that gender models for women and men are not complementary. In recalling old symbols and redefining and adapting their meaning, this group seeks to redefine and reevaluate the domestic sphere through voluntary activity.

Distinctions between formal and informal power, and between domestic and public domains, are useful as emic categories for making sense of the gender conceptions of traditionalist women. Traditionalist women who argue for the primacy of the domestic sphere and the significance of voluntary activities as an extension of that sphere perceive their power as real and autonomous. They perceive their power as formal while distinct from male power and thus have a conception of the domestic as having a formal, public dimension which parallels the nature of male public activities.

Such conceptions permit women, though they lose their reproductive capacities as they move through the life cycle, to continue to define themselves in terms of those reproductive capacities. Their degree of control over male participation and sexuality in reproduction is paralleled by an increasing concern to control the reproductive potential of their children. One way to seek such control is to increase the significance of the female role within the domestic sphere of familial relations. Extending the boundaries of the female role and creating extra-domestic ties reinforces their power as women in New Zealand society. Domestic relationships therefore become an integral part of the structure of society as women work towards "all that makes for the good of humanity" (National Council of Women of New Zealand 1978).

NOTES

Fieldwork was conducted in Christchurch, New Zealand for eighteen months from 1979 until 1980 with a variety of types of women's voluntary associations ranging from tradi-tionalist church groups to radical, feminist, separatist groups. I appreciate the financial support of the National Science Foundation (BNS 781063), and Cornell University's Graduate School and Center for International Studies. I also give my thanks to the editors of this volume, participants in the ASAO symposium, and to Ruth Borker, Martha Gearhart, and Daniel Maltz for their comments. Discussions with Karen Sinclair on her work with Maori women have contributed much to my thinking. This chapter draws on a case study and aspects of chapter two first put forward in my doctoral dissertation (Dominy 1983).

1. Pakeha is the term used to refer to a European, that is, a non-Maori.
2. Elevation in status for aged women based on reproduction and motherhood and marked by an extension of female roles is supported by Amoss and Harrell (1981a:4); Brown (1982:143); Cool and McCabe (1983:62, 68); Dougherty (1978:168) and Kerns (1983:190, 1984:1).
3. The extra-domestic worlds of Pakeha and Maori women parallel each other in three ways: (1) active involvement in church fellowships and the Maramatanga movement (for a detailed discussion of this movement see Sinclair, chapter 2); (2) voluntary activity at the community level, i.e., NCW and the Maori Women's Welfare League; and (3) the predominance of the elderly in extra-domestic activities.
4. Participation demanded at least three meetings per month and more if one was to be an effective delegate, subcommittee and Executive Committee member. Executive Committee meetings were held on weekday mornings, thus limiting the participation of women who worked outside of the home.
5. In my examination of women's roles in structural and conceptual systems, I have examined women's status as a composite of many variables and have argued, following MacCormack and Strathern (1980) and Ortner and Whitehead (1981), for an understanding of sociocultural phenomena in context (Dominy 1983).
6. See MacCormack (1980:18) for criticism of the nature/culture argument and Weiner (1979) for a criticism of examining reproduction only in its biological context.
7. As Counts and Counts (chapter 7) and Sinclair (chapter 2) maintain, the elderly actively negotiate their status in the social world.
8. Kinship supercedes friendship ties which function to preserve the primacy of kinship. In contrast, for Maori women kinship creates friendship which supercedes conjugal bonds (Sinclair, chapter 2).
9. Later the word "prior" was placed before the word "notification."
10. Interestingly, the word "children" applies to both a non-adult or a young person as well as the offspring of parents. Children have no status outside the family unit.
11. The motion passed after an amendment to add "and the unborn child" after "women" was defeated by the meeting. Much later the final phrase "to ensure the welfare of women seeking abortions" was dropped altogether.
12. In discussing birth control in the 1930s in New Zealand, Barbara Brookes (1981) argues that it was seen as a deviation from the maternal role of mothers and there-fore opposed. She supports, therefore, the centrality of motherhood as an ideology by examining stances against abortion and birth control.
13. A remit is a recommendation sent from a branch to the main council of an organi-

zation for consideration.

14. I use representative as a gloss. The assembly is a local group similar to a town council which makes decisions for the locality. Christchurch and environs were divided into at least three districts.

15. DeBeauvoir (1952), Myerhoff (1978), and Wolf (1972) stress in other cultural contexts the role of aging women as social actors who bridge familial and public worlds, often through their involvement in female solidarity groups.

16. In contrast, Maori women attempt to change the status quo. They have greater power than in the past as a consequence of colonization and their involvement in the Maramatanga movement (Karen Sinclair, personal communication; also see Sinclair chapter 2). Involvement in an extended domestic sphere marks both Pakeha and Maori women as mediators and bridges between a female domestic world and a male public world (Pakeha) and a female domestic/public Maori world and a European world (Maori).

17. An extension of the motherhood status also characterizes Maori women's roles as grandmothers and elders (Sinclair, chapter 2).

18. Whereas purity is claimed by Pakeha women, the reverse is true in Maori culture where women are considered polluting. Pollution beliefs in both Maori and Pakeha society exaggerate male and female differences and reinforce the separation of male and female domains.

4

KINSHIP, GENDER, AND AGING ON PULAP, CAROLINE ISLANDS

Juliana Flinn

INTRODUCTION

Recent studies of siblingship in the Pacific have indicated how cultural notions of ideal male and female behavior can relate to notions of ideal behavior among certain categories of kin, such as cross-siblings (Marshall 1981b; Rubenstein 1981; Smith 1981).[1] In Greater Trukese Society, for instance, the relationship between a brother and a sister provides the conceptual model for relations between men and women (Marshall 1981b:203). Sibling relations and gender relations are certainly not identical, and the behavioral expressions of gender will vary between brother and sister, mother and son, father and daughter, husband and wife. Yet when one of these relationships serves as a model for gender relations, kinship and gender are inextricably linked.

Gender relations and gender ideology can undergo transformations or transitions as men and women age. A number of recent studies on gender and aging have focussed on the diminution of gender distinctions with age and the relaxation of constraints on sex role behavior. Keith (1980:351) describes this freedom from sexually defined roles as cultural compensation accorded the elderly for losses they experience as they age. Focussing on elderly women, Brown (1982) points out that older women usually gain opportunities to exercise more authority, explore new avenues of achievement, and behave with more freedom from sexually defined roles. Even in our own society, psychiatrists have described how gender oppositions can become blurred as men become freer to explore female personality traits and women to exhibit male traits once they have reached the end of their parenting responsibilities (Gutmann, Grunes, and Griffin 1980). As gender distinctions fade following the woman's childbearing years, people in many societies are often released from ritual food and language taboos incumbent upon younger adults (Amoss and Harrell 1981a; Amoss 1981:231).

If ideal sex role behavior is associated with a particular category of kin relationship, and if aging modifies sex role behavior, then a shift in gender distinctions and sexuality among the aged may be reflected in a transition in kinship relations. This chapter examines such a change among the people of Pulap, an atoll to the west of Truk Lagoon in the Caroline Islands. From puberty through mature adulthood, the most significant and most valued male-female relationship is the one between brothers and sisters. This cross-sibling relationship is basic to the matrilineal descent system, and the ideology surrounding maleness and femaleness supports the solidarity of descent groups. Once the sexually and economically productive years have passed, restrictions on gender specific behavior are eased for the elderly, as they are in many other societies. Moreover, when sexuality and food production are no longer central aspects of the cross-sibling relationship, certain classificatory brother-sister ties are transformed into 'father-daughter' ties, with concurrent changes in both terminology and behavior, because the 'parent-child' relationship increases in significance as people age.

Joseph, an elderly Pulapese man, about sixty years old, who is the senior member of his descent group, provides an example. His wife was sick in the hospital during the period of research, his only daughter was living on another island with relatives who had adopted her, and his adopted daughter was with her husband elsewhere. Although Joseph no longer went fishing with younger men, he was still an active member of the community, served as head of his descent group, and participated regularly in municipal meetings. Ordinarily he would have resided with his wife and daughters, who are expected to provide the staple foods for the household. In their absence, however, women of his own descent group cooked and provided for him. Even when he had lived with his wife's kin, they regularly sent him food, especially on Saturdays, when a large amount was prepared.

Although not all elderly men face the same situation of having no wife or daughters in the household, no man feels secure that these women will be available when needed, especially if he becomes ill, helpless, or senile. Ties with descent group women, who are all 'sisters', are far more secure; a man can count on these women to provide food. One problem, however, is that constraints on behavior between brothers and sisters place severe limits on other practical assistance. It is difficult for them even to live in the same house together. Even though he was in good health at the time, Joseph was nonetheless concerned about care if he became sick. To solve this problem, Joseph has asked certain women in his descent group to call him 'father' instead of 'brother', thus removing the burdensome constraints on their relationship.

KINSHIP AND GENDER ON PULAP

Pulap is the larger and more populous of two inhabited islets in Pulap
Atoll and lies approximately 130 miles to the west of Truk Lagoon, the
administrative center of Truk in Micronesia.[2] In January 1980, the
population of Pulap was 444; about 59 percent were under twenty years
of age, with about 11 percent over fifty years old (see table 1). During
the Japanese and early American years, the population remained quite
stable, varying between 153 in 1925 (Jupun 1931) and 159 in 1949
(Fischer 1949), but the population has steadily increased since that

Table 1. Pulap Population in January 1980

Year of birth	Males	Females	Total
1970-1979	74(16.7%)	67(15.1%)	141(31.8%)
1960-1969	54(12.2%)	65(14.6%)	119(26.8%)
1950-1959	30(6.8%)	50(11.3%)	80(18.0%)
1940-1949	15(3.4%)	10(2.3%)	25(5.5%)
1930-1939	17(3.8%)	15(3.4%)	32(7.2%)
1920-1929	13(2.9%)	14(3.2%)	27(6.1%)
1910-1919	3(0.7%)	4(0.9%)	7(1.6%
1900-1909	(1.6%)	6(1.4%)	13(2.9%)
TOTAL	**213(48.0%)**	**231(52.0%)**	**444(100%)**

time. Pulapese attribute this increase to improved medical care
provided by the United States administration following World War II
and to the training of midwives, which has considerably reduced infant
mortality.

Pulap is the northernmost of the Western Islands, a group of atolls
acknowledging Puluwat as chief in the area. In the past Puluwat
exacted tribute from the other Westerns and in return protected and
defended them from other islanders. The three atolls comprising the
Westerns are situated geographically, linguistically, and culturally

intermediate between the islands of Greater Trukese Society and the coral atolls of Yap to the west.

One fundamental similarity with both areas is the matrilineal descent system found on Pulap. The matrilineal clans found throughout all these islands are named, exogamous, dispersed descent groups. The members of any particular clan are scattered among a number of islands and atolls, but the shared name theoretically implies that a common female ancestress founded the clan in the distant past. Although the members of a clan never assemble as a group for a particular purpose, form a political organization, or engage in common economic or religious activities, clan membership nevertheless has definite social functions. In principle, marriage is forbidden between members of the same clan, and hospitality is expected from fellow clan members when visiting another island. Excluding the clans of off-island men who have married on Pulap, five such matrilineal clans are represented on the islet.[3] Each is composed of a number of descent lines, whose members can trace their descent through known female links from a common ancestress no more than a few generations back. The members of a descent line are associated with a named homesite and can refer to themselves as the 'people' of the named homesite, regardless of their current residence. Because of customary uxorilocal residence, those actually residing at each named homesite ideally include the women of the descent line, their husbands, and their unmarried children. When a man marries, however, he retains his identity as a 'person' of his natal homesite, while acquiring an additional label as a 'man who comes into' his wife's homesite.

Among the members of a matrilineal descent group, the prototypical relationship is that of siblings, as Goodenough first pointed out for Truk (1951:31), and the Crow-type terminology on Pulap highlights this conception. Kin terms are used only in reference, however, as proper names are used for address. A man potentially refers to any male of his descent group, regardless of generation, as 'brother' and to any descent group woman of his own generation or below as 'sister' (see figure 1). Similarly, a woman refers to a descent group female of her own generation as 'sister' and to a male of her own generation or higher as 'brother'.[4] Although a woman of ego's mother's generation or above is referred to as 'mother', in descent group affairs these women are treated as older sisters, having authority with respect to matters such as land or other property that belongs to the descent group.

Ideally, the strongest, most intimate, and most intense relationships are those between siblings, who are expected to *tumunuw* 'take care of' each other. They should provide mutual support, defend each other,

Figure 1. Kinship terminology on Pulap

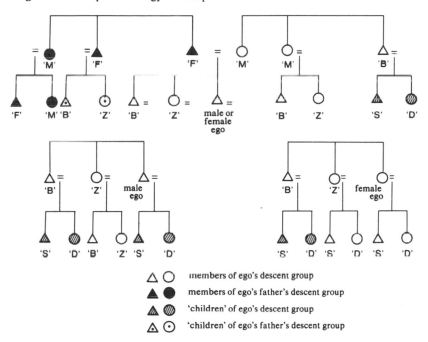

and share food, labor, and property. Marshall (1981b) has described sibling sets as basic social structural units in Greater Trukese Society; fellow descent group members – 'siblings' – share common interests in descent group resources and regularly share food as a symbol of these interests. Siblings should invariably come to the aid of each other and, even when living off the island, people are expected to continue supporting their siblings through regular gifts of food and other goods sent by canoe or ship. The emotional bond among kin is characterized as *tong*, which has been glossed variously as 'compassion' (Elbert 1972:183), 'love', or 'pity' (Marshall 1977:656, 1981a:13, 1981b:207). *Tong* should exist in the greatest measure and ideal form among siblings and is expressed through concrete nurturing behavior, especially the sharing of resources (Marshall 1977).

All descent group siblings are ranked with respect to one another according to sex and birth order, with brothers ranking higher than sisters, and older siblings of the same sex ranking higher than younger ones. Among classificatory siblings, the children of an older sister rank higher than the children of a younger sister, regardless of relative age. Ranking is no mere formality, since it obligates junior siblings to observe prescribed patterns of deference and respect toward their senior siblings. Once they have reached puberty, junior siblings must respect and obey their senior siblings, and in addition, sisters must accord special deference to their brothers. Specifically, junior siblings must never touch the head or shoulders of their senior siblings, they must refrain from standing next to seated senior siblings, and they must substitute deferential terms for several ordinary forms when speaking to or about a senior sibling. Consistent with the emphasis placed on the sharing of food as a symbol of shared kinship, the prototypical deferential term is the one for 'food': *mwéngé* is the common form, *wiih* is the deferential term, and the verb form *(yawiiha)* is commonly used to mean 'speak deferentially'.

In addition to this behavior expected of all junior siblings toward their seniors, sisters must also *yóppwóro* 'stoop' in the presence of their brothers, i.e., bend low when a 'brother' is near and crawl on their knees if a 'brother' is seated. Furthermore, a woman should never step or sit on the sleeping mat of her 'brother', use his clothing, eat food or drink coconuts he has tasted, or smoke his cigarette. Some women are careful even with imported cups, reserving one solely for the use of their brothers. On his part, a 'brother' should never hear sexual innuendos about a 'sister' or witness any advances to her; if and when he does, he is then obligated to fight the offender. As a result of these restrictions, brothers and sisters find it awkward to live in the same house after puberty. Young men who have reached puberty tend to move out and live either in a canoe house or with other relatives.

Although matrilineal descent is fundamental to Pulap kinship, patrilateral kin are also significant, and the Crow-type terminology distinguishes between matrilineal and patrilateral kin rather than between generations. Similar to other areas in Truk, the relationship between members of a matrilineal descent group and the offspring of its men is construed as a parent-child tie, and the offspring are collectively referred to as 'children' of the descent group.[5] Men of one's father's descent group are accordingly referred to as 'fathers' and the women as 'mothers'[6] (see figure 1).

The relationship between a parent and a child is ideally a warm and nurturing one; parents care for small children, and later, as children mature, they are expected to care for and support their aging parents. Children are viewed as resources by their parents, sources not only of affection and eventually of food, but also of assistance, especially in the form of labor. This right to the assistance of children is a significant aspect of the relationship between members of a matrilineal descent group and the offspring of its men: a matrilineal descent group is entitled to the labor and other assistance of its children (the offspring of descent group men). Such assistance is commonly requested in activities such as fishing, collecting coconuts, making copra, providing food for clan visitors, and building a roof, house, canoe, or canoe house. On most occasions it is not even necessary for members of the descent group to make a formal request for help. For example, if they are building a house, the descent group children usually arrive unasked.

In general, a person is expected to nurture relationships with members of the father's descent group. When a man drinks, he invites men of his father's descent line to join him, and from time to time he should send fish and coconuts to the women of his father's descent line. A woman, too, should assist members of her father's descent line, offering her help, for instance, in weaving sleeping mats. When someone is ill, his or her children are expected to join those who move in to care for the patient. Moreover, at the death of a member of the father's descent group, all the children of the group must bring gifts acknowledging their relationship.

Behavior of children which serves to sustain ties with members of their father's descent group reasserts their position as its heirs, especially in relation to land received from their fathers. As the descent group heirs, children also have rights in other property that the father's descent group owns. For example, a man shares rights in the sailing canoe and canoe house belonging to his father's descent group.

Furthermore, first fruits offered by the islanders to the traditional chief are redistributed among the 'children' of the chiefly clan because symbolically they are its heirs. Traditional belief held that even after death the souls of children of the chiefly clan retained special privileges in the form of rights to the chiefly clan's meeting place, believed to be on the nearby uninhabited islet.

Relations between descent group members 'parents' and the offspring of their men 'children' are considered slightly fragile, however, when compared with ties among matrilineal descent group members. Whereas, theoretically, descent group ties cannot be severed, parent-child ties can be weakened or even broken through negligence or poor treatment. In this respect, land is a prime consideration, since the members of a descent group retain a measure of control over land given to any of its children. Although land received through one's mother is never repossessed, land received through one's father can be reclaimed if members of the father's descent group feel the owner has not properly met his obligations to them. For example, if a person fails to offer a gift when a member of his father's descent group dies, he is said no longer to care for his patrilateral kin and may, therefore, lose land given him by his father. The oldest child of a deceased man drapes the body with a white sheet as a sign that he has properly carried out his responsibilities; this act serves to remind the descent group of his claim to land received from his father. Land can also be reclaimed in anger if a 'child' fails to send food to members of his father's descent line or to share his possessions with them, or if he has an affair with the wife of a man in his father's descent group.

Both children and parents must sustain and validate their relationship. If a parent treats his children poorly or slights them in some way, the children may choose to ignore the relationship and refuse to acknowledge responsibility to provide labor or assistance when requested. The bond is not a subservient one; Pulapese take pride in their relations with members of their father's descent group and receive prestige through behavior demonstrating concern, respect, and kindness toward them.

Those who are fellow children of their fathers' descent group refer to one another as 'siblings', (see figure 1) a practice that results in two categories of siblings: one consisting of fellow descent group members and another consisting of all those whose fathers belong to the same descent group. In other words, the children of sisters constitute one set of siblings, and the children of brothers constitute another. (Thus the children of parallel siblings are siblings to each other, whereas the children of cross-siblings are parents and children to each other, with the brother's child a 'son' or 'daughter' of the sister's child.) Furthermore, the ranking of siblings who are children of their fathers' descent group depends on the relative ranking of their fathers in the same way that the ranking of descent group siblings depends on the ranking of their mothers. In both cases children of a senior sibling rank higher than the children of a junior sibling.

Although both categories of siblings ideally entail strong and intimate relationships and sibling respect behavior applies to both, descent group siblings are considered to be the closer of the two. Just as relationships with members of one's father's descent group are slightly tenuous compared to ties within one's own descent group, so too are ties between siblings related through their fathers a bit fragile compared to those between siblings related through descent group ties. Pulapese speak figuratively of a fiber between such kin, a fiber that may be stretched and broken through ill treatment or neglect. For example, although it is supposedly forbidden for any siblings to marry, and descent group siblings rarely ever do, siblings distantly related through their fathers have occasionally married each other. Such marriages are frowned upon, and those who enter into them are said to have 'cut their hand short' because the sibling relationship that had previously existed with the spouse's kin becomes instead the far less significant in-law tie. A person then loses a category of relatives he could formerly have counted on to behave as siblings.

In sum, the sibling tie within the matrilineal descent group is conceived to be the strongest and most binding of kin ties. Ties with patrilateral kin should approach the same strength but are viewed as susceptible to neglect, and failure to share resources is considered more likely to occur among such kin. As Marshall (1977) has indicated, the concrete expression of solidarity among kin is through this sharing of resources, especially of food. Homesite members share food daily, but food is also regularly distributed and shared with other kin, since other relationships must be sustained. In particular, a man should have fish and coconuts delivered to the women of his descent line, and a woman should send food to men of her descent line who have left the homesite. This process in fact defines who is a kinsman, as nonkin do not participate, and a participant is by definition a kinsman. Although other kin may choose to neglect a relationship and fail to share resources, it is virtually inconceivable to Pulapese that descent line siblings would ever do so.

MALE AND FEMALE ON PULAP

Notions of siblingship and brother-sister relations are intimately related to gender ideology and sex role expectations on Pulap. They do not remain constant over the developmental cycle, however, but are most evident during the years of sexual and economic productivity (see Counts and Counts, chapter 1). Puberty marks the onset of this period, and with aging, constraints regarding sex roles are eased and the roles of brother and sister shift with regard to descent group welfare.

Although the onset of puberty is no longer marked by ceremonies (see Krämer 1935:268), it still signifies the beginning of young adulthood and full sexuality. Young men and women undertake proper respect and avoidance behavior toward their siblings, and they become increasingly more active in the economic tasks expected of adults. The Pulap conception of the division of labor requires that men fish and women garden, and gender ideology reflects these basic economic roles. The essential difference between males and females is encapsulated in the Pulap belief that men move and women stay (see Carucci, chapter 6). Men represent mobility, whereas women represent stability and continuity in the system of matrilineal descent and customary uxorilocal residence. Ideally, women reside at the descent line homesite throughout their lives, they produce and care for children to ensure the perpetuation of the descent group, and they produce and prepare the staple foods to assure its survival. As caretakers both of children and of land, women are thus responsible for the fundamental descent group resources. Men, symbolizing mobility on the other hand, change residence at marriage; they give their land over to the care of their wives, and their primary contribution to subsistence is fishing, which takes them away from land. Moreover, Pulap men have traditionally been inter-island voyagers, traveling as far as the Marianas.

Women are thus associated with the land and men with the sea, and Pulapese contend that women should die on land and men should die at sea (see Carucci, chapter 6). The key female contribution to subsistence is the production and preparation of the staple vegetable foods, especially taro, whereas men are responsible for providing fish. Women may gather fish and other marine animals close to land within or along the reef, but only men fish in the deeper water, farther from land. Men also climb trees, movement forbidden to women, to gather coconuts and breadfruit. This association of women with the land and men with the sea indicates a complementarity of male and female roles, represented by periodic exchanges between men and women of fish and vegetable produce that are subsequently combined and shared among fellow homesite members.

Although the male and female domains are conceptually separate, a certain amount of overlap is tolerated, especially for men. Some women have been permitted to learn aspects of navigation,[7] although none have been initiated as navigators. Men encroach more freely on the female domain and occasionally garden in the taro swamp or assist in food preparation. A man may even choose to undertake women's work regularly, either instead of or in addition to male tasks. These rare deviations are acceptable for men; the departure of women from the ideal presents more of a threat to the security of the descent group since women bear responsibility for its resources.

In the Pulap view, male and female roles complement each other, so that both men and women are necessary for the descent group. For example, women support the maintenance of descent group canoes and canoe houses, nominally the male domain, by preparing food when men build or repair one of the structures, or when they embark on a voyage. Men care for the canoes in order to provide fish for women. Consistent with the view of women as responsible for descent group resources and providing stability is the claim that descent group sisters are the ultimate owners of the canoes and that the brothers merely use them in order to provide fish for their sisters.

Relations between a woman's brother and her husband illustrate the manner in which the role of brother supports the solidarity of the women (the sisters) of the descent group. A husband must emulate his wife's deference to her brother and must acquiesce to the brother's requests for assistance or labor that involves the woman's home or descent group affairs. On the other hand, a husband can ask his wife's brother for assistance in virtually any matter because the help a woman's brother gives to her husband is considered assistance to the woman, his sister. The lines of authority thus revolve around the women of the descent line, with husbands obedient to the brothers of the women with respect to her descent group affairs and the brothers subservient to the husbands for the welfare of the women, who are their sisters.

Maintaining the solidarity of the women of the descent group maintains the descent group itself, since the women provide not only new members to the group but also its sustenance. Women impart permanence and stability because they produce and care both for children and for the staple foods. A man does not even retain responsibility for the land he is given when he marries; rather, it is cared for by his wife, for their children. Responsibility for the welfare and well-being of the descent group is thus largely in the hands of the women. In the idiom of the brother-sister tie, male mobility supports and complements female immobility, contributing to the stability and continuity of the descent group.

AGING, ILLNESS, AND DEATH

During adulthood Pulap men and women are both sexually and economically productive, and these are the years during which the prescribed behavior between siblings should be most strictly adhered to. As people age, however, not only are they no longer sexually productive but they also gradually withdraw from active participation in subsistence activities, and their children are expected to provide for them. The process of withdrawal varies from person to person according to their health and inclination. In general, women continue to work in the taro gardens as long as they are able, but younger women in the descent group gradually take over the responsibility. As women age, they spend more time with less strenuous tasks, such as caring for grandchildren, while the mothers tend the taro patches, gather reef animals, or collect pandanus. Older women can also remain active at other lighter work such as weaving and preparing food. Similarly, men gradually withdraw from fishing, spending more time at less arduous work such as making sennit from coconut husks, while younger men climb coconut and breadfruit trees. Thus, although younger adults are expected to take over the subsistence tasks involving hard physical labor, the elderly are far from useless. Only the nature of their contribution changes, as the elderly continue to work and contribute according to their abilities. Old age on Pulap need not entail inactivity or uselessness.

The elderly are less important for their economic contribution, however, than for their control over another valuable resource—knowledge. Beginning with mature adulthood, men and women can choose to become specialists in certain skills or esoteric knowledge; the elderly are those who have acquired the most knowledge and experience in these areas, such as navigation, massage, medicines, canoe construction, house construction, and loom weaving. They can serve as teachers and consultants. Elderly people are respected, not because of their age, but to the extent that they have acquired such specialized knowledge or skills and to the extent that they participate in community affairs. For example, elderly men and women are no longer required to attend weekly municipal meetings, but a number of them nonetheless choose to do so, continue to remain active, and express

their opinions. Moreover, the elderly are the most knowledgeable
concerning events of recent history and are consulted when a dispute
has to be settled. A description of Etal, south of Truk Lagoon, applies
equally as well to Pulap:

> Every fault and foible, every good point and personal character-
> istic of fellow islanders–plus every major and minor event of the
> immediate past–make up a pool of knowledge that grows broader
> and deeper the longer one lives. In a system where precedent and
> a detailed knowledge of the past are vital to dispute settlement,
> every old person can potentially command the attention of
> younger members of the community by virtue of greater knowl-
> edge and experience. This is also clearly one way in which old
> persons can continue to serve society (Nason 1981:165).

In the same vein, Borthwick (1977) and Thomas (1980) have both
pointed out the role that elderly women can play in Greater Trukese
Society in resolving land disputes, due to their knowledge of genealogical details and events of the recent past.

As is common in a number of other societies, the elderly on Pulap
are released from a number of constraints on sex role behavior, especially in the case of women. They feel freer to make their opinions
known publicly, to act the clown, and even deliberately to play out a
male role. At an island feast, for instance, one elderly woman donned a
pair of trousers and uninhibitedly danced in front of the entire
community, to their great amusement. As for men, they tend to
become more sedentary as they give up fishing, thus exhibiting a
female trait.

The younger members of the homesite as well as descent line
members living elsewhere are all expected to care for the elderly and
provide them with food. Ideally, these people include the children of
the elderly; even if they reside at another homesite or off the island,
they should regularly send food to their parents. These relatives should
be particularly attentive when the elderly become ill. An ailing person
is customarily moved to a canoe house in order to accommodate their
relatives who return to attend to them. When an illness is serious or
prolonged, messages are sent to relatives on other islands, who are then
expected to sail for Pulap. Attendants massage patients, cool them with
fans, comb their hair, tell stories, or simply sit with them to prevent
loneliness. They should refrain from any loud or disturbing noises and
attempt to cheer their ill relative. In particular, attendants should
provide the favorite foods they feel the patient craves.

One concern of the attendants is with how the patient intends to dispose of his or her remaining property, since elderly people can choose to reward a solicitous relative with a deathbed gift. In fact, if someone is believed close to death, the relatives feel reluctant to send the patient to the hospital in Truk Lagoon precisely because they wish to be present to hear any final testament.

Increasing ill health is associated with aging on Pulap, and the islanders hold a mixture of beliefs concerning the causes and treatment of illnesses, pragmatically accepting a combination of traditional and modern techniques. They believe that a particular remedy may be preferable or more effective for certain ailments. If one body of therapy fails to work, they try another. Traditional techniques include massage and the use of plant medicines, accompanied in the past by magical chants. Massage, especially by younger female relatives, remains extremely common, resorted to in virtually all cases that involve body aches or require the symptomatic relief of pain.

Although a measure of understanding exists about Western views of disease, Pulapese share with other Carolinians a belief that illness can be caused by sorcery or malevolent magic. They attribute the use of such magic only to other islanders, however, particularly to Lagoon Trukese. A few recent deaths were believed to be due to evil magic practiced by Trukese while the patients were on the island of Moen. Many Pulapese in fact dread eating with Trukese in the Lagoon because they fear the food will be contaminated with evil magic.

Throughout Truk and the atolls of Yap, islanders have traditionally believed that malevolent spirits are prime causes of illness and death (Alkire 1965:115; Burrows and Spiro 1953:215; Caughey 1977:17; Lessa 1950:236). These spirits have been feared because of their reputed ability to eat a person's soul. In the past, magical chants and herbal medicines could drive out the evil spirit and thus effect a cure, but with conversion to Catholicism, they resort to medication without the chants. Holy water and a crucifix have replaced chants to drive out the spirit (or in contemporary usage, the "devil").

Traditional Pulap belief maintained that each person had a soul, which at death became a spirit. Some souls became benevolent spirits while others became malevolent ones. The way in which a person died or the circumstances of the death could influence the type of transformation. For example, if a person died violently, if he was killed or committed suicide, his soul was likely to become an evil spirit, as was that of a woman who died in childbirth. Some Pulapese feel that these souls became malevolent because an untimely death prevented people from continuing naturally into old age. Whereas malevolent ghosts caused illness, benevolent ones interceded for their living relatives. Even today, despite conversion to Christianity, people still claim to have learned recipes for medicines from deceased relatives in dreams. As is common in the Pacific, no distinct boundary separates the domain of the living from that of the dead (see Counts and Counts, chapter 1; Scaletta, chapter 10; Lepowsky, chapter 8). The dead continue to interact with the living, make an impact on their lives, and influence community affairs. Their presence is felt in everyday events among the living, "so that the living and the dead, as it were, continue to inhabit one behavioral world" (Burrows and Spiro 1953:314).

CONCLUSION

We have seen that as people age on Pulap they cease to be producers of children, and at the same time they gradually withdraw from production of food. They can continue to serve their homesite, descent group, and community in other ways, however, the most valuable being as consultants in areas requiring esoteric or specialized knowledge. As they become less involved in subsistence activities, they begin to rely on their children and other descent group or homesite members to provide for them. With age, they also become more susceptible to illness, thus requiring additional care from others. Although expectations about sex role behavior are loosened, the constraints on behavior between 'brother' and 'sister' remain in force, creating potential difficulties for aging men. As in the Marshalls (Carucci, chapter 6) and the Marquesas (Kirkpatrick, chapter 5), aging can be more problematic for men, especially widowers, than for women, who experience more continuity, security, and stability in their roles and relations throughout the life cycle.

As Pulapese age and begin to rely on younger women in particular to provide physical care and massage when they are ill, two categories of younger females can potentially play this nurturing role: daughters and sisters. Daughters, as children, should care for aging parents, and sisters must nurture and support brothers. For an elderly woman, daughters and sisters are readily available from within the descent group; consequently, their position remains secure. An elderly woman has little reason to fear neglect by younger women of her descent line, since those bonds are considered the strongest and most binding of kin ties.

A man, however, faces a different situation. Sisters are available from within the descent group, but the avoidance and respect behavior incumbent upon their relationship makes practical bodily care impossible. A 'sister', for instance, cannot massage most of the body of a 'brother'. Even remaining in the same house with him is mutually constraining and awkward. Moreover, for a man, daughters all come from outside his descent group. And although children are expected to offer assistance, labor, care, companionship, and affection to parents, we have seen that this tie is not as strong as those within the matrilineal descent group. For instance, a man who separates from his wife may weaken ties with his own children. Classificatory children, i.e., children of other men of the descent group, may also have chosen not to recognize or sustain their relationship. Thus, at a point in the life cycle when the parent-child relationship becomes crucial, a man may feel a lack of attentive children. Since the arrival of Catholicism, men have become increasingly concerned about their welfare in old age, because they cannot remarry if they have separated from their wives, leaving them without 'children'.

Although ties with children may have been alienated, a man can always count on descent line 'sisters' to sustain their ties with him. But there remain the constraints on physical care imposed by the requisite avoidance behavior. To circumvent this problem, elderly men can convert certain brother-sister relationships into father-daughter ones. Specifically, elderly men can ask sisters in lower generations to refer to them as 'fathers' and to treat them accordingly. Since the men are no longer considered sexually or economically productive and are thus no longer essential complements to descent line sisters, the sibling relationship and attendant behavior are no longer as critical. Departure from the complementary roles supporting descent group resources no longer threatens descent group solidarity and welfare since elderly men have already withdrawn from active participation in subsistence tasks. Neither is the question of sharing intercourse with sisters as serious a concern.

The need for care and nurture from younger women becomes paramount instead of mutual support sustaining the descent line. Brother-sister avoidance patterns interfere with this necessity and thus become cumbersome. Changing the inter-generational brother-sister tie to a 'father-daughter' one, however, combines in one relationship the support and nurture expected of fellow descent group members together with the rights and duties of the 'parent-child' tie. The care and attention a 'child' shows a 'parent' now is available from within the descent group for both men and for women. Elderly men and younger descent group women can then comfortably reside together. A woman can easily care for an ailing father, since she is able to massage his body, touch his head and torso, and move freely in his presence. Since the man no longer has to support the solidarity of the women of the descent group, the avoidance patterns can be loosened. Here, then, is one more example of a general loosening of constraints for the elderly, but one expressed through kinship relations. Moreover, the ideal pattern for behavior between men and women shifts from the brother-sister model to a parent-child one.

When notions of gender converge with those of kinship and are embodied in one type of relationship, both can shift with aging. Changes in gender roles and loosening of constraints on sex specific behavior can be reflected in the kinship system. Roles and relationships paramount in young and mature adulthood recede in importance when the elderly withdraw from their productive roles, and a different kin relationship may emerge as the ideal for male-female relations. In this Pulap example, the kin terms and norms for behavior are explicitly adjusted in order to convert the one ideal type into the other.

NOTES

The material presented in this chapter is based on fieldwork conducted from January 1980 to March 1981 on Pulap Atoll and among Pulap migrants in Moen, Guam, Saipan, and the United States. The research was supported by a grant from the National Science Foundation (BNS-7906640), a National Science Foundation Graduate Fellowship, and a Stanford University research assistantship.

1. Dominy, chapter 3 in this volume, provides a related example. For the New Zealand traditionalists she studied, the role of mother is central to their identity; to be a woman means to be a mother. And Kirkpatrick, chapter 5 in this volume, emphasizes the importance of relational roles in defining appropriate behavior between men and women in the Marquesas.
2. Pulap lies at the northern end of the atoll and measures 0.262 square miles in area, and to the south is Tamatam, measuring only 0.096 square miles in area (Bryan 1971). The single uninhabited islet is Fenarik (0.025 square miles), which belongs to Pulap's chiefly clan.
3. Howupwollap (also known as *Maasalé*) is the chiefly clan, and the other four are *Pwéél*, *Mongunufaŕ*, *Mwóóŕ*, and *Katamang*.
4. *Pwiiy* refers to 'my sibling of the same sex' and *mwéngiyey* to 'my sibling of the opposite sex' (although a man can also use *yáháákiy* instead of *mwéngiyey* for 'my sister').
5. The term *yafaakúr*, which designates the 'children of the men of a matrilineal descent group', can be used in two ways. First, a 'child' of a descent group can be referred to as *neyiy afaakúr* 'my child of the decent group'. In this case, *neyiy*, which is based on the word for 'child', is the possessive classifier 'my' used with animate beings. Use of the general possessive classifier *yááy* 'my' draws intriguing parallels between *yafaakúr* and *yáynang* 'clan'. *Yááy áynang* 'my clan' parallels *yááy afaakúr*, and the question *yifa yóómw áynang* 'what is your clan?' (*yóómw* is

the general classifier 'your') becomes *yifa yóómw afaakúr*. The answer is the name of ego's father's clan. Moreover, just as 'the people of one clan' are *fóón eew áynang*, all those whose fathers belong to the same clan are *fóón eew afaakúr*.

6. The term for 'my father' is *hemey*, 'my mother' is *yiney*, and 'my child' is *neyey*. Father's sister may also be referred to as *yineyhemey*, combining the terms for 'my mother' and 'my father' to mean a 'female parent on the father's side'.

7. Pulapese believe that the art of navigation originated on their island and that a woman first learned its secrets from a mythical bird.

Part II: AGING, GENDER AND DYING

5

KO'OUA: AGING IN THE MARQUESAS ISLANDS

John Kirkpatrick

INTRODUCTION

The concept of old age is applied when differences between adults are taken to signal important changes in the life cycle. Not only is old age culturally construed, it is also negotiated as people impute, question, accept, deny or reinterpret culturally recognized signs of aging. In the Marquesas Islands, a person does not become a *ko'oua* 'old person' at a fixed date, or when particular tasks become difficult.[1] Although certain signs of old age are recognized, they may be debated, for the term *ko'oua* points to more than just a phase of late adulthood. In this chapter I identify several Marquesan ideas and concerns, and I try to show the problems and opportunities involved in being, or being called, 'old' in the Marquesas. I hope thereby to isolate Marquesan contributions to a broader understanding of aging.

My analysis, which develops in a somewhat roundabout way, deals with social relations, semantics, the pragmatics of labeling, and broad cultural expectations. First, I describe several incidents that express considerable ambivalence about old age and indicate some major ethnographic problems. Next, I discuss the demographic and social context and survey the social position of older people. In order to answer the question of what Marquesans mean by *ko'oua*, I identify cultural views of the life cycle and offer a semantic analysis of *ko'oua*. The analysis in this chapter demonstrates that the situation of older Marquesans is defined, not simply in contrast to other adults, but also in relation to the body of socially upheld norms.

I will show that older people have very little power in the Marquesas. Their position is far less secure than that of older land-holders and political figures elsewhere (see Carucci chapter 6, or Nason 1981 for contrasting cases from neighboring societies). Yet their difficulties are not simply the trials of the old; others face similar problems. Although there are limits on older persons' control over others, such limits affect all adults, not just a few older ones. In a society with few non-domestic arenas of political debate and control – one in which action in such arenas is viewed ambivalently at best – broad questions of social identity loom large. Hence the extent to which older persons can present themselves and be accepted as 'mature', as both enacting and supporting ideas of how human life should be lived, overshadows many other matters.

AFFECTION AND AMBIVALENCE

In 1975, I worked with two Marquesans on Tahiti before I reached the Marquesas proper. One day, one of my teachers spoke of the people in her home valley. She went to find a picture of her *ko'oua,* her deceased fosterer, and a letter this man had sent her. In it he mentioned the pains he was suffering. He hoped that Jesus Christ had allotted them to him, rather than to priests, so that the priests could move about and minister to their congregations. He was glad that Jesus had brought a priest to the valley at a time when he thought he was about to die.

My teacher was visibly moved. Yet she called the letter the 'talk of an old man' *(tekao ko'oua),* 'different' from the talk of ordinary people. She seemed to react deeply and positively to the letter, but she dismissed it as typical of an 'old person'.

During my first months in the Marquesas, I spent much time with older informants. Some had more time free than did other people; some had worked with Henri Lavondès, and were used to ethnographic questioning. Being older, they had a sense of how social life had changed in recent decades, a topic of interest to me. Younger people, including these informants' children, suspected that they were recounting 'heathen' tales and songs, things that were better forgotten. Where I expected knowledge and perspective from elders, younger Marquesans expected 'lies'. Moreover, even when old Marquesans spoke of their youth and of people they had known then, they were likely to call older persons 'heathen'. 'Heathen' times seem to be perpetually about two generations in the past.

'Old person' seems to be an identity about which Marquesans are, at best, ambivalent, so I was surprised to hear people in their forties claim, and even insist, that they were 'old'. Both the apparent alienation of 'old persons' from others and this last, seemingly positive, claim by the middle aged to be 'old persons' need further analysis.

THE SOCIAL CONTEXT

The Marquesas Islands are high volcanic islands, six of which are inhabited. Nowadays, each of these is a commune of France. The population of over 5000 people lives in valleys, each with 80 to 800 inhabitants. Over a thousand Marquesans have emigrated to Tahiti.

Marquesans today are Christians, and are often fluent in Tahitian or French. They are separated from the traditional society of the contact period as a result of depopulation, repopulation, and extensive social change. Marquesans remain distinct in French Polynesia, for they retain their language and a sense that their interests differ from those of Tahitian speakers (Lavondès 1972). Most are pro-French politically, in opposition to the autonomist movement based on Tahiti (Kirkpatrick 1981a).

Nearly all my work was done on one island, 'Ua Pou, which is now the most populous island of the group. With a history of depopulation and repopulation, a young age structure is to be expected. Table 2 combines data gathered in two non-contiguous valleys of 'Ua Pou,

Table 2. Age Distribution, Hakahau and Hakam'i'i Valleys, 'Ua Pou, 1975

Born	Male	Female	Total
Before 1911	11	5	16
1911-1915	5	6	11
1916-1920	4	6	10
1921-1925	6	6	12
1926-1930	16	7	23
1931-1935	15	10	25
1936-1940	26	18	44
1941-1945	19	22	41
1946-1950	22	18	40
1951-1955	20	21	41
1956-1960	29	52	81
1961-1965	75	69	144
1966-1970	94	89	183
1971-1975	81	75	156
TOTAL	**423**	**404**	**827**

Working population: 328   Dependents: 499   Dependency ratio: 1.52
(b. 1911-1960)   (b. before 1911, 1960-1975)
Source: author's survey

covering about half the island population.

Crude birth rates for the island reached or exceeded 40/1000 in the period 1921-1962.[2] Since then, with the emigration of many young adults, they have lessened somewhat. Death rates of about 30/1000 were usual through 1950. After an epidemic in 1951, and a death rate of 65.8/1000 in that year, death rates have stayed below 10/1000. The change is largely attributable to improved medical care. There are now two dispensaries with professional staff on the island. Surgical care is available on Nuku Hiva or on Tahiti.

Men are preponderant in the older cohorts shown in table 2. In part this may be due to women's risk of mortality in childbirth. But the mortality of active women was not much higher than that of men until 1946-1955. It may be that, with improved health care, the risks of childbirth have diminished less than other risks.[3] Another factor of importance is emigration. Widows are more likely to emigrate to Tahiti than are older couples and widowers, for reasons that will emerge below.

Nowadays, most households contain a couple and their natal and/or foster children. Households with single heads or with more than one resident couple are not common (12 percent and 11 percent, respectively, of the 110 households surveyed).

The sample includes twenty-eight persons over sixty, in twenty-one households. Twenty are married; the rest have survived their spouses and not remarried. Table 3 shows that older Marquesans live in a range of household types. The average household population for the two valleys is over eight (households with Marquesan-born heads, N = 98); older people residing with a younger couple live in somewhat larger units. While older couples who live with single young people have smaller households, they still have not abandoned child rearing: fosterage is common.

The extent of fostering relations cannot be shown precisely. Table 3 lists households in which children were fostered by older people, the natal parents being absent from the household. In some cases, the natal parent or parents lives nearby, and may contribute to the welfare of both young and old. In other cases, not covered by the last column of table 3, older persons may see themselves as fostering (hākai, literally 'feed') children who co-reside with their natal parents. Many adult Marquesans remember a particular elder as their tupuua hākai 'foster grandparent', whether or not they were raised exclusively by that person.

The fostering role may be a matter of perspective. For example, a blind old woman who lived alone, with her children in houses nearby, was visited daily by a granddaughter who often slept with her. From her adult children's perspective, the old woman was cared for by them and the girl, but the old woman may have disagreed and seen herself as fostering the girl. Other elders, who can give children food as well

Table 3.   Marquesan Households Including Older People

Marital situation of older person(s)	Total	Number of couples in household		Mean household population	Number of households with children fostered by older person(s) [a]
		no.	cases		
Couple surviving b (husband or both more than 60)	13	1 2	8 5	5.5	6
widow	5	0 1	1 4	1 12.25	0 1
widower	3	1	3	10.3	0

a   Dependent children only counted; only one case counted per household. (This count does not cover cases in which a child resident nearby is viewed by an older person as fostered, or cases in which an older person lives with a child and that child's parents.)

b   Seven couples include both husband and wife born 1915 or earlier.

Source: author's survey, 1975.

as comfort and entertainment, have even more reason to see themselves as nurturing – fostering – one or more co-resident children.

It is difficult to establish whether older people are dependent. Older couples usually claim that they run their households, even when young people do most of the daily work, but a widow who has come to live with her child may do much of the work yet not be seen as the household head. Traditionally, Marquesans depended on horticulture and fishing for subsistence, with breadfruit as the staple food. Contemporary Marquesans continue these practices, but also earn cash income. They produce copra and coffee as cash crops, engage in wage labor – mainly unskilled labor on intermittant public works projects – make handicrafts for sale to tourists, or work in shops. A few specialists – teachers, paramedics, skilled machine operators – draw regular salaries. Older Marquesans rarely take part in these activities. Although a few run small shops, and a few earn wages as janitors, the income of older persons comes mainly from remittances from their children or the owner's share of copra income from land worked by a sharecropper.

Despite the accusation that older persons are 'heathen', they are notably religious. The bulk of the population acceded to Christianity by the 1890s, before the birth of today's old people. Marquesan involvement in Christian activities, such as choral singing of the Gospel of John in addition to regular church services, was extensive around 1920. Nowadays, all Marquesans are expected to be Christians and to participate at religious services at least twice a week. Older Marquesans, Catholic or Protestant, are often more punctilious worshippers than the young. This may, in part, reflect the stronger demands for participation made in the past, but it also can be linked to an increased concern, as people age, with the afterlife. As one old man put it: when one is no longer fit for anything in this world, one thinks of life in the world to come.

The political influence of the Marquesan elderly is small. Marquesan society is not characterized by a large number of enduring public institutions, and older people are relatively marginal to those salient public activities, such as commune construction projects or the Bastille Day celebrations that do exist. While candidates for elective office may spend much time trying to gain the support of a few older men, expecting that they will influence the votes of their children and others in their valley, many Marquesans doubt whether old men have such influence or authority. Perhaps an old man can persuade his children to vote against a candidate – but that is all. A few older men co-ordinate work on house construction or other enterprises by their children, but even their authority is widely seen as commanding only grudging respect and obedience. Moreover, the skills and knowledge relevant to most current political and economic activities are ones that older persons lack. Consequently, it is not surprising that the commune council elected in 1977 includes only one sixty-year-old person, the other sixteen members of the council being in their forties or younger (Kirkpatrick 1981a).

In only one exceptional valley was an old man respected by all as the local patriarch who could co-ordinate activities and proclaim local morality. After his death none of his sons gained the others' respect. Neither the co-operation nor the consensus the old man commanded existed after his death.

Older people do have important roles as landholders, householders, parents or *tupuna hākai*, 'nurturing senior kinsmen'. Many older persons manage domestic subsistence and control resources that younger people would like to use and inherit, but the young have some independence, so long as they have access to land in other valleys or to jobs on Tahiti.[4] Older people may gain affection and loyalty from their children, natal or fostered, but the younger people cannot be counted on to obey, or even to stay close at hand.

DOMESTIC GROUPS AND INTERGENERATIONAL RELATIONS

A couple normally lives with the parents of one or the other spouse for a while after marriage, and one or two children may be born before the couple establishes a separate household. In the new household a simple grouping of parents and children exists for a while, but as the older children grow they go off to school in distant valleys. By age 18, most young people are considering leaving home to enter military service, to work on Tahiti, to marry, or simply to roam. While the young roam, they also return: to visit, to help out their parents for a while, or perhaps to set up their own households nearby. As household heads age, they can expect to call younger workers back to the valley, if not necessarily to the household, but it is not certain just which young people will return. In some cases, the children of an older couple return in sequence, each staying a few months of the year, then departing only to have another move in.

A household need not be economically self-sustaining, if it can count on help from neighbors or remittances from elsewhere. Young Marquesans are apt to leave the islands planning to send back money or gifts. (A planned gift may be magnificent – a refrigerator or a stove – as the giver hopes to show parents just how loving s/he is.) Older Marquesans are rather jaundiced about remittances and returning children. Young emigrants find expensive distractions, while married emigrants find that their commitments to their spouses and children come first. The result is that neither money nor returning labor can be counted on. Despite this uncertainty, older people strive to keep up their own households and even add to their burdens by fostering small children. A pervasive trend in Marquesan household patterns is that dependents must be present, although there may be little chance that they will stay long enough to contribute much labor to the household. Hence Marquesans' careers as caregivers usually continue until their deaths. Adult Marquesans like to see their households as self-sustaining and reproductive units (see Kirkpatrick 1981b, 1983).[5]

With adults engaging continually in social reproduction through nurture, a crucial problem emerges as household heads grow old, a problem that is reinforced by marriage and parenthood beginning at an early age.[6] When older adults are likely to need the help of younger workers, their older children will be in their thirties or older, a time when their own domestic responsibilities are at their height. Tensions between householders and their offspring are hence predictable at two points: (1) when parents need assistance but adolescents want to roam or marry away from the household, and (2) when adult children are

committed to their own families. These tensions could be reduced by
an unambiguous authority structure or by clear rules for recruiting
young workers to households, but both are lacking. Marquesans tend to
muddle through these situations. The most precise and verifiable claims
I heard concerning parental authority applied to situations in which two
young adult couples co-resided. Quarrels are sure to erupt in this case,
Marquesans say, even though one member of each couple is a sibling
to a member of the other. If a parent lives with them, calm can be
restored, for the parent can threaten to evict one couple from the
house. Beyond this limited control, and supervision of ongoing work to
see that all necessary jobs get done, older householders have little
authority over the adult or adolescent members of their households.

The right to evict rests in ownership of the house. Older people
usually own land as well, but control of this resource does little to
augment their power. This is true for two reasons: First, garden land is
abundant, while coconut groves – land that can yield a cash income –
are few. Most men can make copra, on their land or others', for only a
few months per year. Older people usually allot the chance to work
their groves to adult children, the income being divided between owner
and worker.[7] The income does not suffice for more than necessities and
a few luxuries; therefore, to save for a major project, such as house
building, men must find wage labor. A landholder cannot offer an
inducement sufficient to keep workers nearby unless they are otherwise
satisfied with their place of residence.

Second, landholders have little power over potential heirs. French
inheritance law militates for an equal division of property among the
children of a deceased person. Marquesans often make wills and legal
donations of land. They do so largely to give foster children rights
similar to those that legitimate children enjoy by inheritance. The idea
of excluding heirs altogether is unacceptable.

In sum, then, older Marquesans are marginal to most public activities and have little control over others outside their households. Within
the household they can command the labor of pre-adolescent children,
and perhaps co-ordinate the work of older residents. Lacking much
authority, they may complain a good deal, or direct adults who feel
that no supervision is needed. They have rights, as recognized household heads or landholders, but the free exercise of those rights over
younger adults is difficult or unthinkable. Little wonder, then, that
older people may no longer feel they 'fit' in this world, and may look
ahead to life in Heaven. When they die, their lands will continue to be
worked by their children, while their homes, if they have managed to
keep them, may be taken apart so the heirs can divide up the boards

and sheet tin for their own homes. The deceased will be remembered as 'ancestors', and little more.[8]

MARQUESAN VIEWS OF HUMAN DEVELOPMENT

Marquesans' judgments of their consociates often involve what seem to be age categories. People are routinely termed 'young' *(hou)* or 'old' *(ko'oua)*, 'kids' *(tŏ'iki)*, 'young people' *(po'i hou)*, 'errant youth' *(taure'are'a)*, or *'enana mōtua* 'mature adults'.[9] Widespread expectations and premises underlie such ascriptions. These can be discussed as falling under two related headings: physical and personal development.

Physically, children develop until they reach a high point of energy and beauty in their late teens. When photographing family groups, I was often asked for a separate picture of a young person. Parents were proud of their children's looks and wanted them recorded before they disappeared. Throughout adult life, energy diminishes and beauty is lost. Late in life, physical debilitation may bring mental degeneration. Senility is recognized as a potential hazard of old age and is termed 'strong old age'.

Although the physical prospects of adult life are grim, people can overcome them by calling on capacities other than brute force.[10] Limitations imposed by declining energy can be met with increased skill, planning, and calls on the labor of the young. Adults can consolidate their efforts, while the young are expected to be skittish and to fail to follow through on complex projects. More generally, maturity involves a stability of purpose that the immature are held to lack (Kirkpatrick 1983; n.d.).

When 'kids' work, 'the day is done, but the job isn't done'. Adults claim that 'kids' think only of play. As they age, they will become *taure'are'a* 'errant youth', who are concerned with 'bad play': sexuality and dissipation. Eventually, young people marry and 'do not wobble any more'. A married couple may be compared to the hull and outrigger of a canoe: both are needed if the canoe is to travel in a straight line. Marriage does not, by itself, convey stability. It is only about the time that a second child is born to a couple that the spouses are expected to stop 'wandering', to be firmly committed to the marriage and to domestic responsibilities.

Not only skills, but interpersonal qualities as well, are consolidated in adulthood. Although the young may evince *ka'oha* 'concern, compassion' for others at times, this attitude is not 'fixed' in them. 'Concern' – and respect, shame, and even envy – arise momentarily in the young but become enduring capacities of the mature.

Marquesans thus have detailed expectations of actors' competences and proclivities. Adults voice expectations (which the young accept, or at least fail to counter loudly) that sketch out a view of mature people as capable actors who organize an orderly and nurturant life-world. Moreover, the capacities of *'enana mōtua* 'mature adults' that allow them to support a productive life-world – e.g., foresight, persistence, compassion – are precisely those mentioned when Marquesans explain how people differ from animals. The 'mature' are *'enana* 'persons' par excellence. Hence an implication of the everyday claims that the young lack continuing purpose and interpersonal skills is that they are not fully or thoroughly 'persons'.

The categorical distinctions between youth and age, maturity and immaturity are clear-cut, but the interrelations of these oppositions and their reference to particular persons are more complex. Physical development follows an easily predicted course, and occurs at much the same rate for most people. Personal development is another matter, for categories such as 'kid' and 'mature adult' synthesize observers' judgments of a person's activities, relationships, interests and attitudes. Marquesans view the sequence described above as nearly inevitable (although a few people never quite seem mature), but its timing is clearly variable.

While views of the course of personal development are shared, the judgments that are made about the lives and identities of particular persons often are not. A young man of twenty or so may see himself as a dedicated worker who does much to support his family. As such a worker, others may view him as an energetic 'young person' who needs direction in order for his work to be productive. He may see occasional athletics and dancing as his well earned rest; others may be quick to label him an idle 'errant youth', devoted to the pursuit of pleasure. When he marries and establishes his own household, he gives clear evidence of neither maturity nor immaturity, except insofar as *any* evidence of less than total dedication to domesticity signals immaturity.

Maturity is both easy and hard to reach. Any adult couple with normal physical resources can establish a home, have children and provide for them. Over time, most adults will be seen as being at least *among* the mature, the 'folks' of a local population. Yet anyone who would question a person's maturity will find ample evidence in the misdeeds of children, in occasional unfinished tasks, in household disrepair or dirt, and in drinking or other restive behavior.

Maturity cannot be claimed overtly. The mature 'see what is to be done and do it'; instead of claiming a status, they work. Maturity exists in the opinion of consociates, and while one's peers may value ordinary work and domesticity, they are also capable of carping gossip. By the time a person's maturity is obvious to and accepted by all, that person may be so old that questions arise as to whether s/he supports the household or is being supported by others.

Despite these ambiguities, 'maturity' condenses matters of crucial importance to Marquesans, and people are unwilling to relinquish its signs. Older people insist on maintaining their own households, even when their children offer them a more comfortable place elsewhere. They recruit dependents, and thereby prolong their careers as nurturers. Some older people with children of working age cast doubt on the adequacy of the support those children provide, or on their ability to support a household without continuing supervision. One old man spoke of younger members of his household as generally capable, but he saw his authority over them as both the consequence of and the return on his years of work to support his children. Their efforts were, in his opinion, testimony to his own.

THE SEMANTICS OF *KO'OUA*

In the discussion above, *ko'oua* refers to physical development, not personal development. Yet it is clear that judgments in terms of either age or domestic relations easily suggest evaluations of maturity, and hence of personal worth. Before developing this idea, the semantics of *ko'oua* need clarification. *Ko'oua* stands in four oppositions that can be elicited with ease. It is also used relationally.

1. *Ko'oua* may be distinguished from *pakahio*. The latter term applies to old women; the former is unmarked for gender.

2. *Ko'oua* contrasts with *ko'oua oko* 'strongly old' and *ko'oua pē* 'badly old'. Both these phrases apply to persons who are senile. It is better to be *ko'oua* than senile, of course, but the terms for senility are derived from *ko'oua*, so it is clear that the distinction may be seen as a thin one.

3. *Ko'oua* is opposed to *hou* 'young, new'. *Hou* can be used with reference to many objects or events; *ko'oua*, however, is restricted to persons.

4. An adult population may be treated as divided into two categories – *te tau 'enana mōtua* 'mature adults', and *te koko'oua* 'the old persons'. This distinction is not always made: both categories can be subsumed under the more general one of *te tau 'enana* – 'persons', 'folks' or 'adults'.

Relational uses of the term are often heard. A person's *ko'oua* is usually a beloved ascendant, a parent, fosterer or nurturing elder. Also, some adults speak of their spouses as their *ko'oua* and *pakahio,* their 'old man' and 'old woman'. In all these relationships, *ko'oua* can be used vocatively.[11]

THE PRAGMATICS OF *KO'OUA:* SELF ASCRIPTIONS

The anecdotes at the beginning of this chapter were brief; little context was provided. But context may be crucial, as in the following situation.

I am sitting with an informant on the steps of his half-completed house, built of cement, boards and sheet tin. He is forty-five, and the father of eleven children. He has been ill in the recent past, but looks hale and well-fed. We face a garden he recently planted. His wife is cooking. Some of the children are at school; others are at work for wages elsewhere. I make a comment about the pleasant life he has made for himself. He says he is old. He cannot fish or do other work as he could in his twenties. Why, then he was a champion spear fish-erman. Then he had strength and endurance. Now he is past it.

When the informant talks of his youth, he draws on the semantic contrast between young and old (number three, above). He does more, however, than mourn his lost youth. With his successful management of a prosperous household on view, and even mentioned by me, his statements about youth and age convey another message, a message about accomplishments and the competences necessary to achieve them. The explicit statement *e ko'oua au* "I am old" is the vehicle for an implicit one, that his accomplishments derive from mature abilities to plan, direct and complete work, not youthful brawn and energy.

The fact that something rather complex was occurring was evident from several cues: the lack of obvious connection between "I am old" and the preceding conversation; the informant's unusually definitive manner; and his subsequent talk of his children as young, frivolous and thoughtless. But he did not simply make *ko'oua* mean what he wanted it to. Instead, this was an instance of a pragmatic move made possible and even desirable, given Marquesan cultural grounds.

Similarly, others may say that they are tired, dirty, old. As they are no longer young, they come home late from garden work, heavily burdened by their harvest. When they were young they would have gathered these crops, come home, taken a shower, and gone off to play late in the day. Those people make the same sort of claim as my infor-mant, and supply hints about the context in which to interpret it.

Given the value Marquesans find in the competence and activity of the mature, the horror of senility or inactivity in dependent old age is obvious. One changes from being fully a person to being supported by others, being immobile, being evidently less than a fully competent person. Marquesans expectably struggle against both being and appearing to be dependent. They keep working to support themselves and others, and they even recruit new dependents whose presence testifies to their activity.

Why, then, should middle aged Marquesans claim to be 'old'? Two points raised earlier are relevant here. First, physical development is related to but distinct from personal development. Second, the status of mature adulthood cannot be claimed overtly. *Hou* 'youth' is the physical counterpart to an often-mentioned, devalued or ambiguously valued personal identity, *taure'are'a,* 'errant youth', while *ko'oua* is linked to an identity that is valued, but goes largely unmentioned with regard to particular persons. Consequently, *ko'oua* 'old age' cannot function, as *hou* 'youth' does, as a residual category covering diverse qualities and activities that do not fit a stereotype. Instead, its relation to *'enana mōtua* 'mature adults' is ambiguous, and open to specification in many contexts.

To say that someone is old is to comment on his or her life span. A Marquesan hearing this will search for the relevance of this statement of an obvious fact, and will suspect that one is really speaking about the person's competence or loss of competence as a productive householder. To say that one is old oneself, while evidence of past and present mature activity surrounds one, and one's willingness and ability to interact with a strange being such as an ethnographer gives further evidence of maturity – to say this is to invite the hearer to notice one's accomplishments, and the particular attitudes and work that made them possible. One is old, yet capable of doing all this. "I am old" implies a claim to maturity that cannot be challenged because it was not uttered. As challengers to any self-praise abound in the Marquesas, this sort of implicit claim is pragmatically very successful.

THE PRAGMATICS OF *KO'OUA:* LABELING

When others label a person as a *ko'oua* or draw implications about an 'old person' that do not arise with reference to others, *ko'oua* can carry negative value. The two cases mentioned earlier, in which persons were seen as 'old' and 'different' or 'heathen', involve a contrast between 'old' and 'the mature' as a set (semantic contrast number four above).

The force of the contrast lies in that the 'mature' *('enana mōtua)* are easily assimilated with 'folks' *('enana)*. 'Folks' do more than make a living: they support a normative order.

Marquesans treat what we would take to be social rules in two distinct ways. First, 'rules' *(ture)* exist. These are created and enunciated by outsiders: priests and policemen (the word *ture* itself is Tahitian). People follow these rules, more or less, because they recognize God, they respect the priest and they accept French rule. They draw on their mental competence as 'persons' to do so. But these rules are still not the rules *of* Marquesans. Marquesans recognize no such thing as Marquesan law or custom nowadays. Instead, they recognize a second sort of social rule by speaking of things people expectably do, and like to do: activities supported by a consensus of adults. Again, there is no agreed-on rule covering many proprieties, but Marquesans note that 'folks will talk' on little pretext.

While Marquesans view themselves as free agents, 'heathens' in the past are known to have submitted to strange gods. They maintained rules of their own, taboos and the like. They had a code distinct from public opinion, a code that seems benighted to Marquesans today. To act as a 'heathen', then, is to promulgate and follow rules distinct from both the opinion of sensible persons and the laws of state and church that Marquesans have accepted.

With age, people lose the peers who know them in intimate detail; who share memories of past pleasures and accomplishments; who share old jokes; who have, with them, created and followed the good sense of public opinion of times past. This communicative impoverishment may make an elder, in some cultures, a source of arcane wisdom. In the Marquesas, it leaves a person with memories and opinions that are best left unsaid if they show 'what people like to do' nowadays to be a contingent historical product.

An older person who reminds others that Tahitian dancing or wearing colorful clothes to church were once viewed as sinful is open to challenge as a self-appointed source of a distinctive morality: as, in short, 'heathen'. Old people face a choice between silence and the risk of being labeled as marginal, even deviant. Some take the risk. Consequently there is a sense in which there may always be 'heathens' in the Marquesas.[12]

This labeling practice is not based so much on what older persons labeled as heathen say and do as it is on a cultural contradiction. Marquesans claim great ability and choice for themselves as 'persons' or 'folks', yet expect and enforce a considerable degree of self-restraint in social life. The contradiction between freedom and restraint is muted by a view of social controls as produced by good sense, not arbitrary convention or external force. Norms are granted timeless value as the product of human intelligence. Those who experience change most deeply, and hence know well that the here and now is contingent, may find it hard to be up to date.[13] There is, however, little alternative.

AGING AND GENDER

Thus far, I have largely ignored differences between aging men and women. Gender affects peoples' opportunities to maintain valued mature identities in distinct ways (the term "gender" is used loosely here).[14] Strong gender stereotypes are to be found among Marquesans. These are usually more allusive than prescriptive, and they may be reversible in different contexts. I heard that men are more persistent than women, so women give in to men, but I also heard the reverse. Gender expectations do not restrict action so much as establish baselines from which particular persons are likely to diverge. Such divergence is rarely seen as a violation of norms, as the example below shows.

Gender stereotypes set up an opposition between land and sea, an opposition that affects fishing behavior (see Flinn chapter 4). Men fish from canoes or with spear guns; women gather crustaceans and fish with lines from the shore. This opposition may be overturned, however, for women may fish from canoes, and men from the shore, for recreation.

Marquesans sometimes distinguish husbands' and wives' roles sharply, but in practice the distinctions are usually muted. The distinctions do, however, contribute to different opportunities and constraints encountered by aging men and women. The work of supporting a domestic unit may be divided into standard tasks. Husbands are expected to venture from their households to gather food, and to go above ground and below it (gathering breadfruit and coconuts; digging storage pits for fermented breadfruit paste and earth ovens for festive meals). Most fishing is done by men, while women are responsible for tasks at or near the house: cleaning, child care, cooking, laundry.

Everyday work in most households is done by a wider range of inhabitants than just a husband and wife. For example, house yards are cleaned daily, usually by children. Children also often tend babies and run errands, while adolescent girls do much of the cooking and cleaning, and breadfruit may be gathered, with a picking pole, by nearly anyone. Work upland – gathering coconuts and cutting out the meat for copra – is often done by couples with their children, not just by men.

Not only do male/female distinctions fail to map the variety of ways household labor is allocated to accomplish tasks, these distinctions may be contradicted in practice. The most summary statement I heard of the opposition was "It's for the husband to feed, and for the wife to clean." Marquesans take laundry work to be outside husbands' normal duties, but men do such work, and see it as reasonable, in particular circumstances. A single man may do his own laundry, while a married man may see this work as appropriate for him in the context of the resources of his own household. Thus, one man, whose wife was anemic and very sensitive to cold water, washed his family's clothes rather than have her suffer. In another family, an older man who could no longer work regularly away from the house took over child care, cooking and laundry work at the house while his wife secured a cash income and breadfruit for the household. Both those involved and observers agreed that while such task allocations were unusual, they were more to be praised, as being resourceful adaptations to circumstances that got the work done, than questioned as anomalous.

While Marquesans stress the importance of male/female couples for personal and domestic stability, people take pride in managing a household alone. Not only men, but women can accomplish this. Wives whose husbands have departed to work elsewhere, and some single women, support themselves and their dependent children without outside help. This competence brings out the limits on evaluations of gender differences. Men are expected to be, and largely are, more mobile than women, travelling further for pleasure when young and for income in adulthood. Travelling husbands need not place their wives in others' care. These women, as competent 'persons', can do the work necessary to support a household. This is to say that they can meet, on a daily basis, the domestic demands that prompt their husbands to seek out wages elsewhere.[15]

As men and women age, their ability to maintain households changes. Earlier in this chapter, I noted the position of several widows as active participants in households seen as run by younger adults. Older men are likely to be recognized as in charge of a household, but aging men are often incapable of the domestic work linked to their gender. No longer able to do heavy physical labor, a few men are inactive dependents in their children's households, while women of similar age and circumstances are busy caregivers, obviously contributing to the domestic economy. (It should be stressed that Marquesans value both the importation of food and income to a household, and the work to keep the household orderly and clean. While housework is stereotypically women's work, it is not viewed as being of little value in comparison to men's work).

Older women are more likely to move into another's household than are older men, but (a) older women can do more to demonstrate their continuing competence than older men, and (b) it is the survival of a couple, rather than the differential chances of men versus women, that most clearly affects the identity of mature adults. Gender expectations help older women to demonstrate their 'maturity' (this may explain the willingness of widows to emigrate: their work, not a house built in years past, testifies to their abilities). The activities of older men do not *violate* gender expectations. Some men are busy craftsmen or store-keepers: productive but not highly mobile. Others either diverge from gender role expectations in a way that shows both their commitment to domestic continuity and their resourcefulness, or they are inactive. The last group fails to find much to do as productive adults, not just as male householders. They may direct younger people, and claim to be productive by doing so. Their inactivity and the abilities of the young are, however, evident. Observers may see the patient 'concern' of young adults, not sage direction, as assuring the household's 'life'. In sum, then, gender expectations affect the ways in which older couples, widows and widowers enact their 'maturity', but provide different opportunities and problems, rather than a clear advantage, to men versus women.

CONCLUSION

'Old age' is a well-recognized status among Marquesans, but one with ambiguous application to particular persons. Claims that a person is old are often strategic, rather than definitive, for they point to a person's ability to deal with changing resources and situations.

A process of declining social involvement seems nearly inevitable in old age. As people become less mobile, and as youth rise to social prominence, older members of any society seem likely to maintain diminishing social networks. Marquesans, with their concern for demonstrated personal identities and competent productive actions, recognize this process – but they recognize it as a process of adulthood, not just old age. It begins around the time of marriage, when work for one's own household and the establishment of one's own *fāmī* 'family, offspring' overshadow commitments to peers and valley-wide groups (e.g., sports teams). Mature domestic identities are bulwarked by the nurturing of a series of dependents whom a couple bears or fosters, not by consolidating parental, then grandparental, statuses.

This is to say that aging is not so much a process or state of loss as it is one of accomplishment. Loss does occur, both gradually and, with failing abilities or the death of a spouse, suddenly. Aging as a career (Myerhoff 1978: 251) is continuous with mature careers. Marquesans see loss as important long before old age. Mature competence replaces and exceeds in value the energies of youth. People strive to make their old age a prolongation of maturity, not a slow slide into death, but that maturity itself is an accommodation to diminished abilities.

For all its value, the benefits of maturity are not entirely evident. Hard working adults may be esteemed so long as they go about their business, but little public authority ensues. Women dedicated to their households may have no extra-domestic role beyond that of a Christian worshipper. Others may help to enunciate the consensus of 'folks', but can do little to direct it.

Earlier I stressed the risks of expressing opinions and values that call accepted ideas into question. Old people may be seen as 'heathen', or they may be reduced to a silence nearly as complete as that of the ancestors. This silence is not, however, theirs alone: it is the lot of many in a society with few accepted public arenas. In those arenas, public discourse is largely a matter of talk by a few, and muttered assent or disbelief by others. Those who speak separate themselves out from the mass of 'folks' (Kirkpatrick 1981a).

In this chapter, I have tried to avoid applying simplistic concepts of power to a people who look askance at any who try to impose their will on other adults. Equally, I have tried to note the evident disparities, in freedom of action and speech, that exist between the middle aged and many older people, and between men and women. How to interpret the advantage conveyed by the freedom to speak is moot. Perhaps the question of who can make fools of themselves by speaking out in public is less important than the dilemma created by the fact that speaking out makes one seem a fool.

One man who wrote an autobiographical fragment at the request of Henri Lavondès concludes his account with a portrait of himself, sitting amidst his children and watching his island change drastically. The passage reminds me of the conversations reported above, in which I was led to appreciate how much an older person has accomplished. Yet, another perspective is suggested. The writer has raised his children and built a fine house. His work is done, but new tasks loom in the future. He seems irrelevant to that new world, more an ancestral figure than a contemporary actor. The image of a productive householder is easily transformed into one of a figure from the past who can only ask questions of the present. What new things will come? How will the children and grandchildren make their lives in new times? Young adults ask these questions, too. They have no certain answers; they must act on guesses to provide for themselves and their children in a changing world. They may succeed, but that success may quickly fade from view. Many seem to lack, and perhaps cannot hope for, the sense this old man conveys of being rooted in a place that has been made fruitful by his own efforts.

NOTES

Fieldwork with Marquesans was carried out from August, 1975 through August, 1977. The research was suppored by a training fellowship from the National Institute of Health (PHS 1-F31-MH05154) and a grant from the National Science Foundation (SOC75-13983). Sponsorship in French Polynesia, and much further help, was provided by the Centre O.R.S.T.O.M. on Tahiti. Henri Lavondès did much to help me begin my fieldwork. Since then, he has consistently provided much information, perspicuous suggestions, and encouragement.

This chapter combines data and arguments from a paper delivered to the ASAO symposium on Aging, Gender, and Dying and from talks given at the University of Rochester and Connecticut College. I thank the symposium participants, Alfred Harris, Tim Jacobs, and Geoffrey M. White for criticism and suggestions. I also thank Mary Martini, who has contributed to all phases of the research and writing.

1. *Ko'oua* is unmarked for gender, while *pakahio* is the term for an old woman or women. Both terms can take optional reduplicative plural forms: *koko'oua, papakahio*.

2. These data are drawn from the records of the *Etat Civil* kept by the Commune of 'Ua Pou, and from a number of other sources. Rates were calculated for those years in which a population census or estimate for the whole island was available, not for all years. For more detail and a list of sources, see Kirkpatrick (1983). That work contains further discussion of the demographic and social issues raised here.

3. My data on mortality come from communal records. They do not show the cause of death. Nor are off-island deaths recorded. Hence the data cited here and in Kirkpatrick (1983) are at best suggestive of patterns of mortality.

4. Unskilled jobs were fairly easy to find on Tahiti at the time of my fieldwork. The subsequent recession may have changed matters significantly, but I lack current data.

5. Fosterage in Oceania is often seen as a mechanism for recruiting domestic labor (see, for example, Hooper 1970). Marquesan elders often complain that young people should stay to care for those who cared for them. If fosterage is to be explained in terms of labor recruitment, it works rather badly in the Marquesas. A more satisfying explanation can be found in adults' need to have dependents whose existence testifies to their nurturers' competence.

6. The mean age at first marriage is under twenty-two for men, under eighteen for women. Most couples have children soon after marriage.

7. Copra income is officially divided fifty/fifty, unless the worker cleared the grove of brush. Then a sixty/forty division is expected. The actual division may be different, as the owner or worker may choose to take a smaller share out of 'concern' for the other. On this point, reliable data for many transactions are lacking. My impression is that older persons are as likely to be generous to their children, who have many mouths to feed, as vice versa.

8. In the Marquesas, there is little reason to look forward to becoming an ancestor. Ancestors may be remembered for unusual possessions or quirks of behavior; most go unmentioned, and seem irrelevant to their descendants' life (see note 10).

9. *Tŏ'iki* is glossed as 'kid(s)' to distinguish it from *tama* 'child(ren)'. The latter term always implies an intergenerational relationship; the former usually does not. For more detailed analysis of the terms and categories discussed in this section, see Kirkpatrick (1983).

10. 'Life' can be understood in several ways: as physical survival and as social continuity in domestic enterprises above all. Again, 'death' *(mate 'ia)* is a complex matter, one less fully explored than 'life' is in this chapter.

    Death is seen in fairly naturalistic terms by Marquesans, as proceeding from disease or accident, not mystical forces (a death may be prefigured by a *hakatu* 'sign', however). Death is the occasion for grieving, a funeral that many attend, and little more. Messages of condolence are broadcast for a short period. Then the immediate family of the deceased may attend special religious services, while others go back to normal activities. The dead person is apt to be shorn, in memory, of most of his or her biography. The late Mayor of 'Ua Pou, who was deeply mourned by many, was remembered in the weeks after his death mainly in terms of a series of feats. Others are similarly depersonalized in memory, until they are known only as ancestral 'trunks' *(tumu)* or 'insides' *('oto)* from which the living have sprung.

11. The reciprocal terms to *ko'oua* in intergenerational relations include *tama* 'child', *po'opuna* 'grandchild', *po'iti* 'dear boy' and *paho'e* 'dear girl'. Between husband and wife, *ko'oua* and *pakahio* are in some cases used reciprocally.

12. No Marquesan explained to me that people are called 'heathen' as adherents of a specific morality. The inference is mine. I do not claim to have exhausted the meaning of 'heathen' in Marquesan discourse, only to have shed some light on Marquesans' apparently counter-factual claims that their elders are, or are likely to be, 'heathen'. More generally, I suspect that this sort of usage may be widespread in the Pacific, i.e., that many people's willingness to see their ascendants as plunged in heathen darkness follows not so much from their Christian devotion as from their sense of themselves as free and reasonable actors.

13. The process at issue is complex, and hardly confined to the Marquesas. I stress knowledge here, but the work of maintaining ties to bases of personal identity and value when energy fails is also important. Blythe gives a telling example from England:

> ...having to reduce the elaborate intellectual and ethical structure upon which their lives have been built to a formula which can satisfy both themselves and others is the none-too-easy task of the aged, particularly if they have been connected with some great spiritual or political movement. One old bedridden and lonely woman achieved this: asked how she managed to pass the sleepless nights, she said, "I mostly sing" (1979:242).

    This task is, I think, not confined to those who have tried to remake the world; anyone whose world has changed in continuing, complex ways faces the problem, and many may lack the advantages that slogans, songs and declarations give to the politically committed.

14. Gender is a category of doubtful utility, although it is accepted in this chapter. First, in the Marquesas, it is the survival of marital unions, not gender, that is most important for identity-maintenance. Second, the notion of gender, as distinct from physical sexuality, is hard to define for analytic purposes, or as a gloss for cultural categories (see Kessler and McKenna 1978). In another work (Kirkpatrick 1983), I suggest that Marquesans emphasize potentials for relationship in this context: notions of gender, social relations and sexual preference intertwine. Adult men and women differ in more respects than anatomical ones – but so, in different ways, do priests, nuns, and others who combine particular anatomies with distinctive styles of action and relationship. Here, ascriptions concerning 'women/wives', 'husbands', and 'adult males' are treated as data on gender, along with behavioral regularities that may go little mentioned.

15. Labor migration by married men is seen as motivated by hopes to clothe children better, to buy materials for a house – to provide for a household. When wages are spent on drink or amusements on Tahiti, Marquesans are rueful or caustic, but they do not claim that so much effort and inconvenience was sustained with the intention of squandering its fruits. The fact that people often do not meet their enunciated goals does not overshadow those goals, it only shows that people are fallible.

6

CONCEPTIONS OF MATURING
AND DYING
IN THE 'MIDDLE OF HEAVEN'

Laurence Marshall Carucci

INTRODUCTION

Residents of the United States and other western societies often assume that precise boundaries separate life and non-life. In ongoing arbitrations on abortion and life support, lawyers, medical specialists, and concerned citizens of varied ideological persuasion, share in their search for clear-cut definitional features of life (Arafat and Allen 1975:1-15; Jury and Jury 1978; Cincotta 1979:13-31; King 1979:1647-1687; Werner 1979; President's Commission for the Study of Ethical Problems 1980:669-670; Garn 1981: S567-S578; Kart 1981:417-423; Sherwin 1981:21-34; Stinson and Stinson 1981:5-18). In contrast to this quest for rigid boundaries are the distinctions between life and death made by the Enewetak people who live on Ujelang Atoll in the vast stretch of ocean between the western chain of the Marshall Islands and the eastern Caroline Islands.[1] *RiUjelang,* literally 'people of the middle of heaven,' purposely keep the boundaries between life and non-life fuzzy. Contained within that fuzzy area are many types of liminal characters who are neither here nor there (Turner 1969); they remain on the edge (Hocart 1952), and are entities that pass freely between the world of the living and the world of the dead. Enewetak people view birth as a tenuous moment of half-life, half-non-life, and they likewise view aging and dying as processes that unite as well as separate the living and the dead. Death does not represent a sharp break with life – it perpetuates an ongoing transfer of energy (life force) that lends temporal reality to families and clans. The ebb and flow of this energy becomes apparent in the processes of maturing and dying, processes that begin with the birth and growth of a child.

CATEGORIES OF EXISTENCE IN THE MIDDLE OF HEAVEN

On Ujelang a fetus or newborn baby may easily pass back into the world of the non-living because it has no strength. From the point of conception until the *keemem* 'first birthday' it is 'in the space between life and non-life' (Carucci 1980: chapter 5). A child is created by mixing the blood and fluids of the female with the semen of the male. If the combination is good a child will result, but if the combination is *jekaar* 'unfitted', a child may not be created; if created, it will be abnormal. The potential for each child pre-exists in the pubescent female as a part of her clan inheritance. Evil magic, spiritual intervention, or physical illness may prevent a pubescent woman from having children; but each woman who conceives a child becomes the 'pathway' between that child and the clan. Since all children are tied to a matri-clan through the same umbilicus (cf., Tobin 1967:88; Rynkiewich 1972:43), each receives a share of the clan essence. The man, however, also contributes to the creation of the child. Mixing male and female fluids is critical in conception, but the genitor strengthens the fetus through continued intercourse after conception, and his semen mixes freely with the mother's milk to further shape the child. Intercourse with a man other than the genitor at any time before weaning is apt to harm the child and bring about its premature demise (the Lusi of Kaliai, Papua New Guinea have a similar belief; see Counts and Counts, chapter 7).

Spirits often, of their own accord, cause the death of very young children, prevent the birth of a fetus, or cause it to be born unhealthy or with a severe physical impairment. The death of such a child is seen, essentially, as a failure to achieve life successfully. Babies are weak and helpless, and spirits may bring harm to them because they are easy prey, but spirits are also attracted to infants because they are so similar; like spirits, babies have a number of human characteristics, but they are not fully human. Not until a child has attained one year of age is it recognized as a person with significant human faculties. At that point the child is feasted, wished well, and welcomed into the community.

After its first birthday celebration a child begins to move from the status of *niñniñ* 'babyhood' to that of *ajiri* 'childhood'. The transition is as gradual as the route to self-sustenance is slow: from not knowing how to move, an infant learns how to crawl and finally how to walk; from not knowing how to talk, a baby learns how to speak and eventually how to communicate effectively; from being breast-fed, a child learns how to eat like a person. Each of these are important markers of maturity that separate babies from other children. The birth of another baby in the family often completes one's passage into childhood, but the identity 'baby' remains for mothers to use to shame their children into acting in ways that are appropriate to their ages. The identity is also used frequently by children to deride the baby-like actions of their peers. For Marshallese children, any unthinking, inane, or worthless action is typical of babies.

As children mature they are referred to as a group, and often addressed, as *ajiri* 'children', but singly they are increasingly referred to as *laddik* and *leddik* 'male and female youngsters'. These terms may be applied at birth to distinguish the sex of a newborn, but sexual identity for babies and very young children is of little importance. Sex specific terms are more frequently applied to youngsters four or five years of age who are becoming proficient at babysitting, laundering, cooking, running errands, gathering firewood, and at other activities appropriate to their gender-specific identities.

Once past puberty, or when they have lost their virginity, youngsters are called *lekau* and *lijiroñ* 'male and female adolescents', or *iuut* 'youth'. In anticipation of the transition they are said to be *lekaulok* or *lijiroñlok* 'more of a male or female adolescent' or 'closer to being a male or female youth', for youth in the Marshall Islands represents the prime of life. As in Samoa (Mead 1928), youth on Enewetak is a period with few responsibilities and a time when both males and females are approaching their maximum physical beauty. Specific rites of passage no longer accompany the move to adolescence, but physiological changes are clearly marked by significant changes in a young person's cultural classification, and social relations are adjusted accordingly. The disparate activities appropriate to men and women become even more obvious, prohibitions between male and female siblings come into effect, and dissension and schism begin to disrupt formerly close and casual ties between cross-cousins of the same sex as sexual familiarity develops between cross-cousins of the opposite sex (Carucci 1980: chapter 2; Flinn:chapter 4). An increased understanding of clan identity eventually results from the rift cross-cousins experience during their youth.

Entry into adulthood is a gradual process that overlaps with adolescence. People sometimes refer to an adolescent or young adult as a child as a way of bringing offensive childish actions into line, but also as a complimentary way to note youthful abilities. At the other extreme, responsible girls who are nearing puberty are occasionally referred to as mature, though they are not adults nor have they lost their virginity. The categories of aging can thus be used situationally to great rhetorical advantage without the least bit of ambiguity. In different circumstances a married man in his early thirties might be said to be 'like a small child', a *lukuun alab* 'true respected elder or family head', or 'very elderly' 'like an aging ancestor'. These typically Marshallese statements use exaggeration to point out or modify another person's actions; to be meaningful such exaggerations rely on shared understandings about the boundaries between categories of aging and knowledge of the limits of acceptable action for members of each age group.

Rutto 'mature, adult, old, ancestor' is logically opposed to *ajiri* a term that may be glossed as either 'child, immature person' or as 'children'. *Ruttolok (lok,* 'after' or 'more of') not only means 'older', it also represents the process of growing older or aging. Table 4 compares the Enewetak population in 1947 and 1982 by twenty year age groupings.

In 1947 nearly half of the community members were under 20 years of age; but between 1947 and 1982 the percentage of the population under 20 continued to increase from 49.3 percent to 66.07 percent. In contrast, the percentage of the population between 40 and 60 years of age has decreased by 45 percent (even when in-married spouses are included), and the population over 60 in 1982 accounted for less than 3 percent of the total population, down from 8.7 percent in 1947. The phenomenal rate of population increase (4.87 percent/year without spouses) makes percentage comparisons somewhat misleading. In fact, in their 35 years on Ujelang Atoll, the number of Enewetak people over 60 years of age increased significantly (from 12 to 20); this 66.6 percent growth is obscured by an increase of over 550 percent in the number of people under 20 years.

Recent expansion in the number of Enewetak youth has undoubtedly contributed to changing attitudes toward the aged. Changes are evident in a shift in the locus of administrative authority, in a pattern of learning increasingly based on peers and outsiders, and in diminished respect for elders. Nonetheless, perceptions of the aged have not changed as radically on Ujelang as they have on Majuro or Kwajalein (the administrative and economic centers of the Marshall Islands), and changes cannot be attributed to shifts in the composition of the population any more than they can to contact with the outside world. In many respects, the roads men and women take in the process of maturing and dying are much the same as when Enewetak people moved to Ujelang in 1947.

The first step in becoming old, in the sense of becoming 'mature', involves attaining one's maximum physical beauty; it subsequently involves replacement of one's attained beauty with actions and accom-

Table 4. Percentage of Enewetak Population by Twenty Year Age Groupings in 1947 and 1982

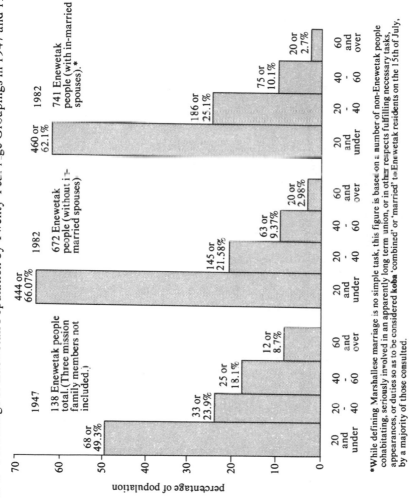

*While defining Marshallese marriage is no simple task, this figure is based on a number of non-Enewetak people cohabitating, seriously involved in an apparently long term union, or in other respects fulfilling necessary tasks, appearances, or duties so as to be considered *koba* 'combined' or 'married' to Enewetak residents on the 15th of July, by a majority of those consulted.

plishments (cf., Weiner 1976). These accomplishments replace one's diminishing beauty and physical prowess. *Karuttolok* 'to make older' refers specifically to the process of making someone sexually mature, a first step toward agedness. When the older village youngsters are spoken of as children, a common response is 's/he is old, (s/he has) already entered the darkness', that is, 'lost his/her virginity'. Growing old thus minimally necessitates being physically mature and sexually experienced; falling from grace and starting a family are critical first steps in becoming old and respected.

Important Marshallese proverbs contend that "a man travels around but women, they stay put," or "a father, and the father of others but a mother, a mother in unity." These sayings are as applicable to the process of aging as they are germane to social and spatial relations for, from mid-childhood onward, males and females grow old differently (Carucci 1980: chapter 2, chapter 7). Young women are proficient at many of the tasks and responsibilities expected of them as adults, and are said to become settled during their adolescent years, but the roots for their sedentary existence are in place by the time they are five or six years of age. In contrast, men's skills change dramatically between adolescence and old age. Traditionally trained as warriors and sailors, young men are now skilled at fishing, sailing, climbing coconut trees, bird catching, and other masculine pursuits. Along the road to respected maturity, young men must sacrifice their transient, semi-nocturnal existences in favor of marriage, children, and the responsibilities of caring for a household and the land to support it.

The ideal young male, still unmarried, provides the prototype for what maleness in Marshallese society is all about. He is physically and sexually mature, he is strong, prepared, and knows ways of moving appropriate to men. Traditionally these movements included warfare tactics, but now are restricted to carousing, fishing, sailing, and the other activities listed above. In times past, chiefly sons and the offspring of religious specialists received different training, but the sons of commoners and workers all pursued the rigors of the warrior to become 'real men'.

Marshallese at one time may have idealized high ranking, highly honored sacred maidens similar to the Samoan *taupo,* but now they much prefer a young woman with one or two children who has attained a pleasantly full figure and who has established her fertility. But to obtain such a woman, a young man must take her as his wife. He must promise to watch over and help the woman, and to do so he must sacrifice some of the freedoms of a 'real man'. The very differences between the ideal man and the ideal young woman thus serve as the impetus to draw young men into marriage and into becoming responsible members of the social order.

As a man becomes older he travels around less, has fewer sexual encounters with young women, and makes fewer trips into the bush, the sky, and the open sea. He will become a man of influence if he continues to increase his accomplishments, if he successfully provides for his family, when he gains a respected voice in the community, and as he becomes a leader of his clan and *bwij* 'bilateral extended family'. Then he will be referred to as *rutto* 'old' or 'old one' or as *alab* 'respected elder'. Often by the time a man has gained such a position of respect he is nearly a senior, with there being only a handful of men more aged than he.

In contrast, the process of maturing for a woman is typified by continuity and stability. A woman should stay on the household lands, have children and care for them. If she has many children she will automatically become important. Sinclair notes that Maori women move to center stage with age (chapter 2). Enewetak/Ujelang women also become increasingly important, but not at the expense of men. They become important because they have accomplished the work of all remembered ancestors – they have extended the life of the society, of their clan, and of their family beyond that of its individual members.[2] A woman with grandchildren deserves honor, for the continuity of her clan and of her bilateral extended family is assured.

A woman may be referred to as 'old' in the sense of being a mature person, an adult. But 'old' is not applied to women as a reference term in the way it is for men – *ewi rutto eo* 'where is the old one' (i.e., a person's father or grandfather)? Instead, mothers and grandmothers are referred to using the appropriate kin terms, though it is permissible to lump women with their spouses as in the utterance, *erri rutto ro* 'where are the old ones' (i.e., a person's parents)? Only very old women are referred to using 'old' as a singular term of reference; in such cases it does not matter, for people claim the stately old women cannot hear the insult.

These terminological contrasts are instructive, for as the youngest of a man's children approach puberty the man talks freely and even jokes about becoming older, and he begins to disengage from active participation in the community by trying to convince men of subsequent generations to take on more responsibility. In contrast, a woman wants to hear nothing of 'being older' until her grandchildren have grown and have begun to have children of their own. At that point, a woman's part in the perpetuation of the clan and bilateral extended family is complete; now an elderly and highly respected family head, she has witnessed the family's success.

Parents and very old members of the community are referred to as *rutto ro* 'human, plural, old folks' or 'ancestors'. The term for 'ancestors' or 'those with descendents' includes both the living and the dead. Persons who are mature, responsible, old people are included as 'ancestors', even if they have no offspring, because they always have a number of adopted children. The names of those without offspring will be remembered if they are crucial to their adopted children's land claims; otherwise, they will be forgotten after a few generations.

The term *rutto* 'ancestors', is related to, and perhaps derived from, the Marshallese term *ri etto ro* 'the ancient ones'. Enewetak people use the term to refer specifically to ancient people who lived long ago, either in primordial times or at least before contact with the west.

Respect customarily accrues to older people, and Ujelang residents use the term *alab* 'respected elder' to refer to them. In other parts of the Marshall Islands the term *alab* denotes persons who headed land-holding corporations (Kiste and Rynkiewich 1976), and in ancient times the residents of one section of Enewetak Atoll known as *Wōd En* had *alab* of this sort. Today, the term *alab* may refer to a respected older person, a household head, or the oldest representative of a clan or extended family. Either men or women may be called 'respected elders', but most often it is men – those who administer the wishes of the women who head the matriclans – to whom the term is applied. 'Respected elders' of very high regard usually head large bilateral extended families or speak on behalf of one of the three remaining clans. Nonetheless, any mature person who embodies some of the attributes of a 'respected elder' may be referred to or addressed as such in order to 'make them higher'. Respect usually accompanies aging, and it is often said jokingly of a groom-to-be or of one newly married, *einwōt kwe alablok* 'it is as if you are becoming more of a respected elder' or, *einwōt kwe ruttolok* 'it is as if you are becoming more of an ancestor'.

WIDOWS, WIDOWERS, AND THE DIVORCED

People who have lost their spouses through death or divorce do not receive the respect due someone of their age; they are truly the unfortunates of Marshallese society. Women survive the ordeal better than do men for, as long as they care for their families, they will be treated as responsible citizens. Brothers and other close relatives will provide for a woman's family, and she and her offspring will become attached to her natal family or, if her parents are too aged, to the family of one of her siblings. As long as a woman cares for her children, she does not greatly disrupt the established social order.

Widowers or male divorcees, however, are in a peculiar structural position, for while they are thrown back into the role of a single adolescent male, their attractiveness has been eroded by age and the responsibilities of a family. A man who fails to care for his children will lose control of them and people will accuse him of being lazy and uncivilized; yet a man who dedicates his time to his offspring will stand little chance of success with another woman. As the provider, a man must be responsible for the nurture of his children. The woman, however, transforms his semen into milk or combines the foodstuffs he brings home into meals. A man cannot perform these transformations himself; they must be carried out by his ex-wife (if he is divorced) or by his wife's sister. If divorced, a man's sister-in-law is unlikely to accept the man and his provisions, for he will surely be blamed for the separation. The sister of a man's deceased spouse is more likely to accept the widower and his foodstuffs, for she is the woman who is most apt to become his new wife. If, however, she is already married, the widower still must decide whether to remain dedicated to his children or to seek out a new spouse.

Sooner or later a widower must try to find a new wife. He will endure the rebukes of society and return to the role of an adolescent male (sans beauty and with ailing masculine abilities). He will travel around, drink with young males, and sleep where and when exhaustion catches up with him. His activities become more nocturnal, and he may sail to another islet without informing others of his whereabouts. He will attach himself to a household of a clan member, most often one of the women of his clan, and he may occasionally attempt to help support that household. If a man is still young and relatively attractive he may soon remarry, but older men are unlikely to find a new mate.

Even if a man's wife has only left temporarily, he will be expected to eat irregularly, run around, and become generally irresponsible. Yet as soon as a man begins to manifest these traits he will be said to be 'crazy', 'unaware', or 'damaged'. He no longer behaves as is expected of a mature adult. Widowers or divorced men receive even more abuse, for their adolescent actions become a way of life.

Leibual

Leibual, a man in his mid-sixties provides a good example of a divorced man.[3] Soon after the move to Ujc'ang he married an attractive woman whose father was from one of the islands in the eastern Carolines. Leibual and his wife had eleven children before their eventual separation around 1970. In the 1950s Leibual, his younger brother, and their wives owned a local store and were among the most respected people on Ujelang. Leibual's genitrix, who is still alive today, is one of four siblings who head the largest and one of the most powerful extended families on Ujelang Atoll. Both his genitor and his father by adoption were respected by the community, and his adoptive mother, who lost her only "natural" child, always treated Leibual, the oldest of her adopted children, as the person who would be the 'respected elder' in charge of her family. In spite of this favorable situation, Leibual has become a person without direction. He drinks regularly with young adolescent males who like to have him around because he never causes trouble. Recently he started a store that imports cigarettes and bootleg liquor from Majuro, the former as 'bait' to attract women partners and the latter to sell to his young male drinking buddies – with the understanding that he will be a member of the drinking party. He has a house of his own, but his older daughters maintain it and care for the younger children. When not out on a drinking binge, Leibual visits and eats with his relatives, and sleeps wherever he may be when storytelling sessions break up and he finds it is too late to return home. In spite of his considerable knowledge, his culturally unacceptable life style causes people to comment: "That guy is really damaged (mentally); he knows only how to drink and smoke but he has forgotten how to work. He discarded his own family, and now he eats and sleeps anywhere like a dog or cat."

Maku

Leibual's older classificatory brother, a 'respected elder' who lost his wife only a couple of years ago, has made a slightly more acceptable adaptation to his misfortune. Nevertheless, his life is quite different than it was during the days when his wife was still alive. Maku, a man now in his early sixties, became the head of his extended family even though he was a member of the youngest line. His older brother's family were among the seventeen local people who lost their lives during the battle of Enewetak. A sound fisherman and able canoe builder, Maku soon gained a position of respect on Ujelang Atoll. Though by one reckoning he married a prohibited relative (which strained relations within that family), he and his wife were the first health aides on Ujelang Atoll, positions that required training on Kwajalein Atoll and that added to their renown. Maku's wife was somewhat older than he. She had previously been married to his cousins' father, by whom she had had four children, and after her marriage to Maku she had another four children. Within a year of their return to Enewetak Atoll in 1980, she died. Following her death, Maku made a trip to Majuro to mitigate his grief. Though Maku had been one of the more dedicated church members on Ujelang, soon after his arrival on Majuro he 'fell from grace' by drinking and keeping company with women. Unlike Leibual, who repeats his trips to the administrative center at least once a year, Maku returned to Enewetak Atoll, regained his position as a church member, and re-established his position of respect in the community. He still associates with young people of the community and has become the unofficial leader of youth activities sponsored by the church. Young men often joke with him about his long period of celibacy inasmuch as it is thought that regular sexual release is required for a male to maintain good health. They contend Maku had an intimate relationship with a woman when he chaperoned the women's church group on a trip to Hawaii in 1982. After all, wouldn't it be impossible to share a room with an available woman without having a sexual encounter? Maku chuckles in agreement with their Marshallese logic, but refuses comment on the incident. Accusations continue, but as a joke, because, without Maku's admission, no one has enough proof of the transgression to have him and his female friend removed from the church. Because Maku's children were all mature before the death of his wife, he is not expected to maintain a household, as is Leibual. In fact, Maku enjoys keeping his own house, and when guests come into the community they are often housed in Maku's home. Nonetheless, like Leibual, Maku spends more time eating and sleeping with relatives than he did before the death of his wife.

Lionto

Women who are without spouses, and whose children are mature, may play cards and bingo, smoke, drink, and pursue other activities in order to contact men. As with men, the community will judge that such women are irresponsible, lazy, or crazy. But a woman's actions are more justifiable than are those of her male counterpart, for her craziness results from *kālok* 'flight', a common illness among women who have lost a person of great importance in their lives. In 'flight', a woman's mental or spiritual being becomes separated from its physical shell and flies away to be near a lover, child, or parent whose departure has brought great sadness.

Lionto, a younger classificatory sister of Maku and Leibual, was deserted by her husband nearly ten years ago. After he left her to return to a sailor's life, Lionto lost all interest in her family. A dedicated mother of five, she had always been a proficient mat-maker and handicraft specialist. She was also renowned for her cooking. Suddenly she became one of the most undependable people in the village. She could often be found playing bingo or cards, sleeping, or simply gazing into space. She lost interest in the church, and her elderly parents, who often took care of her two youngest children, began to have serious doubts about her mental health. Their concern with her condition led them to consult a traditional medical specialist. His analysis confirmed that Lionto's spirit had taken flight and, though the medical specialist performed a healing ritual that would prevent more severe dissociation, he also indicated that she was not likely to return to her former self unless her husband returned to her. Nearly ten years later, Lionto is little changed. Her marriage will never be saved, for her husband has married another woman in Majuro; ironically his new wife is a sister of Lionto's daughter's husband. Lionto roams from the household of one of her daughters to that of another. Often she will begin an important project and suddenly disappear, only to be discovered a day or two later on one of the other islets searching for fish to satisfy her cravings, or playing bingo or cards. Now nearly fifty, Lionto is still respected for her considerable medical knowledge and for her abilities as a midwife, but otherwise her stature in the community has greatly diminished.

Anjoko

Leibual's ex-wife, Anjoko, has adapted much more atypically to her new life style. Unlike Lionto, Anjoko is voluntarily without a husband. When she left Leibual, she moved into a new hut that her kinsmen constructed on her mother's land parcel. Accustomed to the niceties which the family business had provided her, she departed for Ponape and later for Majuro to gain access to the amenities of the western world. In Majuro she met a young man from Kosrae whom she took as her husband. About twenty years her junior, her new mate left her within three years for another Ujelang woman closer to his own age. Anjoko, however, continued to find new short-term partners with such frequency that Ujelang people began to accuse her of being a common prostitute (Anjoko seemed not to be bothered by such comments, for she had always been a very strong-willed and self-directed woman). She returned to Ujelang just frequently enough to maintain her place in the community, yet she would not stay long enough to become burdened with her children (who spent most of their time with Leibual or with other close relatives). In less than two years she was married once again to another Kosraean, this one a couple of years younger than the first. When her young companion mistreated her, she fought back, for she was determined to show him that she could display as many masculine traits as could he. Her third marriage lasted about the same length of time as had her second. This man also left Anjoko for a young Ujelang woman, and Anjoko once more returned to the administrative center to play cards, drink, and smoke in public, largely unsanctioned by members of the Enewetak community. By 1982, Anjoko had established her own business selling gasoline at highly inflated prices on Enewetak Atoll. The profits she realized were generally adequate to allow her to travel, gamble, drink, and live a type of life style that in all respects was most intimidating for Marshallese men. When money ran low, she could always tap the resources of her large family, some of whom lived in the United States, and others of whom were too isolated on Enewetak to stop the 'theft' of trust funds in Majuro before they were sent on to Enewetak. Now in her early sixties, Anjoko sits with the men in council meetings. She openly voices her opinions in the forum while her female age-mates gather around the outside of the council house and express their disagreements in half-audible remarks. While Anjoko is ridiculed for her aggressive style and masculine actions, she has gained a certain respect, especially among the men, for the atypical role she has assumed.

Even in these disparate cases where the course of life has gone awry, people are fitted into the categories of aging outlined above. Early in life these categories allow men greater flexibility than women, but if a woman gives birth to children and cares for them, her position in society in later life is more secure. A man, who must bring himself renown, has less flexibility as he matures, for it is increasingly difficult to relive his life as an adolescent and young adult.

Seen in terms of space and time, a man has the freedom to move about and build his own reputation by travelling and accumulating the overt signs of success. He is best able to do these things as a young man and is increasingly constrained by the limited time remaining in his life. In contrast, a woman is restricted in her physical movements and in her sphere of influence at any one point in time, but her strength lies in her ability to propagate her own line across time. Thus, as a man's time runs out, the time in a woman's life is extended, for she has many children and grandchildren to carry on for her.

OLD AGE, ANCESTORHOOD, AND DYING

Beginning with the birth of their children, Enewetak and Ujelang people take on the status of ancestors, and they remain an integral part of an extended family until long after death. The aged never face the cultural ostracism that occasionally confronts elder citizens of the United States. In fact, one's importance in a Marshallese family increases with age and often continues to increase after death.

The honorific terms *lallap* 'old man' and *lellap* 'old woman' are used to refer to the aged. Only when discussing the very old, or when speaking to mature children or adults about their parents, are the terms 'old woman' and 'old man' used. Kin terms and terms of affection are employed to address the elderly; except in joking, it would be offensive to use 'old man' or 'old woman' to speak directly to an older person.

Old people on Ujelang and Enewetak Atolls remain integrated into the fabric of daily life and, at least until very recently, continue to perform useful tasks. The old men often make coconut sennit or help make simple tools and toys, while the old women prepare materials for handicrafts and help with the construction of sleeping mats. The elderly are a functioning part of the society, and younger members of the community only rarely take special care of them. Respected elders are paid a formal visit on sacred occasions, such as New Year's Day, and they receive food, clothing, and a place to live. Elder widows or widowers live with a child or grandchild and often move about between the house sites of two or three such descendants.

As a person nears death, members of the community gather around to lend support and to witness the event. Women huddle around the death bed while men congregate outside or in the next room and keep curious children out of the way. Notice of death comes with loud wails of women in the room, and the lamentations soon spread to all of the women in the neighborhood. Those who may have returned to their own homes again rush to the scene.

When an elderly person dies, he generally does so in his own home or in the home of one of his children. Ideally, a man should die at sea, or at least out in the bush lands gathering drinking coconuts, and a woman should die on the paving stones of her household grounds. A fitting death is unlikely for an old man because it has probably been years since he fished in the open sea or brought home drinking coconuts. Old men, having expended all of their masculine energies, die – as do old women – in the middle of the village, the core of the women's domain.

The terms *mej* 'dead, death, or the process of dying', *jako* 'gone', and *buk an kakije* 'take one's rest', all refer to dying. For Ujelang/Enewetak people there are a number of indicators of death, but the disappearance of one's breath is the sign of greatest cultural significance. *Emenono* 'breathing/heartbeat' is a critical sign of life for Marshallese, and when taken from a person at death the 'breath/ heartbeat' does not disappear – it becomes the most frequently encountered manifestation of that person's spirit. The breath and the spiritual remains of dead people, which are regularly seen on Ujelang or Enewetak, are all termed *mejatoto* 'air'. Thus, the Marshallese conception of 'life' is perhaps best glossed as 'animate'; used to describe the state of possessing life or of being alive, animate derives from the French *anima* 'breath or soul', and from the Greek *anemos* 'wind' (Webster 1967:35; Oxford English Dictionary 1971:335).

Changes in skin texture and temperature, a loss of brilliance in the eyes, and a change of scent are also indicators of death. Like breathing/heartbeat and wind, these features become a part of the spiritual form of a dead person. Cold, clammy breezes in one particular area of an islet may indicate the presence of spirits (which since early missionary days have been known as *timon* 'demons'). A lackluster stare from a pair of eyes through a window at night or the offensive scent of death often accompany the shadowy image of a dead person, and those who have touched 'demons' say they feel 'dried out' or 'scaly'. While his physical body deteriorates underground, or is consumed by the sea, a Marshallese enters the non-corporeal world clad with the shadowy outline of his physical form. In further interactions with the living, a 'demon' will be seen in its last remembered form – as an insubstantial, revivified corpse; and, as if to disqualify it as a living human being, a 'demon' will bring along all of the associated signs of death.

In addition to the physical components that remain with a person after death, a number of social and cultural components also remain. Spirits have their own social order and they are able to communicate with other spiritual beings as well as with the living. As ancestors, dead people have a direct impact on the course of daily life, for through them social ties are established and maintained and claims to land are substantiated. But the dead also give messages to the living via dreams and apparitions. Many people fear and avoid spiritual entities, but others seek out their advice. Those who are afraid tremble at the thought that association with spiritual beings will draw them into the world of the dead. Many encounters with ancestral spirits are harmless, however, and people who seek advice from 'demons' do so to gain access to the superior wisdom of members of the spirit world. When ancestors enter the world of the dead their understanding grows, not only because they continue to increase in age and experience, but also because their view of the world becomes transcendent and all-encompassing.

Interactions with supernatural entities have a far more critical influence on the course of daily activities than do economic motivations or political maneuvers. While supernatural encounters occur daily, they tend to happen at certain times and locations and are often focussed around particular events. Scenes, occasions, and places where these interactions are likely to occur include the time immediately preceding and following a death, during the yearly renewal celebration termed *Kūrijmōj*, near cemeteries, on the ocean side of the village, or in the bush lands, or on 'the face' of waves. Communication from spirits may also be found travelling on the wind, either free-floating or carried by birds.

Spirits are unpredictable, and those who fear them are generally apprehensive about the element of the unknown; even one's own parents or grandparents may be troublesome under certain conditions. For example, Meila, a daughter of Lionto, was staying at her normal place of residence near the center of Enewetak islet with her four-month-old daughter, her first child. She was watching her sister and brother-in-law play cards with their agemates, but some time after midnight she fell asleep in the room with her daughter by her side. It was a room on the windward side and toward the ocean, on the opposite corner of the house from her normal sleeping location. A short time before dawn she awoke screaming. In answer to her sister's questions she said that her grandmother, a spirit known to be somewhat unpredictable, had come to the window and knocked loudly. Meila could hear her grandmother's breathing and her heartbeat; suddenly she grasped Meila around the neck and tried to pull Meila's baby away and take it to a "better place." At that time Meila began screaming and, as others responded to her cries, the shadowy form of the grandmother disappeared toward the ocean side, whence it had appeared. The grandmother, who considered Meila a favorite when she was still alive, had died on Enewetak about six years earlier. She was known to be a cantankerous spirit even around those she had loved dearly. One old man attributed her actions to her clan affiliation, Ejoa, and claimed that an Ijjidik clan member would never act as she had toward a fellow clan member (his clan was Ijjidik). Though Meila had planned to remain at home, do laundry, and help her sister prepare food for an upcoming church event, she moved to the house of her grandfather in the hope that he could make some medicine that would prevent his deceased wife from acting so unpredictably toward her and her child.

The ceremonies that today accompany death help separate the living from the dead, but traditional death celebrations accomplished the separation more definitively. In ancient times all of a person's belongings, including one's house and trees, were either given to others outside of the bilateral extended family, or they were burned. Corpses, particularly chiefs and *lātoktok* 'persons of rank', were sent off to sea in specially constructed canoes. Neighboring Marshall Islanders bound the corpses of those of very high rank with mats and weighted them with stones to ensure that the bodies were permanently disposed of far out to sea. Similarly, when many spirits and supernatural entities are around to witness *Kūrijmōj*, the 'renewal celebration', the ceremonies of the closing days help drive the spirits from the islet and reestablish order in the village (Carucci 1980:121-131, 507-508).

To avoid 'demons' people skirt cemeteries, and when alone, especially at night, they stay away from the ocean side of an islet, bush lands, and outer islets. Women are more vulnerable than are men, particularly pregnant women, because all of these locations except cemeteries are in the male domain; they are places unsuited to women and potentially dangerous for them. Cemeteries contain only local ancestral spirits. While they may be located in the village and along the lagoon side, both within the women's domain, cemeteries are set apart from areas of constant movement within the village. Most cantankerous persons are also buried in cemeteries away from the main village on Ujelang, which suggests that people suspect that they know who will become troublesome spirits, even before they are buried. In any case, most people go out of their way to avoid locations that are *timonmon* 'demon infested'. Those who must pass, unaccompanied, close by a cemetery after dark are apt to stay at the home of a close relative instead. Ujelang houses that have become the haunts of 'demons' are torn down and relocated, and similarly haunted cement houses on Enewetak may go empty for a few months to allow resident spirits to move to a new location.[4]

There are many ways in which spirits communicate with living people; the message may be indirect, or a spirit may contact a person directly through dreams or apparitions. Dreams and encounters may include spoken phrases, but Enewetak people must also decide how to interpret phenomena such as color, location, or a spirit's decision to appear to certain kinsmen. Meila claimed that her encounter with her grandmother started as a dream, but when the grandmother knocked at the window she awoke, and the dream became a real encounter. Some phrases were spoken, but other elements of the experience, such as the

location of Meila's sleeping quarters and the grandmother's approach
and departure from the ocean side, helped her know that her grandmother's intent was malicious. Even if the entire encounter had been a
dream, it still would have been an important mode of communication,
for Meila is one whose dream sequences are 'true'. Marshallese say
only certain people have dreams that are 'true' while other people's
dreams have no significance: they are 'just dreams'.

Spirits also employ unusual natural phenomena as a means of
communication. News of death and other types of messages may
appear on the face of waves. Waves in the open sea have communicative value for sailors, but not until a wave crests and prepares to break
on the outer fringe of the exterior reef (in an area known as *mejan
etet)* does it transmit information to inhabitants of the land. Just
outside of the exterior reef the face of a transient, cresting wave acts
as a lens to magnify fish; it also becomes a lens to transform the
messages of the foreign spirits who inhabit the sea into interpretable
codes for living human beings. The face of the wave is the point of
entry into the mysterious, male coded, open sea, much as a person's
face is the entry point into the inner self. Thoughts and emotions gain
expression in the human face; messages from distant shores, or from
the sea itself, are displayed on the face of waves. The images of coffins
or of small sailing craft, traditional Marshallese containers for corpses,
always bring news of recent or impending death. When a coffin or
sailing canoe is seen going out to sea near a passage in the reef,
someone on the atoll will soon die. If the canoe or coffin is seen
floating toward the edge of the reef or entering a passage, it brings
news of death elsewhere.

The sounds and movements of birds may also carry messages from
the spirit world to living beings. An ancestral spirit may transform
itself into a bird or it may use the calls of birds to transmit messages
to the world of the living. In combination with other signs, either the
call of a bird on the ocean side at night or a *wunaak* 'flock of birds'
flying in close formation in a leeward direction may be signs of severe
illness or even death. In contrast, a flock of birds flying to the windward along the lagoon reef carries the message *ewor enaan* 'there is
news'. Specific types of birds bring particular sorts of news, and other
creatures, such as oddly shaped fish or lizards, may provide additional
paths of communication for members of the non-corporeal world. The
directionality of winds, of calms, or of the flight paths of birds are
each of key importance in decoding supernatural messages. *Elae*
'calms' on the ocean or in the lagoon are said to mark 'spaces between
the winds'; as entry points into another part of the world inhabited by

supernatural beings, calms carry significant information. Depending on its orientation, a calm may signal to Enewetak people the anticipation of a field trip ship, news of people far or near, or announcement of death. Major weather patterns such as typhoons, sea spouts, or unexpected storms often bring significant destruction and misery to living human beings on earth. They are additional means by which the dead communicate with the living.

In the typhoon of November, 1982, gusts to 135 knots lifted cookhouses and outbuildings from their moorings and deposited them in the sea. Cement homes on Enewetak withstood the gusts, but many town buildings were refashioned into worthless heaps of gnarled and twisted tin. After the storm, residents were disappointed that typhoon relief was not forthcoming, yet they also thought that the damage had been just reward for greed and community bickering. For the past months atoll residents had been arguing about land and quarrelling over the buildings and construction materials that remained on the land. The destruction had left the church unscathed, but structures that had been under dispute were severely damaged or swept into the sea. Ancestors were especially upset with the quarrelling, for they knew the truth about the division of Enewetak lands. When God became aware of the bickering and false claims, the storm inflicted its damage as a form of punishment. While the storm was truly a misfortune, it was also a message to set things straight in the community.

Thus, the ancestors through which people trace their ties to others, and by which people justify claims to land, are active participants in the affairs of day-to-day life; they monitor the decisions of living people and, in consultation with God, chastise those who act unjustly. Beginning in the 1850s, missionaries from Hawaii taught Marshallese that God oversees man's works and punishes those who act improperly. Marshallese accepted this belief, for they already knew that other spiritual beings oversaw and participated in the events of daily life. But even though God may see all things, other spirits are often employed to carry out God's judgments and desires. On Ujelang and Enewetak the ancestors are in the best position to know right from wrong, and they are the ones who usually intervene in daily life. Enewetak/Ujelang people who lie or make false claims suffer misfortune, and bad luck should warn a person to alter his/her course or prepare for even more severe punishment. The popular sermon topics, *Kwe bōn ko jān Anij* 'You can't run from God' or *Kwonaj ko ñan ia?* 'Where do you plan to run to?' hold true, not only for God, but for all non-corporeal beings. On Enewetak and Ujelang, ancestors and other spiritual entities are intermediaries between God and man; they are Marshallese 'policemen for God'.

WOMEN AND THE SUPERNATURAL: MEN AND THE WORLD

Women are much more closely affiliated with the spirit world than are men. The oldest female members of each clan represent the entire clan through each generation in perpetuity. The spirit world is an extension back into the already lived generational time that women perpetuate and push into the future. While women have a greater fear of the supernatural realm than do men, their fear may be based on the intimate contact they maintain with spirits and spiritual concerns. In times of birth, death and grieving, church activities, and medical cures involving spirits, women are brought very close to the sacred world of the ancestors. In contrast, men are more concerned with the administration of earthly affairs, or with the matters of rank and chieftainship that pass through the male line on Enewetak. Also, however, men are wanderers or outsiders who are necessary to the women who provide for families, manage community and external affairs, and procreate. When they are viewed as wanderers, men are not much different from the foreign spirits that women fear most.

From a slightly different perspective, women are always faced with internal danger; the possibilities of dying during childbirth or of losing a maturing child are real perils that women must face. Charged with the propagation of the living, women must protect themselves and their offspring from dangerous outside forces, especially forces from the spirit world. Men, on the other hand, seek out external danger to conquer it; they incorporate a sense of danger within themselves as an indication that they are 'real men'. Men are manipulators of the world but they have few internal dangers with which to deal. Men assist with the propagation of mankind – they are not responsible for it.

CONCLUSION: BOUNDARIES AND PROCESSES

In this chapter, Marshallese stages of maturing and dying have been briefly outlined. Yet the boundaries between categories of maturity are far from rigid, and as figure 2 illustrates, even states of life and death manifest a continuity that baffles western sensibilities. Marshallese distinguish greater and lesser categories of existence, categories that help to segment the process of maturing: Yet the processes override the categories. Referring back to table 4, etic categories indicate that in

Figure 2. Categories of Maturity, Marshall Islands

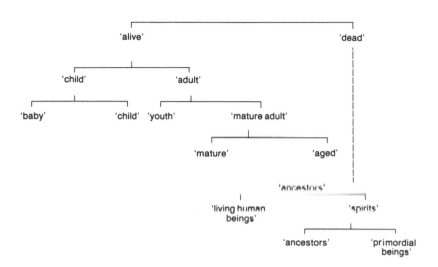

1982 perhaps twenty people, those sixty years and over, might be referred to as *rutto* 'aged'. While in certain circumstances this is true, on other occasions only those who are 'truly aged' (maybe 8 or 9 people) would be referred to as 'aged', while if *rutto* is glossed as 'mature' at least 300 people might be included in the category. Other terms of relative maturity – 'baby', 'child', 'male/female youth', 'ancestor', 'old man/old woman' – are used with equal flexibility. Depending on which criteria are used, these terms may include or exclude certain people. The small scale of Ujelang/Enewetak society contributes to the ability of Enewetak people to consider individuals according to each of their attributes and to fit them into categories in a manner optimally suited to each situation. Nonetheless, aging and dying are processes that occur in different ways and at somewhat varied rates. The flexibility of Marshallese categories, both in their definition and in their use, allows variations in the aging and dying processes to be taken into account.

While concerned citizens and groups of specialists in the United States have an incessant desire to specify and rigidify the boundaries between life and non-life, or between life and death, people on Ujelang and Enewetak are satisfied with a flexible, almost indistinct boundary between people in the living word and spirit beings. A living person's spirit may leave his body and travel around the village as a shadowy image of his face. The body is left limp and seemingly lifeless, yet, as long as the spirit returns, the person is not even temporarily 'dead'. Thus, like each stage of living, dying is not a solitary nor necessarily an irreversible moment in a person's life; as with any other stage of life, death is a process that involves one's state of being and the residence of one's spirit.

In spite of the flexibility of Marshallese categories of maturing and dying, categorical parameters are placed around people at different points in their personal histories. These parameters direct an individual's actions in consistent but generalized ways. As males and females mature they have very different methods of dealing with the world. The approach of death tends to level gender distinctions, but even death itself does not eliminate them. Dead ancestors maintain their maleness and femaleness and they manifest their gender qualities in the way that they interact with people on earth and in their dealings with other people who have died.

NOTES

This chapter is an expanded version of a paper read at the annual meeting of the ASAO in March, 1982. Research in support of this contribution was conducted on Ujelang, Enewetak, and Majuro Atolls between August, 1976 and September, 1978 under a doctoral research grant from the National Science Foundation administered through the University of Chicago. Supplementary materials are from fieldwork on Enewetak and Majuro Atolls conducted between May, 1982 and May, 1983. The latter research, along with three months of library study in Hawaii, was supported by a postdoctoral research grant from the National Endowment for the Humanities. I would like to express my thanks to members of the ASAO symposium for their comments and for continuing to update me on the session in spite of my isolation in the outer Marshall Islands. Most importantly, my sincere gratitude to the Enewetak people who have extended me their hospitality for so long and who have taught me so much.

1. Enewetak people were moved to Ujelang Atoll in 1947 to allow the United States to conduct nuclear weapons experiments on Enewetak Atoll. A repatriation effort was begun in the early 1970s after the similarly exiled Bikini people had been returned to Bikini Atoll. By 1980, a substantial part of the Enewetak community had returned to their radically altered home atoll, and at present the core of the Enewetak/Ujelang community resides on Enewetak Atoll. About 150 residents returned to Ujelang in February of 1983, and a small enclave of Enewetak/Ujelang people also reside on Majuro Atoll, governmental center of the Marshall Islands.

2. In the administrative center of the Marshalls, and on Ebeye, Kwajalein Atoll (economic hub of the area), changes occur more rapidly than on the outer islands; women continue to perform a number of their normal tasks, but men's roles have changed significantly. Often men's activities are reduced to an attempt to provide for one's family through temporary employment or quarterly trust fund payments,

(economic hub of the area), changes occur more rapidly than on the outer islands; women continue to perform a number of their normal tasks, but men's roles have changed significantly. Often men's activities are reduced to an attempt to provide for one's family through temporary employment or quarterly trust fund payments, and to drinking, smoking, and making small talk. Men frequently engage in women's work as they try to perform some useful tasks, but the community respect and recognition that come with age on Ujelang or Enewetak are almost non-existent. Women thus gain greatly in relative power in the new context, since traditional male activities are essentially absent. Men who are able to find and hold jobs may establish new sources of identity and pride, but for others, depression, hypertension, and suicide too often result (Alexander 1978; Health Care Proposal 1980).

3. Each of the short life histories that follow reflects circumstances as they were in 1983. Names have been altered because personal information forms a part of the descriptions.

4. If people are now less concerned with spiritual entities than they were on Ujelang it is largely due to these factors: Enewetak has been essentially uninhabited for quite a long time, the contour of many islets has been altered, and Enewetak lies much farther than Ujelang from the path of dangerous foreign spirits that travel north-eastward from Ponape and the eastern Carolines to the Marshall Islands.

7

I'M NOT DEAD YET!
AGING AND DEATH:
PROCESS AND EXPERIENCE IN
KALIAI

Dorothy Ayers Counts and David R. Counts

INTRODUCTION

In North America old people are frequently stereotyped as being infirm, senile, childlike, and worthless (Berezin 1978:542). This stereotype is exacerbated by the loss of self-respect that frequently accompanies retirement and by the fact that the most pervasive experience shared by the North American elderly seems to be loss – of physical function, of social contact as friends and spouse die, and of self-esteem as people exchange the satisfaction of useful occupation for uselessness and dependency. As a result, cultural gerontophobia – the irrational fear and/or hatred of old age and the elderly both by society and by the old people themselves – is prevalent. This fear exists in spite of the fact that most people age comfortably and in good health *(Ibid)*.

The above stereotype illustrates one widespread misunderstanding about old age. Another is the notion that agedness, frequently undefined and therefore usually assumed to mean decrepitude, begins much earlier among "primitives" than it does among the people of the industrialized world (see for example Cowgill and Holmes 1972:8).

Despite their alleged entry into the ranks of the elderly at an early chronological age, people in non-industrialized societies do not, as a general rule, seem to suffer from the fear of old age that is said to characterize our society. Rather, cross-cultural studies conclude that loss of prestige and esteem by the elderly and negative images of aging are the by-products of urbanization, industrialization, and modernization (Cowgill and Holmes 1972:322; Fry 1980a:4-5). In pre-industrial societies old people often control useful knowledge and hold positions of political and economic power. As a result their status is high and they are respected or feared (Swain 1979).

This is, indeed, a strange situation. Does modernization really result in a state of affairs in which North Americans hate and fear the same condition and category of people who are respected and esteemed in non-industrialized societies? Is a seventy-year-old North American really at the same physical and social stage as a fifty-year-old Melanesian? The difficulty is that the terms 'old person' or 'elder' – or words that have been translated that way – have not been carefully defined so that there is distressingly little content to statements such as "Among the Bugabuga, people are old at forty." Words are taken out of context, the content of the condition "old" is not defined, and no distinction is drawn between being old, however it is defined, and being decrepit, defunct, or socially disaffiliated. Watson and Maxwell note (1977:6) that much of this confusion is due to the fact that little attention has been directed to the sociocultural context of aging. In this chapter we direct our attention to aging, old age, and dying as they are perceived by the Lusi-speaking Kaliai people of northwest New Britain, Papua New Guinea. Specifically, we examine the criteria that the Lusi use to define age categories; we explore the expectations that the Lusi share with regard to the aging process and the role of the elderly; and we demonstrate that old age and death are not necessarily fixed categories. Indeed, their boundaries are mutable and their attributes are complex aggregates of physical characteristics and social relationships that are open to interpretation and manipulation. Consequently, it may be unclear how others should treat an older person, and people may disagree as to whether an individual has begun the process of dying. The placement of a person in the appropriate category may become a strategic act subject to negotiation.

There are about 1000 speakers of Lusi living along the northwest coast of West New Britain. Their social organization is ideally patrilineal, virilocal, and egalitarian. Their *maroni* 'traditional leaders' are men whose economic and social prowess allows them to receive community recognition. In recent years the Kaliai have elected to public office younger men whose experience and education equips them to deal with the political realities of modern Papua New Guinea.

Most of the data for this paper were collected in Kandoka village, the largest Kaliai village and the second largest community in the Gloucester-Kandrian area of West New Britain Province. During the nearly two decades since 1966, we have made four field trips and spent about two and one-half years in northwest New Britain, mainly in Kandoka. There are many advantages to long term field research in a single community (see Foster et al. 1979 for a discussion of these advantages). This is particularly true if the topic of study is aging and dying. First, aging is an experience of change that is best understood if it is shared, and this sharing can only occur over the passage of time. During the past nineteen years we have aged along with our friends and consultants. We have shared and compared this experience with them and we, too, have been reclassified as 'elders'.

Second, people may revise their explanations of socially traumatic events, such as death, as the full effects of such an occurrence become apparent and circumstances change with the passage of time. Long term participation in the village has enabled us to observe the process whereby facts and explanations are adjusted to be consistent with current cultural reality.

LIFE, HUMANITY AND THE SPIRIT WORLD

The Lusi do not oppose life and death in the same way that English speakers do. They have no generic term for 'life'. They oppose existence (*i moro* 'it is') and a condition they call *mate,* a word that may be translated 'dead', 'unconscious' or 'ruined'. The world experienced by the Lusi is full of beings that move, grow, and interact with others in the environment – or at least they have the potential to do so. These beings may take the shape of natural formations such as mountains or stones, or they may appear to be insects, animals, plants or human beings; or they may have no constant form at all. The relevant question to ask about something, therefore, is not "Is it alive?" but "Is it what it appears to be?" There is no empirical test for stones or mountains. Their identity is known through myth, and those that have a history – those that once were pigs, or culture heroes, or malevolent spirits – are identified and their stories told. Occasionally, one of these may identify itself by its actions. If, for example, someone moves a spirit-stone from its resting place to a new spot, say in a village, it may very well remove itself back to its chosen resting place under cover of darkness. Such things are best left alone.

It is not always possible to know with certainty whether a thing is as it seems. Kaliai legend is replete with instances of people mistaking an *antu* 'spirit being' for the animal or human it appears to be. Indeed, the spirit being may consider itself to be a true resident of the substantial world while *iavava* 'humans' are only "those who frighten parrots" (see Counts 1980a for a discussion of the Kaliai myth "Akro and Gagandewa" which explores the concept of a relative reality). Nevertheless, there are clues that aid the Kaliai in their attempts to make positive identification.

Spirit beings do not leave the same signs as do corporeal beings. Ghosts and spirit-pigs leave no tracks, and the songs of spirit-birds sound like human speech instead of bird song. Furthermore, a real animal – a bird or pig for instance – can be killed and the hunter can find its dead body. In contrast, a hunter may spear or shoot a spirit-creature at point-blank range and it will likely melt into the brush and disappear. This does not mean that spirit beings are immortal (a concept that should be distinguished from the notion of life after death, as Rivers noted [1926 in Slobodin 1978:216]), for they do die and they can be killed. However, they do not stay dead, and they seldom allow humans to find and eat them. When a spirit being is eaten, the consumer always suffers: *caveat esor!*

Human beings, as opposed to animals, are defined by the presence of a spiritual component that has two aspects: *-tautau* 'spiritual essence' and *-anunu* 'shadow' or 'image' (in chapter 11, Scaletta discusses similar concepts regarding components of the human spirit among the Kabana of Bariai). The complexity of the notion of spiritual being that is embodied in these terms, used interchangeably by people who are discussing ghosts or spirits, is illustrated by the several meanings of these Lusi words. The term *-anunu* also means 'dream' *(anunugu* 'my dream) and 'reflection', while *-tautau* incorporates the notion of essence and self. The edible meat of a coconut is *niu aitautau,* the fleshy part of a woman's breast is *aituru aitautau,* and our consultants say the portion of something that is called *aitautau* is its 'true' or essential part. The term *aitau* also means 'himself' 'herself' 'itself' as in *aitau iraui* 'he struck himself', while *taugau* may be glossed 'myself' *(taugau ngaraugau* 'I struck myself'). No animals have this spiritual component, while it is a part of all living humans, including the fetus and the mentally incapacitated. Either aspect may leave the body of one who is ill, and either the 'spiritual essence' or the 'image' of a dying individual may be seen by others as far as several miles from the still breathing person. When death occurs both aspects permanently leave the corpse. People disagree about what happens then. From comments that our consultants made in 1966 and 1967, we conclude that many Lusi once believed that one or both aspects of the spiritual component of the deceased person remained near the body until it decomposed (Counts and Counts 1974). In 1981, after fifteen additional years of Roman Catholic influence, the same persons that we talked with in 1966 firmly maintained that the *sol* 'soul'[1] goes immediately to its spirit home. The only circumstance under which the 'soul' might remain near the grave, people now say, would be if the surviving kin failed to pay to have a final Mass said for the deceased. However, death is a social process as well as a physical event, and the Kaliai consider death to be reversible. The spiritual component(s) of an individual may leave and return to the body many times before abandoning it forever.

THE AGING PROCESS

The Lusi recognize a number of named stages in the development of the life cycle: *maseknga* 'new born'; *kekele* 'child'; *iriao* 'youth' and *tamine vilala* 'maiden'; *tamine/tomone uainga* 'married woman/man'; *tanta pao* 'new person' or 'parent of dependent child(ren)'; *tamparonga/taparonga* 'elder or senior female/male'; *tanta taurai* 'decrepit person'.[2]

The criteria for location in the life cycle are egocentric and physiological when the individual is young. For instance, an infant ceases to be 'new born' when its skin darkens and it becomes plump. Childhood lasts until the individual approaches puberty. A girl becomes a 'maiden' when her breasts 'fall' and she begins to menstruate, but there is no agreed upon point of transition when a boy becomes a 'youth'. An initiated but sexually immature boy is not a 'youth' until he demonstrates the secondary characteristics of sexual maturity. After a person reaches puberty, the criteria for movement through developmental stages cease to focus on the individual's physical development and concentrate instead on social events in that person's life and on his relationship with others. As most married people are parents of their own and/or adopted children, and most parents are married, the terms 'married woman/man' and 'parent of dependent children' are usually used interchangeably.

The years that a person spends as a young spouse and parent are the years of peak sexual activity, and it is during this time that the behavioral dimorphism of the sexes is most extreme. All statements by consultants – female and male – confirm that the Lusi perceive gender role behavior to be inseparable from genital sex. Unlike some other New Guinea people (see Strathern 1972:161; Poole 1981:125; Herdt 1981:208, 216) the Lusi consider gender to be fixed in the womb. People responded with puzzlement to the suggestion that a woman or man might wish to engage in activities inappropriate to the individual's genital sex. They commented that while foreigners or whites might do such things, Lusi do not. One man responded by recounting the tale of a person whose genitals and gender role behavior changed from male to female as the result of his encounter with a spirit-creature in the bush.

In fact, dressing and acting like a member of the opposite sex is a way of clowning that is usually done on ritual occasions. Informants readily delineated the tasks and behavior appropriate to each gender, and attributed failure to perform these tasks to the irresponsibility of youth, the poor training given by parents, inexcusable laziness, excessive preoccupation with sexual affairs, or to enchantment.

During the parenting years the ultimate responsibility for the completion of certain tasks lies unequivocally with either mother or father (see Gutmann 1975). These are also the years when an individual's behavior sets in motion the process of deterioration that accompanies aging, for the Lusi consider sexual activity and childbirth to hasten this process in both women and men. The association of sexuality with diminished strength, illness, and aging is common in Papua New Guinea (see Kelly 1976; Meggitt 1964; Jorgensen chapter 10), but the Lusi do not seem to fear sexual contamination with the wholehearted dread that characterizes some other New Britain peoples (see Chowning and Goodale 1971; Chowning 1980; Goodale 1980 and 1981). Sexual activity is potentially debilitating for women as well as men. As do the Kafe (Faithorn 1975), the Lusi consider male sexual fluids, as well as those of women, to be contaminating. The odors of sexual fluids and menstrual blood may cause weakness, illness, and death to vulnerable people: the very young, the very old, the sick, and the newly initiated; and seminal fluid, if ingested in mother's milk, may cause an infant to become ill (see Counts 1984). Fear of female contamination was one basis of the custom requiring initiated boys and men to sleep in the men's house rather than in houses with women. 'Senior' men say that their fathers urged them to space their sexual encounters with women several days apart. They were warned that men who engaged in frequent intercourse would become sickly, thin and desiccated, and would age prematurely.

The effects of sexual activity on women are explicitly described in the Kaliai myth "Akro and Gagandewa". In the story, Gagandewa's mother suspects that her daughter is secretly married because of the physical changes in the girl. She says:

> Gagandewa, the look that you have is not that of a virgin but that of a married woman. Your eyes have lost their lustre. Your skin is no longer bright and smooth with oils as it was. You have the dull eye and the long neck and the dry, dirty skin of a married woman (Counts 1980a:38).

Gagandewa is pregnant and, in fact, frequent sexual intercourse is debilitating to women *because* it is likely to lead to pregnancy. A woman who is too frequently pregnant is likely to be weak and sickly, and to age prematurely because of the physical strains of pregnancy and childbirth, and the hard work involved in caring for several small children. On the other hand, women should not be childless, for the expulsion of the mixture of old blood and sexual fluids present in a woman's abdomen and its replacement by new blood after childbirth is essential for her good health. Ideally a woman should achieve a balance between too many children and none at all, for either extreme renders her vulnerable to disease and premature aging.

THE OLD

People are not classified as 'senior' because of their chronological age; most people do not know how old they are. They are, however, acutely aware of their relative age, of the category and activities appropriate to their contemporaries, and of the progress through the life cycle of their kin in adjacent generations. It is the changing status of these people – parents and children – that defines an individual as an 'elder', for this status is a relational one. Specifically, a person becomes an 'elder' when his parents are dead or socially defunct and when his children marry and he becomes a *tuvu* – 'grandparent' (this reciprocal term may be glossed either 'ancestor' or 'grandparent/grandchild'). These changes are expected to occur coincidentally. Kaliai note that by the time a person is a grandparent his own parents are likely either to be dead or decrepit and dependent. The Lusi terms for 'elder' or 'senior', *tamparonga* for a woman and *taparonga* for a man, are terms of respect and are commonly used by younger people as terms of address and reference. Although no one expects that the achievement of 'senior' status is, in itself, enough to make a foolish person wise, 'elders' are generally expected to be the stable, responsible members of the community. Use of the term 'elder' in address or reference is, in fact, usually restricted to those who are respected. As long as 'elders' are active they are ultimately accountable for the behavior of their children, even those who are married, and the other younger members of their kin group. A married woman may go home to her mother (this is how the Kaliai phrase it), and a man can look to his father to help him obtain a bride, initiate his children, and pay compensation if he is on the wrong side of a quarrel. Two examples from the life of Nathan,[3] whose biography is sketched below, will provide examples of ideal 'elder' behavior.

1.   In 1975, Victor and his parents were declared in village meeting to be culpable in the suicide of a teen-age girl (see Counts 1980b for details). Although Albert, Victor's father, was probably in his early fifties, the ultimate responsibility for both his and his son's behavior was shouldered by the 'elder' of their *kambu* 'patrikin group'. Nathan, classificatory father to Albert and the acknowledged leader of their group, not only insisted that Albert make more generous compensation than demanded, but provided much of the wealth to make the payment.

2.   In 1981, a group of young men got into a village brawl in support of their relative Paul, Nathan's unmarried son. The men were each fined fifty *kina* for their part in the disturbance.[4] Nathan paid the fines for all of them.

There is ambiguity in 'senior' status. The Kaliai share with other New Guinea people the notion that the reproduction of human life and society has a cost (for example see Gell 1975; Kelly 1976; Goodale 1980 and 1981). The waxing strength and knowledge of the younger generation is accomplished at the expense of the waning capability and mental acuity of their parents. People specifically attribute the weakness and senility of the very old to the fact that their vitality has been expended into their children. Older consultants warn that if a man marries before he is old enough to grow a full beard his strength will go into his children and he will never achieve his own potential growth and abilities. They also say that if the first-born child of a marriage is a girl, both parents will age prematurely (girls are thought to develop more rapidly than do boys). The birth of a person's first grandchild is especially significant, for it marks the beginning of the decline into old age. It is not long thereafter, people say, that a person's strength and keeness of thought begin to diminish: in Tok Pisin, *bai ol gutpela tingting i aut i lus* 'the ability to think well is lost'.

The years spent as an 'elder' are the prime years of life. Physical strength decreases, but this loss is offset by the norm that no 'elder' should do a strenuous task if there is a younger person available. The 'senior' years are a time of *-gava-* 'ease' when a person can rest from hard labor but still be active, vital, and respected. Younger people are expected to honor 'elders', and both women and men readily make their opinions known in public meeting. These are the years when a woman is no longer burdened by pregnancy and the care of young infants. She directs her daughters and daughters-in-law in the preparation of feast foods, the care of pigs, and the production of pandanus mats that constitute the ceremonially distributed woman's wealth.

However, embedded in the enjoyment of heightened authority, respect, and responsibility is the knowledge that one's prestige and faculties will soon decline and the fear that the knowledge possessed by the individual may be lost, not only to him but to society as well. The 'elder', therefore has the duty to pass on knowledge, especially secret knowledge, to others so that it will not die with him. He is also obliged to begin deferring to the judgment of younger kin so that when the 'senior's' strength and abilities are spent others will be trained to take his place or, as the Lusi express it, -*kisi aimuli* 'to take his bed'. Our consultants observed that persons who exercise authority invariably make enemies and risk being the victims of sorcery. This is the cost of leadership that an 'elder' must pay, but when a person's grandchildren are born the hazards of sorcery begin to seem oppressive and he starts to think with longing of a peaceful old age. He begins, therefore, to withdraw from those activities that are likely to offend others and create rivals. So it is when a person is an 'elder' and at the peak of his powers and influence that he is likely to begin the long process of withdrawal from active social life.

Once a person is classified as being *taparonga/tamparonga* 'senior male/female', people being to look for and note the physical changes characteristic of old age. These include failing eyesight, dry slack skin, white hair, loss of teeth, and mental decline including forgetfulness, inability to concentrate for long periods of time, and the condition called *vuovuo* 'childishness', 'senility' or 'mental incapacity' – a term used to describe both the very young and the very old.

Under normal circumstances the fact that little girls learn, grow, and mature faster than little boys does not mean that women age more rapidly than men. Instead, tall, skinny people are said to show the signs of old age sooner than do heavy-set people who retain the full-fleshed, plump liquidity that the Lusi associate with youth. There is no special terminology for menopause, nor is the end of menstruation necessarily associated with physical decline or with the unpleasant symptoms – hot flashes, irritability, emotional instability – reported by many North Americans. Postmenopausal women say that they welcomed the end of the burdens of pregnancy and childbirth. However, the end of fertility does not mean that they will no longer mother children, for adults who are well into their sixties and even their seventies adopt and care for grandchildren, nieces and nephews, and other young relatives. As with the women of other Pacific societies, the concern of Kaliai women for young children continues through the life cycle despite their loss of reproductive capacity (for a discussion of the stress that post-reproductive white New Zealand women place on their roles as mothers see Dominy chapter 3).

The end of fertility and the achievement of 'elder' status also does not necessarily signal the end of sexual activity (also see Lepowsky, chapter 8). This seems to be entirely idiosyncratic. As one informant commented, "Some old people itch for sex. Others don't." Adults of all ages have sexual affairs, and widows and widowers may remarry, even though they are well into the 'senior' stage of life and are not strong enough to clear, plant and maintain gardens without the assistance of their adult children. People do not feel that it is shameful for a grandmother to continue bearing children, as Chowning reports for the neighboring Kove (1981:18) or for a male 'elder' to father infants. In 1981 they spoke with amusement of a bent old man from a neighboring village who had married a young wife and fathered several children. They were less amused by the antics of a married grandmother, nicknamed "Frog" because she hopped from one lover to another, who had an affair with a young man the age of her son. Her behavior was scandalous, especially because she was not discreet and she did not limit her lovers to men her own age (the Vanatinai have a similar opinion of lovers whose ages are widely separated; see Lepowsky, chapter 8).

The simplest Lusi term that may be glossed as 'old' is *moho*. People as well as things become *moho* 'old' and worn out, and occasionally a person will refer to his age in this way. Far more frequently the Lusi describe their age/condition by the terms that are best glossed as 'elder' or 'senior' *(taparonga/tamparonga)* or 'decrepit' *(taurai)*. As already noted, one achieves the status of 'elder' following the marriage of a first child, the birth of the first grandchild, and/or the death of one's parents. This status may continue for as long as an individual is active and responsible, even long after the death of one's spouse and without respect to gender or the continued maintenance of a domestic household. The status depends upon the individual's activity level and, as with Donna who is mentioned below, it may be lost by a person's failure to act. While most Lusi are sympathetic with persons who are incapacitated by chronic illness, they express impatience with people who retire from active life and become dependent solely because of their advanced years. Their attitude toward maintaining physical ability and independence is aptly summarized by the phrase "use it or lose it," a sentiment applied to lazy people and sedentary town workers as well as the aged.

The transition to the status *taurai* 'decrepit person' is a gradual progression along a continuum of degrees of physical ability and social interaction. These include mental acuity; physical strength; independence, especially the ability to garden and to meet one's own basic needs; and social activity including effective participation in ceremonial exchanges. Because there is no marked boundary between 'elder' and 'decrepit person', the way in which a person is classified depends largely on the way in which he presents himself to others and the manner in which he permits others to treat him. Some biographies will illustrate the differences in presentation of self (Goffman 1959) that distinguish 'elders' from 'decrepit persons'.

Nathan

Nathan, who was in his late sixties in 1981, is an exemplary case of an active 'elder'. He retired from his career as a policeman and returned to his natal village in 1963 after an absence of twenty-five years. Though widowed shortly after his return from the police, and burdened with the care of a number of young children, Nathan neither remarried nor entrusted the care of his children to anyone else.

Today, with most of his children married and seven times a grandfather, he sleeps in his men's house. He remains an active gardener and is the undisputed leader of his segment of the village. As leader he is responsible for his own children, for those of his deceased elder brother, and for the children of another, more distant, deceased kinsman. All these relatives, taken together, constitute his *kambu-kambu* 'extended patrikin group'. His activities in any given week are varied. He is joint owner and sometimes storekeeper in a trade store venture with two of his married sons who are resident in the village. He keeps the key to the cashbox and he controls the money from the store. Nathan acts as overseer of his sons' cash-crop activity and he has insisted on a policy of separation of their holdings in order to lessen the possibility of conflict between them. He is frequently absent from the village for several days at a time when he goes with his sons and their families to tend distant gardens as part of his policy of maintaining, by continued use, clear title to unoccupied land. His authority is usually undisputed, and he is sufficiently confident in the support of his followers to have publicly faced down one of them whom he suspected of practicing sorcery. When someone commented on his sons' good reputation in the village, Nathan's immediate response was, "Of course! I still hold them in my hands!"

Nonetheless, his age also allows Nathan to present himself as weak and dependent when he considers it advantageous to do so. Fearful of the ramifications should he fail to stop a brewing fight between Peter, one of his sons, and a village leader, he begged that the fight be avoided and the dispute left to the law to settle. Using the keening cry and tears of the very old he clutched at his angry son, alluding to himself as helpless, near death, and desirous of peace. His stratagem was successful and his son withdrew from the fight.

The recognition of Nathan's authority is not limited to his own followers. For example, another respected village elder and the adoptive father of one of Nathan's grandchildren declined to sponsor an initiation rite for the child. He reasoned that Nathan was the appropriate one to make such a decision and that it would be presumptuous of him to intrude, even in rites for his own daughter. Although Nathan continues to be in control of his affairs, he has begun to share his knowledge with his younger kin and to defer to the judgment of his older sons. For example:

(1) He spent several weeks taking all of his children on a trek through the bush to the boundaries of the tract of land owned by his 'patrikin group'. Eventually, he reasoned, population pressures will lead to dispute over unoccupied land, and he wanted his descendants to be clear about the exact location and boundaries of the land to which they hold title so that they will be able to protect their heritage.

(2) He sponsored *naveu,* a ceremonial visitation of spirits, that had not been performed in its fully elaborated form for at least twenty years, so that the procedures, songs, and stories associated with the ceremony would not be lost when he died.

(3) In a public controversy arising out of the polygynous marriage of his oldest son, Nathan refrained from interfering or expressing his opinion in village meeting. He practiced restraint because he regarded his son as fully adult and responsible for settling his own affairs.

Sarah

Sarah, a woman in her mid-sixties in 1981, has been since 1975 the widow of Nathan's older brother. She remains an active, involved member of the community and is often cited by others as an exemplar of the active elderly woman in contrast to Donna, a similarly widowed age-mate who, though healthy, has permitted herself to become an utterly dependent person. As is true of other widows, Sarah no longer maintains her own household. Instead she resides as part of the household of a married son, usually sleeping in the cooking house attached to the main dwelling. Although she is part of her son's household, she is not dependent on him, for her labor continues unabated.

In addition to gardening, harvesting, and food preparation, Sarah often frees her daughter-in-law by caring for her grandchildren. She also serves her own and neighboring villages as a healer. Sarah is highly respected for her knowledge and regularly directs the activities of her daughters and daughters-in-law in feast preparation, food distribution, and the production of pandanus mats and shell money. Her authority and the respect that she commands take on special significance because she is living in the village of her former husband. As a small girl she came as a bride from an interior village whose residents speak a language unrelated to Lusi. She makes regular trips back to her natal village to provide healing expertise, food, and care for ailing elderly kinsmen there. A cheerful and pleasant woman, Sarah has acquired a host of nicknames. Among them are 'Ricebag' from the discarded ricebag that she carries in lieu of the traditional fibre basket and 'Cookie' from the last food request of her dying husband. She accepts her nicknames with good humor and frequently engages in joking repartee with all and sundry about what they may or may not call her.

Sally

Sally, who was in her late fifties or early sixties at the time of our 1981 visit, was the only child of one 'village leader' and the wife of another. It is not surprising, therefore, that she has a life-long reputation as a strong-minded and independent woman. She was actively involved in the negotiations leading to her children's marriages and, during one stormy disagreement with her first-born's prospective father-in-law, she publicly shamed the man so that he tore down his men's house to demonstrate his anger and humiliation. In the early 1970s, Sally began suffering severe headaches and continuous eye infections, and by 1981 she was totally blind. Over the years, Jake, Sally's husband, became increasingly distressed by what he saw as the accelerating level of dissension, violence, and sorcery in the village. When thoughtless children teased Sally about her blindness, he declared this to be the culminating display of the deterioration of public morals and moved with his followers, establishing a new hamlet at an uninhabited point about two miles away. Today Sally and Jake live in this small hamlet with two of their married children and their families, her mother, Jake's brother, and a number of other kinsmen and friends. Sally and Jake have adopted a grandson to be a companion to Jake, and the young daughter of a distant kinsman to be Sally's helper. This girl leads Sally to the toilet area, carries water and firewood, helps Jake in the household's small garden plot, and cooks for her adopted parents. Even though she is blind, physically dependent, and frequently ill with painful headaches, Sally continues to be active. She still weaves fine coconut leaf baskets and she participates in ceremonial exchanges. She has publicly challenged a notorious local sorcerer who, she claims, is in her debt and has not distributed to her the wealth she considers to be her due. In 1981 she attended an important ceremony that was to culminate in the feeding and release of dangerous ancestor spirits. Ordinarily, women must flee the village when the spirits are fed but, because of her age and infirmity, the men classified Sally as a 'decrepit one' and invited her to remain in the village. She firmly refused the offer and left to feast and laugh with the other women, as she had always done.

Koroi

Koroi was the oldest man in Kandoka village in 1981, and one of the oldest Kaliai then living. We placed his age at between eighty and eighty-five, for he had clear memories of the coming of the Germans and the first establishment of indirect rule shortly after the turn of the century.

In the years since our research began in Kaliai, Koroi had become increasingly enfeebled, and restricted to painful walking with the aid of a stick, so that he seldom left the village. Most of Koroi's days were spent in the immediate vicinity of the men's house where he slept despite the fact that his wife was still living and maintained a household. Koroi's daily round seldom gave a hint of his former status as the acknowledged 'leader' of Kandoka. He babysat his grandchildren and great-grandchildren, did household chores around his men's house – including keeping the ground in front of it swept clear of debris – and sat reminiscing with other old men. When, on occasion, he attempted to act as director of ritual events in which his sons were involved, he was gently pushed aside and ignored, though he was welcome to attend as a spectator.

Not only did Koroi suffer from physical disability, but he was generally regarded as failing in mental acuity as well. He was said, therefore, to be *vuovuo* 'childlike' or 'senile', and he described himself as *taurai* 'decrepit'. Though he usually accepted this characterization passively, he sometimes struggled against it. When one of his daughter's children was to be initiated and the men of the village were preparing the shell money for distribution, he heard of it and painfully made his way to where the people were gathered. Seeing his daughter, he began to upbraid her:

Why didn't you tell me what you were doing? I'm not dead yet, so that you can forget to tell me about this kind of work. I'm still your father. If you had finished this and then I had heard about it, it would have made me cry. Why can't you tell your own father about your work?

He had come with eleven fathoms of shell money to make his own contribution, but thinking about how mistreated he had been he became distracted and, instead of giving the money to the organizers, his speech drifted off into complaints about his children. He was always cold, he said, and although he had cared for them when they were young and helpless none of them thought to bring him sugar for a hot drink. Some people in the crowd began to snicker, while others tried to remind him that he came to give shell money and not to get sugar. Finally, one of his relatives gently took the shell money from him and led him, still complaining, back to his house.

During 1981, Koroi's sons began to acknowledge by public ritual their father's retirement from active life. They held the first stage of Koroi's *ololo* 'mortuary ceremony'. Their explanation was that they were doing it "...so that he can see, before he dies, how much we honor him." The final mortuary ceremonies were completed during the summer of 1982 with a reported distribution of hundreds of fathoms of shell money, cash, pandanus mats, clay pots, wooden bowls, and forty pigs. (Scaletta, personal communication). With the completion of his mortuary rites, Koroi was socially dead. His sons had brought to a conclusion the complex of debts, obligations, credits, and social ties that were begun for Koroi by his father and grandfather and upon which he built his reputation as a 'leader'. He no longer had any business; it was finished. The final 'mortuary ceremony' marked the culmination of Koroi's life; his physical death would be 'something nothing' and would be marked by only minimal funerary rites. There would be no public mourning, only the private grief of his family. The completion of Koroi's 'mortuary ceremony' also enabled his sons to become 'leaders' in their own right. They had increased their reputations and validated their claims to leadership by their sponsorship of the ceremony for Koroi, an accomplishment normally denied to men until well after the death of their fathers.[5]

Mary

Mary died in 1976 in her late sixties or early seventies. Like Sarah, Mary had long been a widow but, unlike Sarah, her physical infirmities had made her a dependent person unable to contribute in any way to those who supported her during her declining years. Stricken by blindness more than ten years before her death, Mary, like Sally, required assistance in almost everything that she did. Someone had to lead her to a place where she could relieve herself and to provide and prepare all of her food, drink, and firewood.

Unlike Sally, Mary did not cling to the status of active 'elder'.

Instead, Mary's days were spent huddled in a little cooking house, near but separate from the household of her stepson, and she could be heard at all hours of the day or night keening that she had no water to drink, no food to eat, or no one to help rekindle her fire. Technically, Mary's care was the responsibility of her stepchildren, but both of them had large families of dependent children. On the one hand, Mary's stepchildren could pass her care into the hands of their children, which they did. On the other hand, the fact that both of her stepchildren were responsible for large families contributed to their resentment of the added burden of caring for someone to whom they were but tenuously related. In the final analysis, there was no one person who was directly responsible for Mary, and this ambiguity contributed to her tragic death. Alone in the village on a day when nearly everyone was gone to their gardens, Mary tried to rekindle her fire. Apparently she fainted and fell into the burning embers. She lay there undiscovered for hours until the villagers began returning in the late afternoon. She died a few days later of her injuries. Although no one was charged with culpable neglect in Mary's death, some in the village harbored ill-feeling in the matter for several years, and her fate is pointed to as an example of the tragedy facing the aged who do not have their own children to care for them.

DISCUSSION

There is no clear line separating the 'elder' from the 'decrepit person'. Rather, there is a continuum of characteristics and behaviors defining each status. An aging Kaliai may well decide that it is disadvantagous to be assigned to a particular age category and may, therefore, attempt to negotiate his status. In this case a person may choose to emphasize one or more of a set of qualities and de-emphasize others in his presentation of self. Physical condition and appearance are components in the assignment of one's age category, but they are not definitive ones. Sarah's appearance, for example, is that of an old woman. Her skin is wrinkled, her eyesight is poor, and she is nearly toothless. Nevertheless, her demeanor and life style are consistent with the status of 'elder', and that is how she presents herself. Although an 'elder's' physical condition may deteriorate and he may become increasingly dependent on his children, he is not normally regarded as decrepit until he meets some or all of the other characteristics associated with the decrepit person. Indeed, the term *taurai* 'decrepit person' is usually restricted to those who are too ill, weak or senile by *reason of age* to bear the responsiblities of normal social life. Persons who are physically helpless while still of an appropriate age to think of themselves as merely elderly will resist both the application of the term and the questionable privileges that go with it, as Sally did. Contrarily, the term may be self-applied by a person to whom it would otherwise be inappropriate, as was Nathan's case.

Let us consider the strategies used by Nathan and Sally and the reasons for their behavior. Why did Sally reject 'decrepit' status, and what did she achieve by her rejection? Although we did not discuss with Sally the reasons for her decision, there are several factors that we think are relevant. First, Sally's physical condition is appropriate for a 'decrepit person'. She is wrinkled, grey-haired, many of her teeth are missing, her health is poor, and she is blind and totally dependent on others to meet her bodily needs. Second, the status of 'decrepit person' was imposed on her by others. Considering her physical condition, if she had accepted placement in that category, it would likely have been permanent. Third, a 'decrepit person' is no longer an effective social being. He is not expected to participate in a meaningful way in cere-monial exchanges. He is, in Leenhardt's terms, treated as though he were already defunct (1979:33-34). Therefore, those who otherwise would include him in their wealth distributions may ignore his demands for consideration. If Sally had accepted the appellation 'decrepit person' her rightful claims for reciprocity probably would have been rejected. Finally, the men's invitation to Sally to remain in the village for the feeding of the spirits was not an honor, nor would she thereby have assumed the attributes of, or have been given the privileges of, a man. Rather, she would have lost her status as a socially significant woman and a person to be reckoned with. Sally had nothing to gain and everything to lose by presenting herself, or by permitting others to classify her, as a 'decrepit person'. She, therefore, successfully attempted to negotiate her status as an active and still socially vital 'elder'.

In contrast, Nathan described himself as old and helpless – as a *taurai* – and temporarily placed himself in that status in order to accomplish a specific goal: to divert his son from a fight. Although his appearance – thin to the point of emaciation, wrinkled, white haired, toothless, and partially blind – is that of a very old man, Nathan's mental acuity and his ability to control his own affairs precludes his being classified by others as 'decrepit'. Under normal circumstances Nathan would not present himself this way, but he was faced with a crisis situation. He, therefore, proceeded to negotiate for himself a status that he intended to hold only temporarily and for a specific purpose. Later Nathan explained to us that he had feared that the fight might result in serious injury or death, and he knew that he lacked the physical strength to restrain his angry son. So he resorted to the keening and tears of a 'decrepit person' in order to shame Peter into obedience. Nathan's behavior was a conscious ploy and it worked, for one does not easily ignore the public begging and weeping of an aged and helpless parent. Nathan was not concerned that his self-imposed status would be permanent and, in fact, the next morning he resumed his roles as manager of his trade store operation and supervisor of his sons.

The five people whose biographies we have sketched above provide for us a continuum of the roles of old age as they exist among the Lusi of Kaliai. Sarah is an 'elder' who has no occasion to place herself or to be placed in the 'decrepit' category. Nathan is a 'senior' man who presented himself as a helpless and dependent old person as a strategic ploy. Sally is an 'elder' who resisted the attempts of others to categorize her as 'decrepit'. Mary and Koroi were categorized as 'decrepit' and were treated as though they were already defunct. A 'decrepit one' is a person who has begun the process of dying. This is clearly seen in the behavior of Koroi's children and in his response to them.

1. Koroi's sons sponsored his mortuary ceremony before his physical death had taken place.

2. His daughter neglected to include him in the planning for her son's initiation – in the gathering and distribution of shell money, the principal activity through which leadership is expressed.

3. Koroi was ambivalent about being placed in this category, and was unsuccessful in his effort to negotiate his status. He seemed to accept being categorized as a 'decrepit one' when he danced with the masked figures who came to celebrate his death, but he rejected it when he protested his daughter's neglect: "I'm not dead yet!"

It is possible that the placement of Koroi in the status of 'decrepit person' was a strategic act by his sons who wished to honor him and at the same time to advance their own careers by their sponsorship of Koroi's mortuary cycle. It is certain that Koroi had little room for negotiation. His physical dependency, his lack of mental acuity, and his inability to engage in meaningful participation in ceremonial affairs were characteristic of a 'decrepit person' and placed him squarely within that category.

Mary, too, was regarded as defunct. Unable to care for herself, she was presumed also to be incapable of expressing her wants and needs accurately. Her kin regarded the care they gave her to be adequate.

They ignored her plaintive cries for food, water, or firewood not because they were mean, but because they thought that they, not she, were the best judges of her needs. In this regard their behavior toward her was analogous to that of a parent toward an irresponsible child. The analogy of responsible people behaving toward a 'decrepit person' as they would toward a very young child is appropriate, for the condition of being *vuovuo* 'mentally incapacitated,' frequently an affliction of the very old, is specifically likened by the Lusi to the condition of a child before it is *iavava* 'fully human'. We should stress that *vuovuo* is not adequately translated by the English term 'senile', which has principle reference to the loss of mental acuity as a result of old age. Rather, *vuovuo* means inability to reason, lack of sound judgment often combined with physical dependency. Hence the term is also used to describe the condition of very young children until they are capable of rational thought. One 'elder' commented that he thought of being *vuovuo* as being analogous to having a hole between one's shoulder blades where the thoughts ran out. He anticipated this would happen in his own case, he explained, because "my knowledge has gone to my children. My strength is finished."

'Decrepit' or defunct persons are also like children in the lack of formality with which their deaths are treated. The physical death of such aged persons is, after all, merely the completion of a process begun long before. The point to be made here is that, as in the death of a young child, there is seldom any attempt to assign culpability for the death of a very old person, and that the passing of such persons is usually a matter of concern and grief only to their close kin.

A final point about being 'decrepit', a point only suggested in the biographical sketches, is the declining significance of the behavioral expressions of gender that mark the years of active adulthood. As we noted earlier, the expressions of gender dimorphism are most strongly marked during the years of parenting. As parenting responsibilities decline with age, so also do the behavioral markers of gender until, in old age, even those most strongly entrenched may disappear. Koroi's use of a broom to sweep the area around his men's house – a task usually done by women – and the tolerance of 'decrepit' women at otherwise exclusively male ceremonial events illustrate the fading of rigid gender roles in advanced age. But we must stress that such 'decrepit' men and women do not comprise a neutral or third gender category, and their gender location is not reversed.

DEATH

It is rare for people in Kaliai to die of old age. Death much more commonly strikes people when they are active and vigorous than when they are old and feeble. The Kaliai, therefore, do not usually see death as a natural event. Instead, the friends and relatives of the deceased almost always look for a culpable agent – usually a sorcerer (see Counts 1976-77; Counts 1980b; Counts and Counts 1983-84 for detailed discussions of Kaliai responses to death).

Lofland argues that in premodern society the dying period, the time "between admission to the dying category" and the actual occurrence of death, will typically be brief (1978:18). Lofland suggests several reasons for this brevity. First, premodern societies commonly have a low level of medical technology. This delays diagnosis of terminal illness and prevents people from interfering with the dying process. Second, premodern people usually have "a simple definition of death". When a person enters the dying category, the customary response is for him to commit suicide, or for his kin to kill him or to respond to his condition with "fatalistic passivity" (Lofland 1978:18). This response hastens, or at least does not slow, the process of dying and ensures that, typically, the time that a person spends dying will be short. Analysis of the dying process in Kaliai suggests that Lofland's scenario requires modification.

Lofland does not define what is meant by "brief duration dying" (1978:18) but opposes it to the "prolonged" state artificially maintained by the medical technology available in modern hospitals. Lofland has, however, failed to take into account indigenous definitions of dying and the fact that the length of time a person spends in the dying category depends on the readiness of the people in any given society to diagnose an illness as terminal. The people of Kaliai, for example, are prepared to diagnose as potentially fatal any fever or internal pain or illness that does not respond readily to treatment, either by traditional healers or the personnel at the medical clinic (see also Scaletta, chapter 11, for an extended example from the Kaliai's near neighbors, the Kabana of Bariai). We know of people who were in the process of dying for a period of up to three months. Some of these recovered; others did not. In all cases of which we are aware, the dying person himself made the decision that his illness was terminal. His subsequent activities – moving onto the beach under a tent or temporary shelter, sending for friends and kin to come to say farewell and settle accounts – and the response of his relatives made the dying person's condition a matter of public knowledge and community concern. Contrary to Lofland's generalization that premodern people have a simple definition of death, this is not the case with the Kaliai. The Lusi word that is usually translated as death, *mate,* may in fact be glossed in several ways: to be ruined, fatally injured, or terminally ill *(ngamatene,* 'I'm dying'); to be unconscious or partially dead *(isoli matenga,* 'he's half dead'); to be 'really dead' *(imate gasili)* or 'completely dead' *(imate kuvu).* A person who is *mate* may return to life any time after he begins the process *(imate suvu* 'he dies and returns'), including after he is 'really' and 'completely' dead.

People know that dying is almost complete if any one of a number of the following are present: the dying person's breath smells of death *(aiwari masmasi* 'his salty/sweet smell', 'his death smell'); if he stares without blinking or shame at another person's face; if he is restless and asks to be alternatively lifted and laid down; and if he loses control of his bladder or bowels. Dying is complete when a person stops breathing; when his heart ceases to beat; when his eyes and mouth hang open. The spiritual component usually leaves the body through the eyes or mouth or, if both are closed, by the anus. Burial of adults usually occurs from twenty-four to thirty-six hours after death is judged to be complete. Infants and uninitiated children are often interred more quickly, for there are fewer people in a young child's social network to come to the funeral. The corpse is usually uncovered for public view until it begins to bloat, at which time it is wrapped in pandanus mats and hidden from view.

Even though the Kaliai recognize complete death by the various physical signs, the emphasis in any discussion of *mate* is on the process rather than the event. This process may begin with the social disaffiliation of an aged person, as for example with Koroi, may be reversible, and may continue after the body is buried. Death is processual, reversible, and has boundaries other than the ones we recognize because the separation of a person's spiritual component from his body is not necessarily permanent. The spirit leaves the body during dreams and visions, during serious illness, and in death, and it may return under all these circumstances. We know of a number of people of all ages who have been defined as 'completely dead' only to return to life. Three of these people were men for whom mourning ceremonies had already begun and who report having "near death experiences." (see Counts 1983 for discussion and analysis of these experiences). It is sufficient to note here that no one related having experiences identical to those reported by Moody (1975), such as hearing one's self pronounced dead; feelings of peace and quiet; finding one's self out of one's own body, being able to see and hear but not communicate with others; having unusual and often unpleasant auditory sensations; being pulled through a dark tunnel; and encountering a "being of light". Kaliai did report meeting friends, kin, and supernatural beings; finding a boundary they could not cross; and being required to return to life – experiences that Moody reports are common among North Americans who are near death but return to life. It is also noteworthy that although return of the spirit to the dead body is not uncommon, no one expressed any fear of being buried alive, nor do our consultants report the occurrence of live burial in the past.

If a person's spiritual component permanently separates from the body and burial takes place, the ghost may remain near its home village and appear to its living kin and friends. These appearances usually occur at dusk and are most likely to take place if the death has not been avenged or no compensation has been paid. The disembodied spirit (of a still living person as well as of a dead one) may also appear as a signal to the community that a death is about to occur. Someone (people do not yet know who) is dying, and villagers wait anxiously until the identity of the dying person is revealed.

The Kaliai do not ordinarily respond to death with the passivity that Lofland suggests is characteristic of people living in societies with premodern technology. We know of no instance when a terminally ill Kaliai committed suicide and of no case when others hurried the process by killing the dying person (but see Scaletta's discussion in chapter 11 of a case in which the Kabana, who live in Bariai to the west of Kaliai, argued that death should be hastened for a woman who was dying in great pain). Furthermore, the public acknowledgement that an individual has begun dying in no way implies that his kin passively accept either his fate or the inevitability of the process. Indeed, relatives and friends will probably work frantically in an attempt to change the course of the illness and promote the victim's recovery. This is true even for the old if the individual has not been categorized as 'decrepit' and if the onset of the illness is sudden.

If, however, the dying person is *taurai* 'decrepit', if he is physically dependent and mentally incapacitated and his dying is seen as the result of his gradual deterioration, then his kin are fatalistic about his death and passively accept it. On the rare occasions when a person dies of old age *(imate ngani i taurai)*, 'he died of being old', his kin do not attribute culpability or seek an external cause, nor does mourning go beyond the quiet grief of his immediate family. Informants who have witnessed death from old age say that the family gathers around to talk with the dying person and to hear his bones loosen and break one by one, beginning with the ribs. Finally the backbone breaks, the dying person crumples, and he is wrapped in pandanus mats and soon buried.

SUMMING UP

There are three points emerging from this consideration of the Kaliai experience of aging and dying that we believe deserve emphasis.

First, some of the confusion that exists in the literature on aging and death derives from generalizations by scholars who have failed to take into account indigenous concepts or the sociocultural context. We are not original in recognizing this problem (for example see Watson and Maxwell 1977). However, it is important to call attention to the fallacy underlying the assumption that there is a necessary relationship between a people's technology and the way in which they define and respond to aging and death. A simple technology does not imply a simple cosmology.

Second, Kaliai provides a contrast to societies, such as those in the New Guinea Highlands, where sexual opposition and gender reversal are pronounced. The Kaliai say that sexual activity is debilitating and that sexual effluvia is contaminating, and their public norms clearly distinguish between the behavior and tasks that are appropriate to males and females. However, in Kaliai as elsewhere, individuals often depart from ideal standards. When the parenting years are over, sexual division of labor becomes flexible and sexual dimorphism fades. When we compare this situation with the Highlands we are tempted to speculate that societies characterized by strongly polarised gender distinctions during youth and the parenting years may balance that polarization by moving to pronounced gender role change for the aged. Conversely, in societies where sexual opposition and role distinctions are more balanced or muted during the parenting years, gender roles roles are likely to undergo much less dramatic change in old age (Lepowsky, in chapter 8, also argues and presents data that document this point). Instead, people in these societies superficially resemble a more common pattern, one that Gutmann, Grunes, and Griffin call the "normal androgyny of later life" (1980:122). Our data and that of Lepowsky (chapter 8) suggest that the term "androgyny" may be inappropriate for analysis of the processes of gender changes in old age in some Melanesian societies. Very old Lusi do not enter a third gender category. They are not without gender, nor are they at once both male and female. Women and men remain distinctive, but their separateness is muted in old age and, as in young children, may be of little practical consequence in everyday life.

Finally, if we are to develop hypotheses about aging and dying that have cross-cultural validity we must treat aging and dying as dynamic and processual. Old age and death are not rigid, biologically determined categories with fixed, immutable boundaries within which people are frozen. Instead, old age and death are descriptions of social categories. The old and even the dead may have vital roles to play, roles that are defined in terms of relationships with others. If we would understand why old people in Kaliai, or any other community, behave as they do and why they are treated as they are, we must ask the same questions about them that we would ask about any other social group. How, for instance, is a person identified as an old person; or as a defunct one? What are the criteria by which one kind of old person is distinguished from another or from the dead, and what difference does this identification make to the individual and to his kin? Can a person negotiate his status? Does he have the option to define or redefine himself, as Nathan did, and can he refuse the category imposed upon him by others, as Sally did? If a person has choices and can decide how to present himself, what factors influence his decision? What strategies are available to the old?

So we end this study of aging and dying in Kaliai with questions. But this is appropriate, for if the old and even the dead are to be seen as involved in ongoing processes then we must ask of them the same questions about identity, activity, ideology, and relationships that we ask of the other members of human society.

NOTES

We collected the data on which the study is based in northwest New Britain in 1966-67, 1971, 1975-76, and 1981. Our research was funded by predoctoral research grants from the U.S. National Science Foundation and by Southern Illinois University in 1966-67; by the Canada Council, Wenner-Gren Foundation Grant 1809, and the University of Waterloo in 1971; and by the Social Sciences and Humanities Research Council of Canada and by sabbatical leaves from the University of Waterloo and McMaster University in 1975-76 and 1981.

1. The term *sol* is a Tok Pisin term; there is no Lusi equivalent of the unitary concept that is glossed 'soul' in English.
2. In 1981 there were 360 people living in Kandoka: 186 infants and children born in 1965 or later; 53 unmarried people born before 1964 or who were married but childless ; 81 'parents of dependent children'; 33 'senior' or 'elders'; and 7 *taurai* 'decrepit persons'. Of the 'elders', 18 were women and 15 were men, while 6 of the 'decrepit persons' were women and one was a man.
3. All personal names are fictitious.
4. The *kina* is the unit of currency in Papua New Guinea. In 1981 it was valued at

about $1.60 (U.S.).
5.   Koroi died in 1984.

8

GENDER, AGING, AND DYING IN AN EGALITARIAN SOCIETY

Maria Lepowsky

INTRODUCTION

In a society where adult women as well as men participate publicly in significant political, economic and ritual activities, there is no marked rise in status or prestige as a woman reaches menopause or passes into old age. Rather, the status of elderly women closely parallels that accorded elderly men, being determined predominantly by age and personality as opposed to gender. This paper examines the experiences of aging and dying for men and women on a remote and culturally conservative island in southeastern Papua New Guinea where there is considerable overlap in the range of roles and behavior considered appropriate for members of each sex.

Despite the surge of interest in the last ten years in analyzing gender roles from a variety of cultural settings, few authors have attempted to compare systematically the status and the experience of women versus that of men in a given culture throughout the life cycle of the individual. The logic of such an approach was first pointed out by Robert Lowie (1920), who discussed the structural significance of age- and sex-based social categories, emphasizing the "artificiality" of attempting to analyze the "sex dichotomy" and "age classes" separately from one another. Linton (1940, 1942) introduced the concept of age-sex categories, "the building blocks of the society," which he believed are more important than "family systems" in determining the place of the individual within the total social order (1940:872). He made the observation that "[t]he current neglect of this aspect of social organization is no doubt due in part to its deceptive appearance of simplicity" (1940:872). Linton suggested ranking age-sex categories on the basis of their differential prestige, which he defined in his 1942 article as "social influence."

This chapter focuses upon the age-sex categories of 'old man' and 'old woman' on Vanatinai, Papua New Guinea, but the cultural meanings and social influence of these categories only become intelligible when they are seen as end-products of earlier stages of the life-cycle. The categories "adult man" and "adult woman" are, therefore, discussed first to provide a context for understanding the cultural treatment of old age. Indigenous attitudes toward death, dying and the relations between the living and the dead are then discussed.

The island called Sudest or Tagula by cartographers and government personnel, is known as Vanatinai to its inhabitants. Vanatinai literally means "motherland" or "mainland" (Tagula is the name given to the island by its neighbors from the more populous island of Misima, 70 miles to the northwest). Vanatinai is the largest island in the Louisiade Archipelago at 50 miles long by 8 to 15 miles wide and lies about 225 miles southeast of mainland Papua New Guinea. It and neighboring islands mark the boundary between the Coral Sea to the south and the Solomon Sea to the north. Vanatinai is surrounded by one of the world's largest lagoons, and its extensive coral reef systems impede the progress of Western motor vessels, contributing to the island's lack of integration into the world economy. Per capita income on the island is under $20 per year. The inhabitants plant yams, sweet potato, taro, manioc and other crops in their gardens; prepare the starch from the abundant stands of sago palms in the swamps; collect shellfish and fish from the reefs and streams; hunt wild pig, crocodile, monitor lizard, possum and other game; and forage for a wide variety of wild fruits, greens, tubers, nuts and legumes in the rain forest. They also participate in an elaborate system of intra- and inter-island exchange extending as far as the mainland and connecting with both the *kula* region to the northwest and the exchange networks of the southeast Papuan coast (see Lepowsky 1983).

GENDER ROLES

Vanatinai is a matrilineal society. Women are described as the "owners of the gardens" by both men and women, and they make key decisions about the allocation and distribution of garden produce. Women and men inherit land and valuables equally.

Girl children are valued as the future mothers of lineage mates. There are no puberty or initiation ceremonies for either sex, no men's houses or associations, and no residential segregation of the sexes.

There is very little emphasis on the concept of female pollution. People have intercourse during a woman's menstrual period, but a menstruating woman must not enter or pass near a garden lest wild animals eat the crops. A related taboo extends to both sexes at the planting of a new yam garden: both menstruating women and people of both sexes who have had intercourse within the last two or three days are barred from participating or the new yams will not grow properly (also see chapter 7 for discussion of a similar belief by the Lusi of Kaliai, West New Britain).

Men and women often work side by side on the same subsistence tasks, and the activities considered appropriate for men and for women are largely overlapping (see Lepowsky 1981). Vanatinai women learn significant forms of garden, exchange, and healing magic and often function as clan leaders, hamlet managers and ritual experts. They speak out at public meetings, and their words are listened to with respect by both men and women.

Men have a virtual monopoly on the practice of sorcery, although a few women have been adepts, dressing in male traditional dress while carrying out their rituals. Only men use spears, either in warfare (in precontact times) or in hunting, although women formerly knew war magic, carried spears for their brothers, and removed the dead and wounded from the fray. Women presently hunt game – possums and fruit bats, for example – by climbing trees and sneaking up on them. People say that "women are the life-givers and men are the life-destroyers", but many women are alleged to practice witchcraft.

Both women and men may organize and lead exchange expeditions, traveling on foot, paddling, or sailing canoes to distant hamlets. These expeditions are equivalent to the *kula* journeys undertaken in the islands to the north and west of the Louisiade Archipelago, except that there is no rule mandating that certain valuables (shell necklaces) must circulate in a clockwise direction among islands while others (armshells) travel counter-clockwise. The shell necklaces, stone axe blades, and shell currency pieces circulating on Vanatinai and nearby islands are called *une* or *ghune,* cognates of the term *kune,* which means *kula* in the southern islands of the *kula* ring (see Lepowsky 1983).

The primary stimulus for exchange journeys on Vanatinai is the mortuary feast. After a death, surviving kin and affines must organize a series of increasingly elaborate feasts in honor of the deceased. The feast-givers ritually transfer yams and other garden produce; sago; pigs; household goods such as pots, sleeping mats, personal attire; accessories such as coconut-leaf skirts, armlets, betel nut baskets; and a variety of ceremonial valuables such as shell-disc necklaces, shell currency pieces and greenstone axe blades to a designated patrilateral heir of the deceased. The deaths of men and women receive equal ritual weight, both men and women host or substantially contribute to mortuary feasts, and both men and women receive valuables at feasts as heirs (see Lepowsky 1981 and 1984a).

Every adult is expected to contribute labor, foodstuffs and/or goods and ceremonial valuables to a mortuary feast for a deceased individual to whom s/he is linked by ties of kinship, marriage, co-residence, or exchange partnership. Contributions are also expected if one is linked by any of these ties to a feast host or hosting lineage. Therefore, the impending mortuary feasts on the island in any given year obligate virtually every adult to some sort of contribution. However, the degree of participation beyond a minimum contribution of labor and foodstuffs is at the discretion of the individual and is a function of individual personality and resources. Some men and some women strive to earn the title of *gia,* a gender-neutral term that literally means 'giver' and can be translated as 'bigman' or 'bigwoman', by hosting more feasts and contributing more lavishly to the feasts of others than the minimum demanded by custom. Such giving obligates others to future returns in kind and builds personal prestige. While more men than women are extremely active in exchange activities, a few women are far more active and have a wider reputation for their exchange activities than the majority of men. Other women and men may concentrate their energies on being good gardeners, skillful healers or loving parents.

There is no separate arena of exchange for women and men as in the Trobriand Islands (Weiner 1976), where women exchange skirts and banana leaf bundles in a mortuary rite and men monopolize overseas *kula* exchanges. On Vanatinai women and men frequently exchange valuables, pigs and foodstuffs with each other, and individual women and men may compete against each other to obtain a prized valuable from a mutual exchange partner.

Vanatinai women, therefore, have access to their culture's primary avenues to prestige and social influence; the mortuary feast/exchange complex. The participation of women in a culture's major prestige system has only rarely been reported. Numerous authors have suggested that a division of social life into a public and a domestic sphere, with the relegation of women's activities to the domestic sphere, lowers female status and influence in a particular society (Hammond and Jablow 1973; Sanday 1973, 1974; Rosaldo 1974; Sacks 1974, Bacdayan 1977, Leacock 1978). Ortner and Whitehead (1981) believe that the public domain is significant in understanding cultural constructions of gender because it is the locus of prestige systems dominated by men. In light of these arguments, the Vanatinai case, where both women and men participate in the same, *kula*-like exchange and prestige system, is an important ethnographic example of female participation in the public, prestige domain. This female participation and influence is an indication of the sexually egalitarian nature of Vanatinai society (see Lepowsky 1984b).

GENDER AND AGING

Anthropologists have observed that in many societies where the status of women is lower than that of men or where women's sexuality is considered dangerous, the postmenopausal woman enjoys a rise in social standing or an increased access to certain privileges or activities concomitant with her loss of the ability to bear young and to menstruate (see, for example Sinclair chapter 2 and Dominy chapter 3). In some societies an older woman is presumably seen as being more "man-like" (e.g. Simmons 1945:64-66). Ruth Benedict (1953) discusses the concept of "discontinuities in cultural conditioning," although she applies it primarily to the discrepancies frequently found in human societies between the roles of child and adult. On Vanatinai there is no discontinuity between the status or influence of premenopausal and postmenopausal women, because adult women already hold considerable authority and influence over the lives of others, authority that often extends well beyond their own hamlets. As both men and women age, the nature of their social participation and influence changes, but the changes are parallel for members of each sex.

In an article published after the first draft of this chapter was written, Judith Brown (1982:143) also uses the concept of discontinuity in the context of the female life cycle, discussing "the discontinuity of women's lives as they age beyond the childbearing years." After an extensive survey of the cross-cultural ethnographic literature, she describes "amazing unanimity in the findings. Women's lives appear to improve with the onset of middle age. In some societies this change is dramatic and in others moderate.... Middle age brings fewer restrictions, the right to exert authority over certain kinsmen, and the opportunity for achievement and recognition beyond the household" (Ibid.).

Even before Vanatinai women have adult children (Brown's definition of "middle aged women"), their lives are relatively unrestricted by custom or taboo, they hold authority within the hamlet group, and they participate in prestige-garnering exchange activities to the extent that they personally desire, giving them an avenue to extra-domestic achievement and recognition.

While it is true that pregnant or lactating women are restricted in their mobility by the demands of offspring and thus are less likely to participate extensively in exchange activities, the fathers of young children are also rarely involved in exchange beyond the minimum that custom demands of every adult. They feel the same constraints as their wives: their labor must be available to provide sustenance for their dependent children, and they feel vulnerable to sorcery or witchcraft attacks on their children if they become too prominent or successful in exchange activities and invite the envy of others. Thus middle aged adults of both sexes, people whose children are adult or nearly adult, are likely to be most active in traditional exchange.

The Vanatinai case does not contradict Brown's findings. It does suggest that there is a continuum in the degree of continuity or discontinuity in the female life cycle. In egalitarian societies such as Vanatinai, there may be little or no discontinuity because the status of the premenopausal woman is already high. In societies with an overt ethic of male dominance, the discontinuity is likely to be greatest as the woman moves beyond her earlier identity as potential childbearer whose sexuality involves the danger of shame or pollution of male associates (see, for example, the Maori case discussed by Sinclair, chapter 2). These societies should have the most "dramatic" change, in Brown's terms, while societies with a less pronounced or fully elaborated ethic of male dominance should have a more "moderate" discontinuity in the female life cycle.

The Vanatinai case also suggests that in societies where the roles and behavior considered appropriate for men and for women are largely overlapping, the gradual diminution of gender distinctions with advancing age until the attainment of "the normal androgyny of later life," postulated by Gutmann, Grunes and Griffin (1980:122), will be less apparent. Gender distinctions are not highly marked in adult life on Vanatinai, although it is true that the elderly no longer reproduce, older women do not menstruate or lactate, and older men no longer hunt with spears or, in former days, would no longer have made war. There is, then, on Vanatinai, a greater congruence between male and female life styles in old age than in youth or middle age, as Gutmann and his colleagues would predict. However, the difference in the overlap of gender roles between adulthood and old age is relatively small and undramatic compared to societies with an overt ethic of male dominance.

THE ELDERLY

The Vanatinai terms *laisali* and *mankwesi* are synonymous and may be translated as 'old woman'. Significantly, they are used as terms of respect for any woman of influence above the age of about twenty-five or thirty. Similarly, on Misima Island, 70 miles northwest of Vanatinai, the term *nevenak* means both 'old woman' and 'important woman' and is used as a respectful term of address, just as the male equivalent, *tanoak,* is. 'Old woman' has rarely been reported as a term of respect in the cross-cultural ethnographic literature, and may, indeed, be an insult (see Carucci, chapter 6).

Since it is taboo for anyone on Vanatinai to address an affinally related woman (or man) by name, a person is often called 'old woman' as an alternative to 'X's mother', 'Y's wife', or 'that woman there'. *Amalaisali* similarly means 'old man', but this term is rarely used. Instead the pidgin expression *olman* 'old man' is commonly heard.[1]

It is difficult to say when 'old age' begins on Vanatinai. Mature adults are addressed as 'old woman' or 'old man' interchangeably with the terms of address for 'adult woman', *yola na,* and 'adult man', *amala na.* The descriptive term for adult woman or female is *wevo* and for adult man or male is *ghomoli. Taiyauwiya* means both 'old' and 'before' or 'in early times', while *toa* means both 'young' and 'new'. There is no separate term for the extremely aged or for the decrepit aged, a phrase first used in the cross-cultural study on aging by Simmons (1945), just as there is no separate term for newborn or infant.

Table 5 indicates the population of one Vanatinai village plus its outlying hamlets classified by age and sex. The data are derived from a census conducted, while I was present, by government personnel. I observed that one man older than seventy, a second man older than sixty and two women above the age of sixty did not travel from their hamlets to be counted in the census. Three of these individuals were in poor health, and two of them died within a few months. The islanders regard the function of the census as the construction of the tax rolls. At the time all adults between ages eighteen and forty-five were expected to pay a head tax, which was collected immediately after the census was taken (the head tax was subsequently eliminated). Since the elderly did not owe any taxes, some of them saw no reason to appear for the census. My own records therefore show ten individuals above the approximate age of sixty rather than the six recorded by the census. The number of elderly is probably similarly undercounted for other parts of the island as well as other parts of Milne Bay Province.

Table 5. Population of Jelewaga Village, Sudest Island and Outlying Hamlets by Age and Sex[a]

Age[b]	Male	Female
70+	1	0
60-69	2	3
50-59	14	13
40-49	14	11
30-39	19	9
20-29	17	22
10-19	33	27
0-9	16	29
TOTAL M and F	**116**	**114**

a. Data are from Papua New Guinea government census for June, 1978. One man older than 70 and one man and two women older than 60 did not appear for the census and are not included in the table.

b. No dates of birth were recorded prior to the 1960s, when only some births were recorded. Ages of other adolescents and adults are based on written estimates by government patrol officers or census officials of approximate year of birth.

People in their forties are usually most actively involved in exchange activities. They host and attend the largest number of feasts, for they are still building their reputations and accumulating (and giving away) wealth. It is men and women in their fifties and early sixties who are most renowned as 'bigmen' and 'bigwomen' and who hold the greatest number of ceremonial valuables. They tend to conserve their energies and their wealth, contributing heavily to the feasts for people most significant to them. But both men and women continue to attend and participate in mortuary feasts until the end of their lives if they are physically able.

The activities of the elderly vary according to personality and physical fitness. Some people are active gardeners into their seventies, walking long miles through swamps and streams and over mountains with heavy loads of produce. One old man who died in his eighties in 1978, and whose vigor was greatly admired, often walked the 8 miles over the central mountain range to visit his relatives on the north coast. Another old woman never stirred from her place by the household fire and was pitied for her poor health (also note the "use it or lose it" attitude toward physical vigor in old age expressed by the Lusi of Kaliai in chapter 7). She was, I later learned, only in her late sixties, the same age as a number of other far more active men and women who were blessed with better health and strength. But even this woman was taken by sailing canoe to attend a feast on another island about 30 miles distant. She had a central role in the mortuary ritual as the only surviving adult female member of the host's matrilineage and was publicly draped with valuables in the key ritual called *mwagumwagu*. The excitement and attention of this trip seemed to invigorate her and spurred her to remember and recount the extensive exchange and ritual activities of her middle years.

Except for those who are extremely infirm, even aged men and women attempt to make a contribution to hamlet life. They often live with or adjacent to an adult child. Those who are retired from active gardening and food collecting care for grandchildren and other young kin while the parents are away from the hamlet on subsistence tasks. They may collect small loads of firewood or gather fallen ripe coconuts, and they tend the fire, seeing that it does not die during the day, an important function in an area where there are no matches available and fire must be rekindled by the tedious fire-plow method. Tending the fire and remaining in an otherwise deserted hamlet is valued by others as 'keeping the place hot', thereby keeping malevolent sorcerers away.

Young grandchildren are often assigned by their parents to live with a grandparent who is alone and to assist him or her with tasks such as cooking, fetching water and firewood, and working in the garden. The foster child may remain with the grandparent until adolescence or or until the latter's death, or else return periodically to live with the parents while a sibling is sent to the grandparent (the Lusi of Kaliai, West New Britain have a similar custom. See Counts and Counts, chapter 7).

Grandparents show a special love for their grandchildren, saving them choice tubers and fruits, teaching them traditional customs and stories, and defending them against a parent's anger at some childish misbehavior. Grandparents and grandchildren call each other by the reciprocal term, *rubugu*, or use the affectionate diminutive, *bubu*.

People are expected to remain sexually active well into old age. Unlike many other parts of Melanesia which have an ethic of male dominance and a belief in the polluting power of women, the people of Vanatinai regard sexual activity as healthy rather than health-threatening or depleting. It is a privilege of the sexually mature individual that need not be given up in old age. The Vanatinai case suggests that societies that tend toward equality between genders have a positive attitude toward sexuality in general and thus toward the sexuality of the elderly.

A widowed man or woman is expected to remain celibate until the entire sequence of mortuary feasts has been completed, a process that normally takes several years, but individuals are often widowed in middle age and sometimes before. Thus many people who survive into old age have been widowed for a number of years, have satisfied their mortuary obligations, and are free to take lovers if they wish. Some occasionally enter into liasons with one another, and a few remarry. Only a minority of couples survive together into old age.

The elderly usually enter into liasons with people who are from approximately the same age to as much as twenty years younger. Since sexual attractiveness is believed to depend largely upon knowledge of the appropriate love magic, old people who succeed in sleeping with young partners are admired for the potency of their magic, but their age difference is considered scandalous (the Lusi of Kaliai, West New Britain have a similar attitude toward sexual liasons between people of wide age difference, see Counts and Counts, chapter 7). I was taught one magical technique for obtaining a lover by a young man who explained that he had gotten it from a male relative. Its efficacy was demonstrated, he said, by the fact that his kinsman, then in his late sixties, had used it to seduce a fourteen year old girl, a relationship that at the time had been the subject of shocked and disapproving gossip. An elderly widow told me when I was asking about the use of an aromatic white root called *wughulumo* that, "If we make our *bunama* (sweetly scented, magically-enhanced coconut oil) with it and put it on our bodies, we can sleep with youths *(zevazeva)."* Friends teased this woman about a suspected romantic relationship with a man fifteen years her junior. As do other islanders, the elderly try to be discreet about their sexual activity.

The active elderly and the decrepit aged are equally well treated by their descendants and other hamlet residents, who try to see that they are warm enough and have water, tobacco, and their favorite foods. People state that the primary reason for having children is so that there will be someone to care for one in old age. At one childbirth a childless, middle aged female birth attendant who declared that she wanted no children was asked rhetorically, "Who will fetch your water and firewood, and who will cook your food when you are old?" Even young children seem to be aware of the expectation that they will eventually reciprocate by caring for their parents in old age. One day a woman friend complained in front of her three children about having to carry them every night from where they had fallen asleep in the center of the house after the evening meal to the tiny side room where the family slept. Her six-year-old daughter immediately retorted, "Don't complain about carrying us, because we will have to carry you around when you are old!"

Although people commonly express their affection and indebtedness to aged parents and show no overt resentment at having to care for them, the considerate treatment of the aged is ensured by another factor. On Vanatinai all health and prosperity is believed to stem from the ancestors, who are appealed to through magic and ritual. An elder who is badly treated at the end of life will retaliate in the afterlife by refusing to aid living descendants or by visiting misfortune upon them, for it is deceased parents and other close kin who are the most important magical allies. Furthermore, by the time a Vanatinai person reaches old age, he or she is very likely to know sorcery or witchcraft, and it would be dangerous to anger such a person (see McKellin, chapter 9, for discussion of a similar belief among the Managalase of Papua New Guinea). Therefore, despite the claim that children are necessary for security in old age, even old people with no immediate living descendants are provided with the necessities of life.

Although no specific instances of angry ghosts who were neglected in old age and revenged themselves upon descendants were recounted to me, I was told of several cases where elders who thought themselves poorly treated brought misfortune upon offenders. In one village I visited to attend a feast, an old woman who lived alone was discreetly pointed out to me as a witch by my companion, who warned me that we must be polite to her and not walk in front of her, for she had caused fellow villagers who acted disrespectfully toward her to fall sick. For this reason, the woman was said to be provided with food by unrelated neighbors. Another old man, known as a notorious sorcerer, was said to have crippled the spine of a three year old boy (with tuberculosis) because the child accidentally kicked sand into the old man's eyes while playing near where he sat on the ground talking to other adults. This act was also interpreted as revenge against the child's adult caretakers for not being respectful enough to have prevented the boy from playing nearby.

The following accounts briefly describe the lifestyles and activities of two representative elderly individuals.

Wonamo

Wonamo (not her real name) a widow in her early sixties, lives in a small house adjacent to that of her son and only child. Two young granddaughters share the house with her and help her by gathering firewood, cooking, and washing dishes. She is frequently seen on the paths leading from the coastal village to the garden areas en route to one of her gardens or returning with a heavy basket of produce balanced on her head. Her daughter-in-law has many young children who are close in age, which limits her gardening activities, and Wonamo supplies a sizable proportion of the family's food. One of her gardens is on the gravelly soil of the coastal ridge. Another smaller garden lies inland just beyond the brown, stagnant waters of a sago swamp. A third garden is 4 miles from her house on the far side of the steep central mountain range that bisects Vanatinai. This garden, which she visits once every few weeks, is not far from the small, isolated hamlet where her sister lives. Wonamo makes the strenuous climb across the mountain pass to the upland plateau where her garden and those of her kin fill a sunlit clearing cut in the rain forest. After weeding her plot or gathering ripe tubers she usually spends the night with her sister before returning to her home on the south coast.

Wonamo had to spend an exceptionally long time, more than twenty years, in mourning for her husband. She had few close kin and only one child to help her obtain ceremonial valuables to present to her husband's kin and heirs to complete the mortuary feast sequence. From the time that she and her kin finally made the feast that liberated her from widow's garb, she almost always plucked a red or pink hibiscus to stick into her hair while she went about her business, enjoying her release from the taboo on self-decoration for a widowed spouse.

Wonamo is admired for her industriousness and her cheerful temperament. I once accompanied her on a trip across the mountain to attend a small feast intermediate in the series honoring her deceased mother's brother. After the long walk through the swamps and over the mountain, we arrived at the clear stream just below the hamlet. We bathed, as is customary before visiting. Wonamo then pulled from her basket two fine shell-disc necklaces, put one around her neck and gave me the other to wear for the duration of the feast, for the kin of the deceased are supposed to decorate themselves and look as attractive (and wealthy) as possible during mortuary feasts. She and her sister supervised the cooking and the feeding of the guests. Those related by marriage to the dead man publicly presented valuables to his heir, his sister's son. An elderly widow, the deceased's sister's son's wife, was the major contributor. She gave one fine greenstone axe blade in its carved, 'seven'-shaped handle; one carved, wooden ceremonial lime stick decorated with shell discs; and one orange shell currency piece.

Kariboki

Kariboki (not his real name) was a quiet, soft-spoken gray-haired man in his sixties. Divorced long ago, he lived alone in a small house near two adult daughters of his deceased sisters. Their young children were often seen with their great uncle (MMB) line-fishing or gathering shellfish on the fringing reef. Kariboki also tended a small garden plot adjacent to his nieces' gardens on the coastal ridge about fifteen minutes' walk from the village. His only child, an eighteen year-old daughter, lived with her mother in an inland hamlet on the far side of the sago swamps, but they rarely visited one another.

Kariboki owned the largest and strongest outrigger paddling canoe in the village. Many of his neighbors relied upon borrowing it for fishing, for trips to the hamlets on the other side of the bay, and for the occasional day-long trip to the government station and tiny trade store located at the western tip of Vanatinai. They showed their appreciation with gifts of fish or a few sticks of tobacco.

Kariboki sometimes passed the long afternoon hours, when most people were away from the village, sitting with an elderly widow, a clan sister, by the smoldering fire in front of her son's house. The two of them, having lost most of their teeth, would pound their betel mixture with wooden mortars and pestles and amuse each other with gossip and stories of old times. Kariboki was a gifted story-teller and extremely knowledgeable about local customs and history, but he was a shy man and would only talk when in the mood. In the evenings he often sat on his verandah and played haunting, mournful melodies on the bamboo flute he had made, an instrument he had learned to use in earlier years when working on the mainland. He was too embarrassed to permit me to record his music.

When I returned to the island in 1981, I learned that he had died the previous year. The eyes of all of his former neighbors, not just his kinfolk, still filled with tears when they talked about the loss of this kind and gentle man.

These Vanatinai cases confirm several predictions made by Cowgill concerning the status of the aged in human societies (1972:7-13). He hypothesizes that the degree of disengagement of the elderly from ordinary social relations that has been described for American society (Cumming and Henry 1961) is a function of the degree to which a society is modernized. The elderly of Vanatinai are not disengaged, "unceasingly groomed by ... society for total cultural withdrawal," nor are they "deculturated" as are American elderly according to Anderson (1972:210, 213). Vanatinai elderly remain an essential part of the social framework, participating in economic, political and religious activities as well as in domestic relations. Their high status and degree of social involvement conforms to Cowgill's predictions that the elderly will have a high status in "preliterate" societies with a low rate of social change where they retain property rights, perform valued economic and cultural functions, and retain leadership roles, particularly roles of religious leadership considered appropriate due to the perceived closeness of the elderly to ancestor spirits.

The Vanatinai case suggests further, related hypotheses concerning the status of the elderly. Their status is likely to be higher in small-scale societies where the status of women is high and where there is little or no social stratification by rank. In these egalitarian societies, as in Vanatinai, individuals are evaluated on the basis of personality and temperament rather than by sex, age, or rank. When social prestige is concentrated by ascribed class or rank, it also tends to be concentrated in the hands of a core of middle aged men belonging to the dominant social group. A cultural ethic of male dominance or of female pollution or inferiority may be accompanied by an age-based system of social prestige favoring prominent middle aged or elderly men and devaluing the aged of both sexes.

Observations of the roles and status of the elderly on Vanatinai lead to an appreciation of the importance of individual personality in evaluating social position. Although it is often overlooked, the personality of the individual is significant in shaping both social activities and the perceptions by others of the elderly individual in large-scale societies as well as in small-scale ones (cf. Simic 1978a).

Clark (1972) discusses as a cultural problem the issue of the dependence of the elderly upon their younger kin. A growing dependence upon others may lead to decreased self-esteem, particularly in members of cultures that, like American culture, place a high value upon individual autonomy and self-reliance. Clark notes that in simpler societies the dependent elderly may have compensatory functions as, for example, "guardians of cultural values" (1972:268). On Vanatinai, where the young and the vigorous depend upon the superior knowledge and wisdom of the elderly and the ancestors, elderly individuals who are dependent for their sustenance upon kinfolk remain confident and assertive in their relations with others.

The dependence of the elderly may lead to intergenerational tensions, particularly when an extended family lives in the same household or compound (LeVine 1965; Simic 1978b:16). Such tensions are occasionally found on Vanatinai, taking the form of disagreements over individual comportment, child rearing practices, and contributions to household maintenance. Courteous relations are maintained in part through fear of sorcery attacks or the withdrawal of ancestral good will. Nevertheless, the elderly remain firmly integrated into social life, and their contributions are valued by people of all ages.

DEATH AND DYING

The term *mare* means not only 'die' but 'faint' and 'have a seizure (and metaphorically, as in many other parts of the world, 'have an orgasm'). Recovery from unconsciousness is, therefore, regarded as a return to life after having been dead, and some islanders thus 'die' several times. Sometimes the expression, *imari moli,* meaning 'S/he has truly died' is used to indicate that someone has actually died and will never recover.

When someone is seriously ill and possibly dying, s/he may call kinfolk together to bequeath possessions or to resolve old disputes over ceremonial valuables that might otherwise lead later to quarrels among descendants. Individual men and women who possess a knowledge of healing magic and associated medicinal plants will attempt to treat the sick person, and the house is kept tightly closed with the fire heavily stoked.

Death is often and tragically not an event restricted to the elderly. Infant and child mortality on Vanatinai are high, and adults are often cut down in the prime of life. As in many other Melanesian societies (see Counts and Counts chapter 7, McKellin chapter 9, Scaletta chapter 11) death or serious illness are almost always attributed to sorcery or witchcraft, though on rare occasions they may be thought the result of a taboo violation. The death in 1978 of the man in his eighties was attributed, however, to his extreme old age. It was said that he had lived so long because he was a good man who had never worked sorcery against anyone else and that, therefore, no one had ever tried to kill him by sorcery (for a reverse of this belief see McKellin chapter 9). His was the only death on the island in recent memory attributed to natural causes, but it was ritually treated no differently from other deaths.

Because almost every death is assumed to be due to the malevolent action of one individual, a death creates great tension, fear and anger, as well as grief, in the Vanatinai hamlets. Recent events in the deceased's life are analyzed privately for clues as to who might have been angry at or envious of the victim or a family member, for sorcerers are often said to revenge themselves by killing close kin of the object of their ill-feeling. Some sorcery killings are thought to be random events that occur because someone is merely trying out a newly-learned killing technique. Sorcerers are called *ribiroi,* 'poison', but their usual technique is said to be the firing of a magical projectile into the body of the victim, who then sickens and dies. Sorcery is a crime in Papua New Guinea, and several Vanatinai men in recent years have been convicted of killing through sorcery, usually after pleading guilty, and sent to prison for up to eighteen months. Their release from prison then engenders further terror among their neighbors.   Almost all sorcerers are men. The islanders regard killing through sorcery as a modern substitute for the former custom of killing in warfare, which was also a male activity. Some women and a few men are supposed to know witchcraft, a killing tradition which is said not to be indigenous to Vanatinai but to have diffused from the islands to the northwest (Lepowsky 1981).

The affines of the deceased must compensate the kin and heirs of the dead person through an elaborate sequence of mortuary feasts and the presentation of ceremonial valuables, pigs, and foodstuffs. In some cases the surviving spouse or his or her close kin are suspected of the supernatural attack on the deceased. In other cases, someone else may be blamed for the death, or the assailant is not known, but the deceased's affines, who will be released after the mortuary feasts from their extensive obligations to aid the deceased and his close kin with goods and services, must demonstrate through their mourning and their generous contributions to the feasts that they are not happy to be liberated from their affinal obligations. The mortuary ritual sequence and mourning customs are fully discussed in Lepowsky (1981 and 1984a).

When announcing a death, the islanders never say, *"Imare"* '"S/he is dead,"' because such a direct form of speech would indicate that the speaker killed the person through sorcery and was boasting of the crime (compare with the Kabana terminology of death and dying, Scaletta, chapter 11). Most deaths are revealed to neighbors by the wailing of mourners which begins as soon as the death occurs or is discovered. Others then hasten to the scene to learn who has died and to join the wailing. When messengers inform others of a death they employ euphemisms such as, 'S/he has left us' *(Iloitete ghida),* 'S/he is sleeping *(Ighenaghena)* or 'The tree has speared its leg' *(Ghubwa ivwe ghei).* The tree referred to is the totem tree of the deceased's clan. To inform kinfolk of a death, the messenger may pluck a leaf from the deceased's totem tree and, without speaking, let it fall at their feet.

SPIRITS

Death on Vanatinai is a transition to another state of being rather than an endpoint. Spirits have their own community, located on (or within) the summit of Mt. Rio, a pyramid-shaped peak that rises above the rest of the island and is often shrouded in clouds. These clouds are said to be the smoke from the cooking fires of the spirits. The gardens, coconut palms, and pigs of spirits look like wild plants and animals to mortals, and their community life parallels that of the living.

The spirits of the dead oversee the lives of their descendants, responding to magical petitions and sending advice in dreams about such matters as healing, growing good gardens, and obtaining ceremonial valuables in traditional exchange activities (compare the Marshallese relationship with spirits described by Carucci, chapter 6, and the Telefol interaction with spirits discussed by by Jorgensen in chapter 10). Male and female spirits are equally powerful. My neighbors used to call out to the spirit of the husband's deceased mother, who was buried nearby, when they were leaving the hamlet and ask her to 'keep the place hot' in order to discourage the presence of living sorcerers. I was told that this spirit could frequently be heard grating coconut for dinner and rattling dishes when there was no one else around. An elderly woman used to ask the spirit of her dead husband to warn her, by talking or making a scratching sound, if any invisible sorcerers entered the hamlet. Spirits may also warn of sorcerers in the daytime through the cry of the bird whose call also indicates the imminent arrival of a visitor, or at night by the blinking of a firefly.

Spirits on Vanatinai are usually regarded as benevolent by their living kin, who have little fear of these spirits if good terms were maintained while they were alive. People may, nevertheless, become frightened upon seeing a ghost, and children are particularly afraid of grave sites. Spirits may be kept away by chewing ginger, a 'hot' substance, and spitting it into the corners of a room.

The 'owner' of the dead, who is in charge of the spirit community on Mt. Rio, is Rodio, the creator spirit, who lives there with his two wives. Rodio sends a canoe to pick up the spirit after someone dies. This canoe is called *Maigoigo,* or 'noisy', a reference to the idea that 'only bones' travel in Rodio's canoe. The canoe is also called *Matawikenu,* which means 'eyes are sleeping' in the language of Misima Island. This canoe must always circle the island in a clockwise direction. It stops first at an uninhabited, swampy peninsula called Tevaiwo on the southwest coast of Vanatinai. Local islanders scrupulously avoid the area, calling it 'the spirits' place' *(kaka ghabai).* The spirits 'sign in' at Tevaiwo, marking their separation from the world of the living and entry into the afterlife. One man said that spirits know how to write, although most living islanders do not. Then the 'bones' of the deceased are reconstructed into the shape of a human being. The canoe continues past the western tip of the island and travels east along the north coast until it reaches a place near Araida Village. At this point mortals might see the spirit walking inland carrying a white sleeping mat and a white basket, for white is the color associated with death. The spirit pauses at a big rock called Egina, which has a panoramic view of the north coast and the lagoon, to rest and to weep for the living relatives it is leaving behind. Here the spirits of its dead kin meet the new spirit, admonish it not to weep because it is moving on to another life, and lead it the rest of the way up to the summit of Mt. Rio (compare the Telefolmin land of the dead in chapter 10).

Snakes, which shed their old, withered skin, symbolize the immortality of the spirit in Vanatinai culture. Rodio, the supernatural patron of the dead, sometimes takes a snake's form, as do many other supernatural beings and living sorcerers. For this reason, although snakes are not believed to be poisonous, the islanders are afraid of them, and never harm or molest them for fear of angering a supernatural being, a localized spirit *(silava)*, or a sorcerer who has temporarily assumed this shape. People say that if new spirits arrive at Mt. Rio without pierced noses or ears, Rodio will pierce these holes himself with his tail to make them properly snake-like, for otherwise they would have to be turned back and not allowed to join the community of spirits. Nose-piercing in infancy was discontinued about forty years ago but, except for a few children, all islanders have had their ears pierced as infants.

While the spirit of the deceased is in transit to the summit of Mt. Rio, the corpse is prepared for burial. The primary burden of dressing the corpse and of mourning falls upon the affines rather than the kin. A surviving spouse and other close affines suffer a form of "social death" which lasts until the final mortuary feast is held some years later. They are blackened with burnt coconut husk and may not bathe or comb or cut their hair or beards.[2] A widow *(wabwi)* wears a special, ankle-length skirt of coarsely cut coconut leaf called a *yogeyoge* and a widower *(sibawa)* wears old and dirty clothing. The widow(er) is secluded in the house and attended by kin of the deceased, who must feed her/him by hand until the first mortuary feast is held. Afterwards s/he may not court, dance or travel away from the hamlet except to obtain ceremonial valuables for the mortuary feasts.

Just before burial, the affinal mourners dress the corpse in its finest garb: a new coconut-leaf skirt or sometimes a garment made of white cloth. The deceased's skin is carefully oiled with scented coconut oil and the body is decorated with flowers or scented leaves stuck in its armlets and hair. The face is carefully painted as for dancing at a feast, and ceremonial valuables are placed on the chest or forehead or in the hands. It is said that if the corpse were not beautified, the other spirits would refuse it admission to their world. The valuables are removed and given to close kin before the actual burial, but their essence is said to remain with the spirit "like a photograph." These burial valuables constitute one part of an exchange between the living and the dead, who are later expected to reciprocate by aiding their descendants in finding good health and prosperity.

According to myth, in ancient times the living were able to journey to the summit of Mt. Rio and conduct mortuary exchanges with the spirits themselves. A supernatural named Mwajemwaje, who lives in the forest and is the patron of various types of food magic, once became angry with his mother for refusing to give him a small bunch of bananas and permanently closed the 'door' to the land of the dead. Modern islanders fear the spirits and, therefore, rarely travel to the top of Mt. Rio, although one young couple made the journey out of curiosity while on a hunting trip. People say that when hunters or other visitors sleep in two caves located some distance below the summit (one cave is restricted to single visitors and the other to married people), they hear the spirits whispering to one another: "Be quiet, our friends are sleeping."

Since World War II, many islanders believe that America, too, is the land of the dead and that the spirits of the dead turn white and go there. The corollary to this belief is that one day these spirits will return to Vanatinai, bringing with them the material goods that America has in such abundance, and will give them to their descendants. This belief arose when the young island men, conscripted during the war to labor for the Allied soldiers on the mainland, met American soldiers who, they report, were friendly to them and gave them food, money and tobacco. The men also noted that black and white American soldiers sat down and ate together. They concluded that the American acts of generosity meant that the Americans were, in fact, their own ancestor spirits.

I learned after a few months on the island that most of the people above the age of forty believed me to be the returned spirit of an important old woman who had died a few years previously and who was buried about fifty feet from the house where I lived with a local family. Proof of my status as a spirit was my generosity in giving food, tobacco and trade goods to the islanders, who said I had returned to 'help the place'. Although I denied being a spirit, most older people did not believe me and refused to accept that I was mortal and would one day die just as they would. They were at first afraid to talk about their beliefs because of the "cargo cult" overtones, which they feared would get them into trouble with the government. Even as a presumed spirit, I was treated with great friendliness and even intimacy. I did have trouble eliciting some kinds of information about the land of the spirits: every time I asked for more details about life on Mt. Rio, one old man, an expert on the matter, would laugh and say, *"You* know!"

None of the younger people shared this belief, even though most of them had never been to school. They regarded me simply as a 'European'. When I returned to the island in 1981 after an absence of two years, I asked if people still thought I was a spirit. I was told that the older islanders had now concluded that I was just a 'European' after all, since I had left the island instead of remaining there permanently.

The primary means by which the living contact the dead is by magical petitions for assistance with a specific problem such as conceiving a child, having a successful yam crop, curing a serious illness, or obtaining a particular ceremonial valuable from an exchange partner. The most essential ingredient for this magic is a relic taken from the corpse shortly before burial or obtained secretly by digging up the corpse after some time has elapsed. The individual, usually a child or sister's child of the deceased, speaks privately to the corpse and asks for permission to remove the desired relic and for future assistance. The relic, called a *muramura,* may be a tooth, skull, jawbone, or lock of hair. Relics are also obtained by digging in the graves of long-dead individuals who were renowned for their prowess in trade, warfare or love. Such relics are sometimes exchanged secretly between living individuals. Relics are extremely potent and make the place where they are stored supernaturally dangerous or 'hot', a condition that may cause illness in those living nearby. They are therefore usually hidden in secret locations in the forest.

Possession of relics is strictly illegal and is considered to be evidence of sorcery by the government, even though many people who take relics do so in order to maintain communication with dead kin and to receive assistance in positive endeavors rather than to destroy the life or health of others. The jawbone of one convicted sorcerer's mother's brother was confiscated and is stored in the government station. People refer to it as 'the memory of his uncle'.

The taking of relics was a more widespread custom before the intervention of the colonial government. The islanders say that in precolonial times skulls circulated between exchange partners the way that ceremonial valuables do today. Skulls of war victims were specially decorated for a feast, at which the brain might be ritually eaten, and then stored in shallow caves or other special locations. Some people say that in early times a person's death obliged his affines to kill someone and offer the corpse as compensation to the deceased's kin in the same way that pigs are presented today. The body might be eaten and the skull either preserved or shattered. Furthermore, *bagi,* the shell-disc necklaces that circulate in exchange both in the Vanatinai region and the *kula* region to the northwest, are said to have originated as decorated human skulls. Nowadays the part still known as the 'head' of the *bagi,* to which shell pendants are attached and which hangs from the necklace itself, is made of white helmet shell. The exchange of skulls or bones has been reported in other parts of Papua New Guinea (Goodale 1983).

CONCLUSION

On Vanatinai living islanders and the spirits of the dead each have their own domain, but the realms of the living and the dead are intermingled rather than completely separated. Just as there is little discontinuity between adulthood and old age in the life cycle of the living, there is little perceived discontinuity between the social relations and activities of the living and those of the dead. Behavior in the spirit community parallels that in Vanatinai hamlets. Spirits oversee the lives of their descendants and communicate with the living through dreams and animal messengers (compare with the Marshall Islanders described by Carucci, chapter 6). The living speak directly to the dead and address them through ritual and magic. Spirits may take animal form or even return to the island in the shape of an American anthropologist.

Social ties are not completely broken by death: they merely take other forms. Ancestor spirits, in particular the spirits of close kin and the recent dead, protect the living, watching over their activities and sending them aid as needed. The living address them as 'my mother', 'my father', 'my uncle' and so on; honor their memory with mortuary feasts; and expect assistance from them in human endeavors, just as they would expect assistance if their kin were still alive. Spirits are the 'owners' of the living, controlling their destinies, causing good fortune such as births, good harvests, and luck in fishing, love, and exchange, or sending crop failure, illness or death if they are angry or if they do not wish to prevent misfortune caused by a living sorcerer. The spirits of the dead on Vanatinai are in fact the givers of life.

NOTES

This chapter is a revised version of a paper presented at the annual meetings of the ASAO held in Hilton Head, South Carolina in March, 1982. I would like to thank Dorothy and David Counts and the other participants in the session on aging, gender and dying in Oceania for their helpful comments on the earlier version.

The field research upon which this chapter is based was carried out on Sudest Island, Papua New Guinea, from January, 1978 to March, 1979. My deepest thanks go to the people of Sudest Island for their assistance and friendship during my residence on the island. The research was supported financially by the United States National Science Foundation and by the Chancellor's Patent Fund and the Department of Anthropology of the University of California, Berkeley. Support during the writing of this chapter was provided by the United States National Institutes of Health. All of this financial support is gratefully acknowledged.

1.   The islanders speak a pidgin they call *Vanga Lumo*, or 'the language of Europeans', that was originally learned by the men who were taken to work on the Queensland sugar plantations in the early 1880s and subsequently reinforced by conversations with white gold-miners, traders and storekeepers from 1888 to the early twentieth century. Dozens of pidgin words have crept into the daily speech of the islanders, but only older men and women can actually speak *Vanga Lumo*. It is not intelligible to speakers of English, Tok Pisin, or Solomon Islands Pidgin.

2.   These taboos in theory should be adhered to until the final mortuary feast is made from one to twenty years after the death, but most people begin to bathe again after the first mortuary feast. They blacken their bodies after the first mortuary feast when there are visitors in the hamlet, when they are on exchange visits, when attending mortuary feasts, and when they are feeling particularly sad about the loss of the deceased.

Part III: AGING, DEATH AND DYING

9

PASSING AWAY AND LOSS OF LIFE: AGING AND DEATH AMONG THE MANAGALASE OF PAPUA NEW GUINEA

William H. McKellin

Where any was ill you went your round,
Right many a corpse left home feet first
But you came out of it safe and sound,
From many a gruelling trial – Aye,
The helper got help from the Helper on High.
　　　　　Faust (Part I) – Goethe

INTRODUCTION

Managalase men, women and children are aware of the presence of death that surrounds their daily affairs. Death casts its feral shadow over every pregnancy, birth, feast, garden clearing, planting, hunting expedition and even over simple strolls to fetch water. Ideologically, death is fundamental to Managalase concepts of fertility, reciprocity, prestige, and power. The threat of death and the participation of the dead in society play a constant counterpoint to the affairs of the living. The dead participate in the daily and ritual affairs of this dualistic community.

The Managalase, who live in the Hydrographer Plateau region of Papua New Guinea's Oro Province, rarely attribute death to old age. Most people who survive infancy lose their lives near the peak of their social and political careers in attacks by sorcerers, magicians, or malevolent spirits. Consequently, few people live to see their great-grandchildren; few simply pass away of old age.

The elderly have a powerful but ambiguous position in Managalase society and culture. Managalase dead as well as the living are thought of as members of the society and, indeed, the two groups might well be conceived as moieties. The elderly share in the activities of both the living and dead. As they grow older they move back and forth between the moieties of the society, eventually to be transformed into the spirits of the dead. In a society where few people reach old age, the longevity of the elderly needs explanation. Rivers' discussion of death in Melanesia captures the sense of the position of the elderly in Managalase society.

> It is true that the word *mate* is used
> for dead men. ....(it is) also used for
> a person who is healthy, but is so old
> that, from the native point of view if
> he is not dead he ought to be (Rivers 1926:40).

An elderly person's longevity raises crucial questions about his or her power and social responsibility. Why did these men or those women outlive their age-mates? Who is responsible for their survival? Having survived so many trials of sorcery and magic, who will, in the end, be responsible for their inevitable demise? And finally, what are the social consequences of a person's unusual longevity for others in the community? Weiner (1980) has suggested that an examination of death and mortuary practices is perhaps a better key to understanding social regeneration (social organization in its processual aspect) and exchange than is the study of marriage.

In looking at Managalase society, the cultural and social roles of the majority who lose their lives while they are still young or middle aged clearly contrast with those of people who reach old age before they pass away. The survival of the elderly interrupts the dominant patterns of social regeneration and strains Managalase cultural ideology. The survival of the elderly highlights the often ambiguous interplay among power, morality, and mortality. These questions will be examined by considering several concepts in Managalase ideology: the nature of life and power, the interdependence between the dead and the living, and the relationships between illness and loss of life and between old age and passing away.

CAREERS

A long life reveals something about the trajectory of a man or woman's career within the community. And, the fact that a person has survived to old age significantly colors interpretations of his or her social, political and spiritual biographies. Two men, Anero and Bui were the senior men in the Managalase village of Siribu. They were not the only elderly people, but each was the eldest in his faction of the village and the most influential survivor of his cohort.[1]

These men witnessed profound changes to life on the Plateau from first contact in 1904, through pacification and the end of cannibalism, to Papua New Guinea's independence. The most important single change in Managalase society during their life-times however, was the decline and end of young men's initiation, the focus of Managalase ritual life. The year-long cycle of seclusion, tattooing, dancing and plateau-wide feasting came to a complete halt in 1951 under continued pressure from the government, the Anglican mission and plantation labor recruiters. Unlike many of their successors, Bui and Anero had the opportunity to continue learning the songs used by numerous clans by participating in additional initiations until marriage. They were also members of the last cohort to direct an initiation ceremony.

Bui

Bui was undeniably the elder of the two and the oldest man in several inter-related villages. He was only a small boy when the first government patrol passed through the plateau. Anero was born soon after this first contact with Europeans. Their fathers were cross-cousins (joint members of a clan) and their mothers, who were from the same distant village, were considered siblings.[2] Anero's father died soon after his birth, and Anero was raised by Bui's father and mother. The two men were raised as siblings, though they developed different principal clan affiliations in adult life.

Bui was primarily affiliated with a group having a long history of traditional political power. His close kinsmen re-enforced their established political positions as Village Constables (McKellin 1982). As a young married man of about thirty, Bui went on a government patrol that was ambushed by his traditional enemies. During the fighting, he was crippled by a blow to his knees. For the remainder of his life, Bui walked with sticks or crawled from place to place. In spite of his disability, Bui continued to develop his own extensive exchange alliances throughout the Managalase area by arranging marriages among his kinsmen and kinswomen, managing feasts with affines, sponsoring the massive multi-village dances that formed part of initiation and by becoming a skilled tattooer of initiates. He also assumed responsibility for his brothers' political alliances after they died.

Bui's children, four sons, were also prominent men as both traditional and government political leaders. One son was the first president of the Afore Area Local Government Council which spans the census division. Bui outlived two of his four sons and witnessed the birth of two great-grandchildren. He died in 1979 of an illness that was diagnosed as an attack of pig hunting magic by enemies to the south of the Managalase.

Anero

Anero, who died the year after Bui, had a less spectacular political career than Bui, yet he too developed his own network of exchange alliances, depending more heavily than Bui on his maternal affiliations. Despite his less extensive political connections, Anero was also respected and, to some extent, feared. The cause of his death is in dispute. While they lived, both men were recognized for the political power they had wielded in the past, but in their last years exchanges were arranged by younger men.

Seniority played an important part in the social relations of Bui and Anero. No longer active participants in negotiating political alliances, they exercised power as authoritative sources of information for the younger men who managed exchanges and day-to-day political affairs. They served as links to historical events in the life of the community. In disputes over the ownership of trees or land, they were two of the few people who could claim to have seen trees planted or garden sites cleared by the disputants' predecessors. Because Bui and Anero were the contemporaries of deceased members of other clans, they also knew the tabooed names of these dead people: names that were unknown to many of their own descendants. Bui and Anero were each thought, by their own kinsmen, to be more knowledgeable and, as a consequence, more powerful than the other.

The inherent power of these two men, evidenced by their mere presence, meant that they could not be dismissed in spite of their physical disabilities. A key to their authority and continued political influence was simply that they had the power to outlive their contemporaries.

The position of the elderly in Managalase society is based on their understanding of *ajide* 'physical and spiritual strength'. The Managalase conceptualize life and power as the possession of a *kaven* 'soul' or 'soul-substance' which is centered under the sternum while a person is alive, awake and well. The 'soul' or 'soul-substance' is a man's or woman's strength and character. Shadows, body heat, breath, saliva, excrement, blood and semen (and now photographs), are also imbued with the 'soul' of the individual. A person's 'soul' is powerful or weak, potentially dangerous or innocuous in direct proportion to his or her physical strength, intellectual brightness, emotional balance and mental potency. The ability of an individual to act and influence others is directly related to the nature and vigor of his or her 'soul-substance'. A bigman, bigwoman or manager has a powerful, highly animated 'soul' while the 'soul' of a person who is less important is not as strong and is less potent.

Both men and women possess powerful and potentially dangerous 'souls'. A woman's natural fertility is her initial source of power, enabling her to bear children and to aid the growth of crops. For men, gardening magic is a partial counterpart to women's inherent fertility. But, a woman who has borne children must plant the first yams in any garden for it to be productive (Faithorn, 1975; Kelly 1976). The strength of a woman's 'soul' is measured largely by the gardens she tends, the children she bears, and her role in exchanges. As men and women mature, marry and have children, parenthood and its associated exchanges takes a gradual toll on their strength, and causes aging. The loss of procreative substance and the physical and spiritual stress of providing goods for exchanges drains the power of a person's 'soul' during the years when they are most socially and politically active (Counts and Counts, chapter 7; Scaletta, chapter 11; Goodale 1983). This loss of power is countered by the acquisition of magic.

Magic makes the 'soul' of the magician highly animated. When magic is performed the magician draws on the forces of kinsmen's spirits and mythological beings for power. In gardening magic this power is passed on to the crops to produce the large yams and taro suitable for exchange. Hunting magic is revealed to men during dreams by their spirit familiars. The spells they learn from these spirits gives them strength and helps them to hunt game.

EXCHANGE AND POWER

The various kinds of feasts and exchanges that are basic components of Managalase social and political life are directly related to the growth and regeneration of society. Both men and women begin their formal, active involvement in exchange with their marriages. The girl's contribution to the marriage is her willingness to participate. The typical prospective Managalase bride is characterized as aggressive. She chases her boy friend and forces her parents' marriage negotiations with the threat of eloping (McKellin 1984). The groom and his siblings, parents and age-mates prepare the feast and accumulate the goods for brideprice. They are also assisted by his patrilateral and matrilateral kinsmen who want to establish affinal alliances with his wife's family. The gifts include traditional items such as shells, women's tapa and pandanus mats; trade store goods; pigs; yams; sugarcane; game; and money. The gifts are received by the bride's brothers and parents and are soon reciprocated with a feast and comparable gifts of slightly lesser value given by them to the husband's kin.[3]

Married couples must also participate in intervillage feasts. Men organize exchanges with their wife's brothers and their sisters' husbands. Women may also sponsor feasts for their brothers. These exchanges, which depend on complex political arrangements for their success, are negotiated by several men from one village under the leadership of a bigman. The sponsors time their yam feasts and pig exchanges to coincide and invite their affines for several simultaneous dances. Their affines may ask their allies from other clans or villages to help them sing and dance at the feasts as repayment of a previous debt.

The birth of the first child is an important event for the community. To insure the growth of the child and future siblings, food is prepared, exchanged, and eaten at the child's home by the parents of the child and the members of the households of the mother's brothers. This is the first of a series of *siribe inan,* 'maturation feasts' where the child's father, father's brothers, and mother's brothers exchange cooked food and eat together. The naming of each child is also celebrated in the same way. In the past, these meals culminated at adolescence in feasts given when girls and boys had their noses and ears pierced and boys were tattooed.

These formal exchanges, which occur every three or four years, are augmented each year when a couple gives to the wife's brothers and parents small, informal gifts of food consisting of small game, and bananas, beans, sugarcane and other crops as they ripen.

In addition to the personal obligations that stem from marriage and parenting, an aspiring bigman in monogamous Managalase society helps to negotiate marriages for his kinsmen and kinswomen. This furthers his career with new affinal ties and increases the demands on his strength. A man also makes his mark by taking the responsibility to coordinate feast giving and to redistribute to his allies the feast foods he receives .

Seasonal giving of produce and game, the feasts for rites of passage, and large political exchanges increasingly tax the 'souls' of men and women. This is mitigated somewhat by the internalization of magic and by the assistance of spirits and mythological beings.

Managalase dead play an important part in sustaining the community of the living through their roles in exchange, production and reproduction. Death does not sever the bonds between the living and the dead that were established during a lifetime, but it does transform their nature. The dead lead a parallel existence to the living in villages in the bush that are only visible to mediums. These places are referred to as an individual's *aranj*, his 'real' or 'base village'. Just as living individuals of different social statuses perform different activities, the dead also act in accordance with their age, sex, social maturity, and their previous relation to their living contemporaries as collaborators in reproduction, exchange and social regeneration (Barth 1975; Lepowsky, chapter 8).

The spirits of young children and preadolescent boys and girls remain near the houses and gardens they visited with their parents and guardians while they were alive. As small children they travelled perched on the shoulders of their parents. Now, as ghosts, they may return, take up their piggy-back position and possess the body of their caretaker-host. These children, the medium's spirit familiars, assist the living by diagnosing illnesses.

The spirits of adolescents also help their surviving kin and friends by lending their untapped fertility to increase the yields of yams, taro and other garden crops. In the past, before the government burial regulations were fully enforced, the bones of single men and women were placed in garden houses with seed-yams to increase their garden's fertility.[4]

The spirits of older married men and women also contribute to the welfare of the community. They appear to relatives near villages in the forms of animals, such as birds and snakes. At night, they also appear in dreams. The dead reveal magical spells for hunting to their living male associates and locate game for them. These ghosts also disclose the future, give advice, and protect the land from intruders. In exchange, they receive a portion of meat originally presented to their living relatives.

An offering of food is also made to the spirits of the previous cultivators of a garden plot each time the site is cleared and replanted. This small feast is first shared among the gardeners and their families, then the remainder of the yams, taro, bananas, game and areca nut is left for the spirits who continue to frequent the garden. Their role in the commensal community will be to care for the garden in the absence of the living gardeners and to contribute their strength to the crops. By providing game and assisting with the growth of gardens, these spirits assure prosperity. These spirits may also identify enemies who are responsible for deaths and play a part in the revenge. Consequently, as seers of the future and protectors of the land they help in the community's defense.

Spirits in each of these different stages of maturity receive food from the living in exchange for their assistance, and they also share in the food received at the larger, intervillage, affinal feasts. Because they helped to provide crops and game given in exchanges, the spirits are entitled to a portion of the food received at other feasts. Feasting on a large, village scale brings together the spirits and living members of many different households and social groups. Together they form a large commensal community of consociates. Those who shared food while they were alive continue to do so after death. The relationship between the living and the dead is at once both one of exchange and of cooperation in the same way that the relations within the household, territorial, or lineal group are based on interdependence and complementarity.

The elderly, however, do not take complete or leading roles in gardening, hunting or as principal givers or recipients at exchanges in the society of the living, nor can they fully assume the roles of the dead within the community. Instead, they move back and forth, participating to limited degrees in each of the moieties.

LOSS OF STRENGTH

Life is a constant struggle by a person to control and enhance the strength of his or her 'soul' against the drain of exchange obligations, illness and death. A person loses strength when his or her 'soul' leaves the body during sleep, illness, some cases of possession, and death. The Managalase, like others in Papua New Guinea, believe that while a person sleeps, the 'soul' leaves the body (Barth 1975; Counts and Counts, chapter 7; Scaletta, chapter 11). It goes out of the village and encounters the spirits of dead relatives in the bush who may reveal the future or direct a man to game. When a person sleeps the connection between the 'soul' and body is tenuous and the sudden wakening of a sleeper could prove to be fatal.

The 'soul' also leaves the body during particular kinds of illness, for example, *kine'e jakihan* 'spirit attack', or when it is abducted either by the ghost of a dead ancestor or by one of many wild spirits who inhabit the bush. In the first instance, the spirit of a dead relative takes the victim's 'soul' away to the hunting territory where it resides in a village with other ghosts. These abductions are interpreted as retribution or warnings by ancestral spirits who are not satisfied with their portions of food from feasts. The sickness they cause reminds the living of the control that the dead can exercise over the frequency and timing of exchanges.

Bigmen, to gain recognition and political power, must remain healthy and able to demonstrate physical and magical strength (Burridge 1975).   An aspiring bigman who is vulnerable to chronic illness can undermine his own claims by exhibiting physical evidence of his weak magic and poor relations with his ancestral spirits.

In addition to illness, these assaults on the strength of individuals may leave a woman infertile, restrict a child's growth, ruin crops, or prevent success at hunting.

Ambushes by bush spirits of various kinds also cause illnesses. People who are alone in the forest, and therefore susceptible to attack, are said to be either foolish or purposely hiding theft or sorcery.   In most cases that are actually diagnosed as assault by bush spirits, however, the victims reportedly either failed to take proper precautions through carelessness or suffered because of the carelessness of their companions.

Spirit attacks, both those by ancestral and wild spirits, are potentially fatal because they result in the loss of one's 'soul'. The illness can be cured if the abducted 'soul' of the patient is located and returned to its proper place through the intervention of an asi'in 'spirit-possessed medium'.

When familial ghosts are responsible for the attack, the curer has little difficulty finding and retrieving his patient's hostage 'soul' because the sites of spirit communities are well known to local mediums.   Capture by bush spirits is more dangerous because the attackers do not reside in spirit villages and are therefore more difficult to locate.

The victim, as long as his or her 'soul' is controlled by either an ancestral or bush spirit, is in a weakened condition and is vulnerable to illnesses from other sources.   The compounding of illnesses further complicates attempts to cure the patient.   Although the 'soul' is often separated from the body, its loss at death is usually the result of a direct attack on the victim.   The ultimate departure of the 'soul' from its center under the sternum is marked by the victim's final breath.

LOSS OF LIFE

Sorcery, attacks by bush spirits, suicide, and murder are the most frequent explanations for loss of life; among these sorcery is the most common verdict. Attacks by sorcerers are usually accomplished by one or a combination of two basic methods. In the first, the sorcerer steals an object imbued with the intended victim's 'soul' (eg. excreta, blood, saliva on food refuse), carefully places it in a container, and hides it in a secluded place.

The second basic method involves poisoning an object of the victim's with juice from a particular kind of ginger root, *sia,* from which this method gets its name, and throwing the object into a stagnant pool. In both methods, the 'soul' of the victim, contained in his leavings, is drawn from his body. Sorcery causes either a short illness and an unpredictably quick end, or a slow wasting away and death as the 'soul' is extracted.

There is also a third form of sorcery. It robs the body of its 'soul' and, rather than creating illness, it induces the person to commit suicide. This is similar to the assaults of some bush spirits, who take the 'soul' of their victim and replace it with a poor imitation.

Sorcery is virtually impossible to cure. If sorcery is diagnosed by a medium, all but the closest relatives, who attempt to find the sorcerer, give up hope. Short illnesses leave no time for intervention and long illnesses, although they allow plenty of time for treatment, are rarely cured. The only possible remedy is to locate the sorcerer and his paraphernalia and to douse it in water, cooling its potency and releasing the victim's 'soul' from the sorcerer's control.[5]

Sorcerers use essentially destructive power on behalf of themselves and their community. Even where sorcery is used for revenge against a community's enemies, the sorcerer acknowledges his inability to retaliate through other channels. Magicians, on the other hand, have elected to use magical knowledge and power that is basically productive and rooted in society and its ancestral spirits. Still, magic can be both beneficial and destructive, and magicians who have grasped the ambiguous nature of their power can, for a time, both control it and make use of it.

Death may also result from warfare and murder. In the past, warfare, either by ambush or open battle, pitted the strength of groups and of individuals against one another. The 'soul' of each warrior, strengthened by the appropriate kinds of magic, made him elusive to his enemy, and guided his spears at his opponents. Both the physical and supernatural vitality of the combatants was tested. Warfare no longer accounts for many deaths. In the past, warriors renowned for their strength and skill were the targets for opponents who sought their own recognition. Murders are rare but, when they do occur, revenge is sought through sorcery as well as the national courts.[6]

When assault by sorcerers, bush spirits, warriors, or murderers cause death it comes as a shock, even though such attacks from outside the community are a constant threat. A death that clearly has its source within the village is devastating for the bereaved relatives and the village because it is unexpected and disrupts the harmony of the entire community.

In suicide the victim is the agent, though perhaps not the cause, of his or her own death. Suicide by a person of either gender is a last, desperate attempt to force a kinsman or fellow villager into action on one's behalf after a life in which direct, personal persuasion was ineffective. In a sense, the suicide's 'soul' only has the strength to rally one last time to meed its adversary. For a Managalase woman whose relations with her husband are beyond repair and whose brothers are either unable or unwilling to help, divorce is not an alternative. In Managalase society, suicide is her final, strategic option. Her suicide forces her brothers to break off exchange alliances and take revenge against their affines who are held responsible for her death (Counts 1980b). A man commits suicide when he is publicly shamed and finds himself unable to effectively refute a false or half true accusation. A young man will commit suicide if his desire to marry a particular girl is frustrated, or if he is falsely accused of promiscuity. Disappointment in love affairs leads to most of the suicides by adolescents. In these instances parents, whose duty it was to protect their children by training them properly and arranging their marriages, are responsible for their children's deaths. A young person of either sex also may commit suicide out of grief at the death of a boyfriend, girlfriend, or spouse.

A suicide creates drastic social disruptions. The act of a single person has the potential of converting affines into enemies. Not only are social relations destroyed, mourning is restricted to close relatives, mortuary feasts are perfunctory and the spirit of a suicide does not return to assist his or her surviving kin. Instead, if the spirit returns or appears in dreams, it causes further trouble.

THE SOCIAL AND MORAL IMPACT OF DEATH

The responsibility for a person's death or loss of strength does not rest just with the agent – the sorcerer, the warrior, the bush spirit, or even (in the case of suicide or violated taboos) with the victim. Responsibility is also attributed to the social and moral failings of the victim, his kinsmen and the members of his community. Even a death that is traced to sorcery is an indictment against members of the community who failed in their obligation to protect the victim from assault.

The fact of death, and questions of responsibility for it, are dominant concepts in the ideology of the Managalase. This dominance is apparent in the way in which death exerts a force to regulate exchange. Not only do satisfactory exchanges and offerings to ancestral ghosts prevent them from causing illness, they also oblige these ghosts to protect their kin when they are assailed. The responsibility for, and the impact of death, is directly related to the deceased's position in the developmental cycle of exchange.

The death of a child has its greatest social and emotional impact within the household. Parents and siblings are held responsible by their social and spiritual communities for the death of a child. Each family member searches his or her own conscience for the misdeeds and events that led to the child's death. A father who has not satisfied his exchange obligations, who has violated mythological injunctions against a tabooed place, or a mother or older siblings who have left a child unattended and open to attack hold themselves and each other accountable for the death. Though deaths among young children are frequent, each child's death has a distinct and profound impact upon the family and the community.

People are most likely to attribute the death of an adolescent to the capture of his or her 'soul' by bush spirits or, occasionally, to sorcery and the violation of taboos. Suicide also accounts for a number of adolescent deaths. When adolescent suicide occurs, not only are parents' expectations for their children destroyed, but guilt is added to their grief. The death of an adolescent who is at the peak of his or her physical strength also raises doubts about the ability of the adults to provide guidance and protection for the community. It is not his or her household alone that is affected by an adolescent's death. Its impact is also felt by other kinsmen, age-mates, and prospective spouses and their families.

When an adult dies, the impact is felt by his or her household, gardening partners, exchange associates, affines and other exchange partners. The death of a woman may end an alliance. If she dies and leaves young children, however, the father may continue exchanges with his wife's brothers until the children are full grown and not susceptible to interference by maternal ancestral spirits who might interrupt their development. The death of a man in the affinal exchange network may have less impact than that of a woman because his siblings may easily assume his position. Whether they can successfully maintain their own obligations as well as the ones they inherit is another matter. Young widows and widowers, still in their reproductive years, may remarry and continue old affinal ties while older widows and widowers with adolescent children usually do not remarry.

A Managalase man is responsible for his own welfare and for the well-being of his wife and children. He wards off illness and postpones death by fulfilling his obligations to his affines and exchange partners. He avoids unnecessary exposure to foreign spirits, uses his magic carefully, and prudently selects those exchange partners whose strength and magic matches his own. Finally, he courts assistance from ancestral spirits to pre-empt attacks from bush spirits and sorcerers.

Although all adult males, particularly the eldest of a set of brothers, are the protectors of their kinsmen, the bigman of a village is obliged, because of his acquisition of excessive magical knowledge and power, to be responsible for all the members of his community. Using his extensive knowledge of magic, he strives for political ascendancy, but not without opening himself and those who are dependent on his protection to a rival's attack. The prominence of a bigman is measured by the prestige of his enemies as well as the power and potential menace of his exchange partners, and the strength of his magic should be sufficient to repulse their assaults. When a bigman risks his reputation, pigs, and valuables by arranging exchanges, he is also risking his life and the lives of those around him. If he can successfully protect himself and them in the process, his superiority is confirmed. But if he should fall ill or die, or if a number of his followers succumb, not only is his reputation discredited, but the survival of the community is jeopardized.

The average, less ambitious man who merely performs his obligations to his affines, and who does not have a particularly strong 'soul', has less to fear from his own exchange partners, but he must rely upon more powerful sponsors and allies for protection from magical attack.

The death of any man leaves exchange obligations dangling. His brothers and other associates must meet these obligations as best they can, and they inherit the support of his remaining dependents. His yam gardens are left untended and the fruit of his trees is allowed to rot.

When two or three village members die, the village itself dies. The houses of the deceased are abandoned. The living leave to form new settlements and the dead go to their villages in the bush. For example, after the death of Bui's son, who was the village councillor and area bigman, the whole web of political alliances in Siribu and surrounding villages began to unravel. After two or three more deaths, the village was pronounced *derahar* 'dead', and over the course of several years the people dismantled their houses and established three new villages at different sites.

OLD AGE AND THE ELDERLY

The survival of people such as Bui and Anero into old age demonstrates the strength of their 'soul'. This spiritual strength is offset by
the visible signs of physical decline that begin with parenthood and
mark advanced age. Mature men and women in their prime take pride
in their emblems of experience and power: gray hair, grown children,
and – for the men – baldness and tattoos. The Managalase, like the
Marshallese (Carucci, chapter 6) and the Pulapese (Flinn, chapter 4),
associate the signs of age with social accomplishments and the control
of knowledge. Missing teeth, failing vision, decreased mobility, slack
folds of skin and memory loss mark physical decline and the transformation into old age.

Socially, the elderly undergo a transformation that is more significant than even physical change in defining their status. People are
identified as fully mature and elderly by their position in the developmental cycle of exchange and not by their chronological age.[7] During
the course of a person's lifetime the nature and position in his or her
exchange partnerships and associations is constantly changing. Each
birth, marriage, and death in one's social group or network of exchange
partners alters the pattern of social relations. A person's basic
exchange relations, which are established at marriage and soon after,
begin to expand as women bind together groups of affines. These relations continue to grow as members of a generation marry, become
parents, and as their children approach marriageable age. During the
childbearing and child rearing years, however, the number of deaths
within one's own generation increases and the expansion of exchange
ties slows. One's successors (their children, and others of the following
generation) reach marriageable age and establish their own affinal ties
in conjunction with their parents and guardians. Until the birth of
children/grandchildren, the two generations share responsibility for the
affinal ties established through the marriages of the younger generation.

As children/grandchildren are born, however, these exchange obligations shift to focus on the development of the children who become
the exclusive responsibility of the second generation. When conflicts
arise over the priority of exchange relations, the older ties give way to
those of the younger generation. Maintaining recent alliances prevents
infertility, sickness, and the death of children, tragedies that might
result from interference by affinal spirits. There is less to fear from
failing to re-enforce the mature ties of people with grown children.
Therefore, the oldest generation is supplanted in political and social

interaction by the two younger generations and prepares to take up the role of ancestral spirit in the exchange cycle. They become *ame* 'old men' and *barana ma* 'old women'.

The attitudes of the younger members of the household towards the elderly are ambiguous. Sometimes young people perceive the old to be proud, essentially resilient people who have survived all the perils that killed their contemporaries. At other times, however, the elderly are simply annoyingly demanding individuals with dangerously powerful 'souls' who are on the verge of becoming active ancestral spirits and who can either assist or cause trouble for their descendants.

Most people die before either their grandchildren mature or their great grandchildren are born. If they do not, they postpone the next stage in the cycle of social regeneration. Their participation as spirits in the cycle of exchanges between the living and the dead is delayed as they remain with the living, dependent on them for food and shelter. Their longevity retards the social and magical maturation of their grandchildren, for adolescent and married grandchildren are partially deprived of ancestral spirits to whom they can directly appeal in the performance of magic. Instead, they require assistance from their parents who know ancestors from a yet earlier generation.

The mature person is distinguished from the elderly by the number of living exchange partners, for an elderly person outlives most or all of his or her affines and other exchange partners. The death of contemporaries affects the social position of the elderly in two ways. First, the demise of partners curtails direct participation in intergroup alliances and ritual exchanges. With the decreased involvement of the elderly in exchange, they become increasingly dependent on their younger relatives for the meat and yams that must be obtained through exchange. Their position within the household is similar to that of dependent children. Though they may use their accumulated magic and familiarity with ancestral spirits to protect gardens and cure illness, the elderly lack the power of spirits. They are, however, similar to their contemporaries, the spirits of the dead, who only receive food when it is redistributed after a feast.

Second, the impact of the death of contemporaries on the role of the elderly is clearly demonstrated by the difference between mortuary rituals for the young and for the elderly. When younger people die, opposite sex siblings and affines are responsible for the deceased's body. They visit the deathbed, wrap the body for burial and carry it to the burial site. Because they have performed these duties, they join in the mortuary feasts that follow and maintain relations between the groups.

The death of an elderly person often cannot be dealt with in this way.   Affines and siblings may be dead or unable to perform their duties.   Consequently, they cannot participate in the cycle of mortuary feasts given by the dead person's surviving kin. When an elderly person dies, the burial and mortuary rites are restricted to immediate kin – the children of the deceased and their families – who take the places of affines in the burial of the body and in the mortuary feasts.   The deaths and mortuary rites of the elderly, therefore, involve the same restricted range of people as do the deaths of children and deaths from suicide.   All three are dealt with inside the person's kin group and the cycle of mortuary feasts, that could have extended alliances, ends.

The ambiguous existence of the elderly is further evidenced by their relationship to magic, strength, and spirits.   Old age brings irregular sleeping patterns.   The elderly sleep more during the day and fewer hours at night.   During sleep, the 'soul' of an elderly person departs to wander with ghosts in the spirit villages.   The elderly are gradually transformed into spirits, passing from one half of the community to another. Children are warned to avoid the houses of sleeping old people who in their sleep may assume the likeness of particular birds, snakes and other animal forms used by the spirits of the dead.

As people grow older, age itself is treated as proof of power by those who are younger.   Magical knowledge is considered necessary to stay healthy and to achieve old age. The strongest – those who maintain their positions of prominence – are also those who achieve old age (compare the association by the people of Vanatinai of old age and magical knowledge in Lepowsky, chapter 8).   Less powerful men and women may also have long lives, but their achievements may be ascribed   to   the   protection   of   more   powerful   contemporaries. Furthermore, their lower political profile simply makes them less likely targets for rivals.

The perceived connection between power and survival is supported by instances in which men, who were not extensively involved in exchanges as youths, outlive their brothers and acquire and maintain their alliances.   A man who does this may emerge from political obscurity as he reaches old age.

It is also generally assumed that people who are old were either more prudent or had more potent magic than their contemporaries. Within a cohort, the ownership of this particular kind of magical knowledge, *kús,* is uniformly denied as is the case with other forms of magic.[8] *Kús* magic has general application.   It can be used in hunting, to aid crops or to destroy the gardens of rivals and make them ill. Like other forms of magic, *kús* requires both a spell and some implement. There are two related kinds of *kús*.

The first kind of *kús* is the product of the continued possession and internalization of hunting, bird trapping and/or war magic over the course of a lifetime. The spells are initially taught to the magician in a dream by a spirit of a dead relative. They invoke the names, places and words of mythological beings. By memorizing the spells, performing them, and sharing portions of the game with the spirits, the power of the spirits and the magic is internalized by the magician. This potent knowledge and power results in an alteration of the magician's 'soul'.

The implement used in this form of *kús* may be the body grime that builds up on the arms and legs of a magician who avoids washing while using his magic. This dirt, which derives its strength from the 'soul' of the magician, is rolled into a ball and used with other paraphernalia, such as bark to perform *kús*. Other personal possessions of a magician, such as a bag, lime spatula, or a stone, that have absorbed the power of the magician's 'soul', may also be used. Once the magician dies, the ball or stone is inherited by one of his kinsmen and his name is used as part of the spell.

The power of *kús* has its roots in the mythological and spiritual spheres rather than the domains of social and physical life. The power of the mature magician, who has internalized the power of spirits through his magic, is likened to the power that inheres in the dangerous, tabooed names of deceased handicapped and single people. A handicapped person is considered to be an incomplete human, for he lost a portion of his 'soul' to a spirit while he was still in his mother's womb (McKellin 1983). The spirit of an elderly single person is powerful because his or her 'soul' was not expended in social reproduction. An individual who has inherited the personal belongings of one of these persons can invoke his or her name to repulse a spirit attack on a garden or human being, or the name can be used to cause illness among one's enemies.

Though men are most likely to inherit *kús*, particularly if its source is hunting magic, a woman may acquire it from her husband or from her parents if she is the eldest child.

Too much magical knowledge and power may tempt an ambitious man to use his power arbitrarily. He may become blinded by political self-interest and fail to see the effects of the magic on himself or his community. Instead of using his magic to meet social obligations, he becomes inclined to personal self-aggrandizement and, ultimately, to social destruction. Acting as does a Tangu sorcerer, he may use magic increasingly as a coercive rather than as a productive power (Burridge

1975).

As magicians age, their magical powers intensify their integration with the incorporeal world. For instance, in recognition of his power and authority, Most people believed Bui to have had *kús* while he was alive. People avoided sharing eating utensils and lime spatulas with him for fear that his *kús* might make their teeth fall out or make them sick. After his death from pig-hunting magic from an enemy source, only nonrelatives maintained this belief. There was less agreement as to whether or not Anero possessed *kús*. His close kinsmen claimed that he was powerful and did have *kús*, while his detractors disputed this, despite his old age. The cause of Anero's death is debatable; some contend that he died from a spirit attack while others think that it was old age. All who agree that he had *kús* carefully avoid speaking his name.

PASSING AWAY

Death from old age is passing away. It is the failure of the 'soul' to return to the person's body after long and extensive travels to the bush. Death in this guise is very different from that which results from some form of attack. It is not preceded by illness and lacks the physical symptoms of other forms of death. Passing away marks the end of the elderly person's metamorphosis from being an active, if peripheral, participant in living society, to final, unambiguous membership in the society of the dead (compare death of old age among the Lusi of Kaliai, Counts and Counts chapter 7, and the Vanatinai, Lepowsky chapter 8).

A person's final breath ends life and begins death. It marks the permanent severance of the body and the 'soul'. Though it will remain near the body until decomposition is complete, the person's 'soul' will eventually leave the village and take up permanent residence with the dead in the hunting territory, interrupted by visits to former gardens and other places frequented while alive.

The death of an old person brings his or her participation in society to a much more conclusive end than does the death of younger person. Surviving kin have already established exchange relations with ghosts of siblings and others and are not heavily dependent on ties with the recently deceased old person. Though the very old may maintain ties with society, the significance of the elderly is reflected in the simplified mortuary rituals and feasts customarily held for them, and in the fact that if the person possessed *kús*, the deceased's name and other words that sound like it are *kŭs e savu* 'permanently taboo'. The person is identified instead by reference to some personal characteristic such as hair or skin color, or by his or her relationship to a living person.

The death of an old person is an anti-climatic end for one who, although powerful, lived beyond his or her ability to be productively involved in the activities of society.   Women and men leave as legacies their children, the trees they planted, and the songs they composed. Men may be remembered by the decorated bodies of those they tattooed. Their personal names, however, may only be known and used by those who maintain exchange relationships with their ghosts.

CONCLUSION

Among the Managalase, death from old age, 'passing away', is distinguished from 'loss of life' during one's prime. The latter abruptly ends a person's development and disrupts a whole network of social obligations. Loss of life is considered to be the result of an assault by a bush spirit or by a representative of a rival group against a member of the community. But the community itself is held accountable to some degree for not protecting its member. A life has been stolen. The person or group who is held responsible for the death is now itself a target for revenge. The single consolation is that the spirit of the person whose life was taken remains active and may return to assist his fellow kinsmen and women.

Death from old age, on the other hand, comes after a person has passed through his most active years of social activity. An elderly person has survived attacks by others thereby demonstrating those his 'soul' is stronger than those of his assailants. But the magical powers which he once controlled, the the powers that helped him achieve political success during his younger years and to which he owes his longevity, at last consume him. His close familiarity with and internalization of magical power ultimately draws him to its source in the other world. The old person, therefore, controls his life to the end. Only he and his spirit familiars are responsible for his death.

If we consider the bigman as one who demonstrates a strong 'soul' during his lifetime we would also expect him to reach old age, unless he succumbs to a more powerful rival. Burridge (1975) suggests that the bigman or manager transcends the contradictions inherent in the ideals of magical power and knowledge, mutual obligation and the quest for power through the extension of exchange ties. Such a person synthesizes these opposing concepts of power and obligation which encumber less successful men and he symbolically embodies the cultural ideals. This characterization of the manager is as an ideal type who stands in contrast to the sorcerer, to the average man, or to the rubbish man.

Burridge notes that in actual cases bigmen may become sorcerers as well in an effort to retain declining social control. In the Managalase case, a man does not need to become a sorcerer to coerce others; the possession of magic is itself sufficient. This magic wields the same destructive force as sorcery. Burridge's ideal manager is a man at the peak of his power still able to fuse the contradictory aspects of his power and social obligations. A Managalase bigman at his zenith fits Burridge's ideal type, but, as he grows older he is no longer able to maintain control of his own magic, his position with its obligations, or his temperament. Eventually, the magic he possesses overpowers him. The extensive magical knowledge he has acquired gradually changes him from an old but live elder into a spirit. His quest for magical power and prestige reminds one of Faust, a doctor and scholar who, not satisfied with the learning that was available to others, sought more power to transcend ordinary limitations and therefore brought about his own destruction.

Why does a person outlive his contemporaries? The answer lies in the strength of his or her 'soul'. Enhanced by magic, his 'soul' is empowered to avoid or withstand lethal attacks. Why, then, does an old person die? Who is responsible? The elderly die because their own magic transforms their 'souls', an inexorable process they can no longer control. They alone are responsible for their deaths.

Those who die young or in middle age leave society abruptly, in the midst of their social, economic and political activities. Their untimely deaths disrupt the social and political activities of their living kinsmen and exchange partners. In Managalase ideology, however, they are still active and valued participants in the community as spirits of the dead.

By the time they die, the elderly are socially and economically dependent, relegated to a minor participation in exchanges, political negotiations, gardening and hunting. Their limited social contribution is their social and magical knowledge. Death finally dissolves the ambiguity of their double existence in the societies of the living and the dead. At death they regain their independence and influence over the living community.

NOTES

Research was conducted among the Managalase of Oro Province, Papua New Guinea, during 1976 and 1977, funded by the Canada Council and the Social Sciences and Humanities Research Council of Canada, and in 1984 by the Spencer Foundation of Chicago, Illinois.

1. The following represents the approximate age structure of one Managalase village:

70+	1
60-70	4
50-60	14
40-50	20
30-40	27
20-30	32
15-20	23
10-15	24
5-10	39
0-5	29

2. Clan membership is traced to the principal affiliations of each of four grandparents, enabling individuals to have several clan affiliations. Actual membership is dependent upon the participation with other members of each clan in exchanges.

3. Since cash crops were introduced in 1957, there has been a growing tendency for brideprices to increase while the amount of goods returned to the groom's family have decreased. This is caused by the government's insistence that cash crops be planted on land inherited patrilineally in the mistaken belief that this was the pattern of customary entitlement. This policy reduced the incidence of the traditional practice whereby husbands were expected to garden with their wives' families in order to establish relations with the spirits of previous users of the land and secure claims to maternal gardening land for their children. Now, women and their children have increased difficulty retaining claims to maternal land and are thought to be lost to their maternal clans. The increased payments retained by a bride's kinsmen are treated as partial compensation for this loss.

4. Traditionally, bodies were wrapped in pandanus mats and exposed in trees or placed in small shelters while the flesh decomposed. This practice was last followed in the 1950's.

5. Scaletta, chapter 11, also discusses the dilemma faced by a victim of sorcery and her family who refuse to release her spirit and allow it to die in the vain hope that they can find the sorcerer and effect a cure.

6. One murder occurred in 1976 when a man from Siribu, who was working at the government patrol post at Afore killed the bigman from that area with a blow to the head during a melee. This was the first murder in the region in about 8 years. Since   1976 there have been no other murders.

7. *Givas* 'single men' and *kasura* 'single women' whether they are young or old, occupy essentially the same positions in exchange networks. Single men and women who do not marry at approximately the same time as their cohort are referred to as *givas got* and *kasura got* respectively. In failing to marry and have children, they drop out of the cycle of social reproduction and exchange. With their deaths, their names become taboo, and the crops will die if the tabooed name is spoken near a growing garden.

8. The term *kús* is not replaced by an English gloss in this chapter because it has no accurate English equivalent.

10

FEMSEP'S LAST GARDEN: A TELEFOL RESPONSE TO MORTALITY

Dan Jorgensen

"Unlike beasts, men do not merely live but also have a conception of life. This is not something that is simply added to life; rather, it changes the very sense which the word 'life' has when applied to men." (Winch 1964:322)

"...Laudomia, too, will disappear, no telling when, and all its citizens with it; in other words, the generations will follow one another until they reach a certain number and will then go no further." (Calvino 1974:142)

INTRODUCTION

In this chapter I delineate the place of death in the traditional culture of the Telefolmin of Papua New Guinea. Death never seems very far from the preoccupations of Telefolmin, and one of my aims is to show how Telefol views of death are relevant to the conduct of life. We tend to see death as anomalous, a disturbance of the normal pattern of things. When death overtakes those around us – parents, friends, co-workers – it is mainly relevant to those most intimately connected with the deceased, often described as the immediate family. For us death is an intensely personal matter, and by this token it is less consequential for those beyond the range of close personal ties; put somewhat differently, this means that we are able to keep an awareness of death at arm's length precisely because of the distances between us. Thus it is possible for us to see death as an unusual event only sporadically touching our lives, and it also becomes possible for us to insist in a broader and more anonymous way that life moves on despite individual deaths. In such a view, the social order has a life of its own, a life apart from that of its members. By virtue of this, death becomes largely irrelevant in our collective understanding of how the world works.[1]

Matters stand very differently for Telefolmin: society is not an abstraction, but rather assumes a known form. Telefol society comprises a score of villages, each with a population of up to 200 or so. Most people are known to each other by sight and reputation, and members of one's own village are on much more intimate terms. Thus individuals have a large network of significant others in the context of a society that is both considerably smaller and more concrete than our own. In these circumstances it becomes virtually impossible to remain ignorant of or unaffected by the deaths of one's fellows, and it becomes impossible to maintain that death is somehow unusual, no matter how unwelcome it may be. So it is that death for Telefolmin is at once a personal and collective issue, and we should not be surprised that mortality is a theme that receives a great deal of symbolic elaboration in Telefol culture.

TELEFOL SOCIETY

Telefolmin are slash and burn horticulturalists living in the mountains of the Sepik headwaters of Papua New Guinea. Telefol social structure is based on small but permanent villages that serve as home bases for a mobile population cultivating numerous and widely scattered gardens on a household basis. Telefol kinship is bilateral, but in most contexts friendship is more important as a determinant of behavior. Though there are named cognatic kinship categories, these are nonexogamous and do not form the basis of corporate groupings. When compared with societies from the Highlands to the east, Telefol society is notable for its extensive development of ritual forms and for the relative underdevelopment of ceremonial exchange (Jorgensen 1981a). The villages are endogamous and are organized around men's 'spirit houses' (Telefol: *yolam*, Tok Pisin: *haus tambaran*). Such houses are the focus of a men's cult marked by a series of graded initiations. The men's cult is partitioned into two moiety-like divisions referred to as *iman ilo* 'Taro Side' and *un ilo* 'Arrow Side'. A striking feature of the cult is the centralization of senior initiatory rites in the village of Telefolip, said to have been built by the ancestress Afek. Telefolip has endured since the beginning of things, and each of its houses is rebuilt on the same site from generation to generation. The village takes its name from the paramount spirit house with which Afek inaugurated Telefol society.

This house is the focal point for taro rituals whose efficacy affects garden fertility for all Telefolmin and neighboring peoples, nurturing taro as a mother's milk nurtures her children.[2]

A STORY ABOUT DEATH AND FEMSEP'S LAST GARDEN

Telefolmin tell a light-hearted story, a folk tale, about one man's curiosity concerning death. He wondered where the flesh of dead people went, and so he came up with a scheme to find this out. He had his friends bundle him up like a corpse so he could feign death. He clasped a bamboo knife in one hand and a stone adze blade in the other, both carefully concealed. Then his friends took him to a cave and left him there.[3] He waited. Nothing happened. He waited longer, and there was something stirring in the cave. Soon he heard whispering. There were two beings, a father and son, in the cave with him. They were monstrous rats, and they soon began sniffing the "corpse." The son said to the father, "I'm hungry! Hurry, let's hurry! Can I eat his balls?" But before the father could reply, the man fell upon both of them and killed them. Then he went back home to his village and told this tale to his friends.

He died long ago.

This story tells us something of the Telefol understanding of death: it may be confronted or even attacked, but it is inevitable.

An acquaintance with old Femsep will also tell us something about such things. In his earlier days Femsep was a man of some note. Europeans still widely believe that he masterminded the Telefol rebellion against the Australian administration in 1953, though he was not imprisoned with the others arrested at the time. Ryan, in his book *The Hot Land* (1969), styles Femsep as the headman of the Min tribes. Though headmen (and bigmen) are alien to Telefol life, Femsep always made a point of being the first on the spot when Europeans arrived in Telefolmin, and he rarely failed to impress. He was one of the first to learn Tok Pisin, was one of the first government-appointed village officials, and had otherwise made himself prominent in local affairs.

When I met Femsep in 1974 he was getting on in years, though he was not certain just how many had passed (Telefolmin do not reckon the passage of time in this way). His joints were beginning to pain him, and he complained of trouble getting around. He nevertheless led an active life, even by demanding Telefol standards. He continued to garden, and surrounded himself with a flock of children whom he fed and put to work in his cultivations. One day he invited me to accompany him to one of his gardens. We arrived at a beautiful spot on a hillside overlooking a stream where a huge clearing had been freshly planted. It was the largest Telefol garden I had ever seen. When I expressed surprise, Femsep beamed and said, yes, it *was* big. This, he explained, was because he was an old man, and this was his last garden.

ENTROPY AND BECOMING NOTHING

The basic Telefol view of the world and of man's place within it is simple: man's world is on the wane. Telefolmin will eventually pass out of existence as a people, and their world will come to a close. In the Telefol understanding of the world, death and the problem of mortality are two particular instances of a much wider and more general process which I call entropy. The notion of entropy is encompassed in the Telefol term *biniman,* a word whose literal meaning is 'to become nothing.' 'Becoming nothing' is the general drift of the world, a discernible tendency in events and processes. This is particularly evident when Telefolmin address the relation between past, present, and future. In the past, Telefolmin were more numerous than they are now; men were taller; taro was larger, pigs fatter; gardens grew more quickly. By comparison, men of the present are short and do not live as long as men did before; taro is now smaller and takes longer to grow; today's pigs are mere possums; and the villages are nearly empty of people. These tendencies will continue into the future. At the scale of the Telefol conception of history, entropy spells the ultimate dissolution of Telefol society as a whole.

The end can come about in different ways. Should a woman give birth to a boy already wearing the *sel* headdress of the fourth initiatory grade, the world will be finished. Should so many have died that Bagelam, the land of the dead, becomes full, the world will be finished. In any event, the Telefol cosmos will come to its inevitable close after the twenty-seventh rebuilding of the central 'spirit house' at Telefolip, or if men ever fail to rebuild it.[4]

This view contains a statement about the ultimate fate of man and his projects, but its relevance to Telefolmin is much more immediate than a mere stipulation that in some remote future all things will end. Our own cosmology tells us that eventually the sun and even our universe will finish and that there will be a final end to human existence. But this is of little concern in daily life. Mortality remains an issue fundamentally unconnected with society at large, and so we can in some sense balance the implications of mortality with a conviction that things will get on without us and that our culture will grow through a cumulative process that sums individual achievements and innovations. All of this, however, is quite alien to the Telefol sense of things. For Telefolmin the ultimate fate of man and his world is simply a logical extension of his more immediate condition. This is part of the terms of experience bound in such deeply rooted notions as ideas about time and space and verified by patterns in events.

SPACE, TIME, AND ENTROPY

Telefol spatial orientations are marked by a heavily concentric bias (Jorgensen 1981a:238f). These notions are implicated in the Telefol discrimination between the realm of the *abiip* 'village' and the *sep* 'bush.' This is especially evident in folk tales where a bush locale signals human order in jeopardy. The existence of *kundunang* 'cannibalistic amazons' serves to underscore the point. 'Cannibalistic amazons' inhabit the peripheries of the known world. Doing without men, they take wild dogs as husbands, and when they give birth they eat the boys and female pups they bear. Such beings turn the human order on its head. In more homespun and concrete terms, men speak of various kinds of loss as departure, a kind of dissipation or dispersion from the center. Domestic pigs are notorious for running off and becoming feral; poor taro yields are understood as the flight of the crop from the garden to the bush. When young women elope with men from beyond the village, this breach of endogamy is a loss to the village as a whole and to the parents of the bride. In the same vein, Telefolmin speak of death as departure and abandonment.

Villages are linguistically equated with clearings *(abiip)*, and the distinction between bush and village carries with it the sense that entropy varies directly with distance from the center. Entropy is also figured in the invasion of the center by that which lies outside. In the old days the predominant image of this was the spectre of enemy warriors raiding villages. Other instances remain relevant: the depredations of wild pigs and other bush animals on crops; the invasion of gardens by grasses and bush seedlings. Telefolmin are scrupulous about plucking out stray grasses invading their village plazas. The sight of grass overrunning a village clearing indicates more than simple neglect. It is instead a sign that all the people have gone to the bush and that the bush is overwhelming the village.[5] Such quiet but assiduous weeding is simply one more way of resisting the encroachment of the bush and asserting the integrity of the human world in the face of what lies beyond it. Finally, it should also be added that Telefolmin often see *bagel* 'ghosts' hanging about the edges of villages shortly after a death has taken place, for at such times the dead draw nearer to see how many more of the living will join them.

When we consider Telefol temporal orientations, the sense of entropy once again becomes marked. It is easy to find in this a glorification of the past at the expense of a less satisfactory present, and it is tempting to speculate that these views are a recent reaction to the loss of Telefol autonomy in the face of outside power. But while this accords with the Telefol view of their own history, it is a mistake to dismiss these notions as epiphenomenal, for they are in fact part of the foundation of the Telefol view of the world. It is not simply that history conforms to the pattern of entropy, but that this sense of the world's trajectory is invoked when experience would seem to run counter to the pattern. For example, when Welagim explained to me that each generation of Telefolmin would become progressively smaller and less numerous, I pointed to his son Tegemsep as evidence to the contrary; Tegemsep stood a full head taller than his father. But Welagim beamed and said this was simply the exception to prove the rule: Tegemsep was as tall as he was because Welagim had done exceptionally well in providing meat for his children, thus beating the system. Others had similar replies to similar evidence that – to my eyes – Telefolmin were in fact becoming bigger all the time.

The notion that the world is somehow running down is evident not only in abstract discussion or responses to my queries: people would spontaneously remark about everyday events in these terms. On hearing of a friend's untimely death, Olmamsep remarked that this was because the man had fathered too many children while young: the man aged prematurely and died because his bones became 'wrinkled'(for similar descriptions of aging see Counts and Counts, chapter 7, Scaletta chapter 11). I went with a friend to visit a particular village and noticed two relatively young men limping around. The matter-of-fact explanation was that this was because there were fewer old men now than in the past.[6] This being the case, the infirmities of old people – stiff joints, arthritis – begin to increasingly afflict the young. The sense here is that an end approaches, and that it draws nearer at an accelerating pace. For example, men may under certain circumstances enhance taro fertility by eating *kuyaam* 'terrestrial cuscus.' A whitish grey marsupial, 'cuscus' is associated with old men and may only be eaten by men whose fathers and elder brothers are dead. To do otherwise would hasten their elders' demise. Similarly, old men may help the growth of a stunted or sickly child by feeding it a little 'cuscus'; but a child who eats more than a small amount risks premature aging. 'Cuscus' shortens the distance between the beginning and the end. For this reason it is not surprising that when Uunsep bagged two 'cuscus' in a nocturnal hunt he should have returned immediately: as everybody knows, if you find 'cuscus' at the beginning of your hunt you will find nothing further that night.

All these instances are tied together by a common thread: the notion that things are on the wane and that this is a normal property of the world as experienced. This much is implicit in language, for size, quantity, and time are bound up together: *afek* means 'large', 'numerous', 'old', 'important' and refers to ancestors, while the word *katib* means 'small', 'few', 'young', 'unimportant'.[7] The notion that the passage of time amounts to diminution is embedded in the categories with which Telefolmin apprehend temporality.

MORTUARY AND MOURNING

The traditional means of disposing of the dead was to place the body on an exposure platform in one of the deceased's gardens.[8] After the corpse was in place no taro might be harvested from this garden; it is still the practice today to uproot a dead person's taro and burn it, stalk and all. At the same time any pigs belonging to the deceased are killed and distributed to mourners, while payments of cowries are made to friends and kin with outstanding claims. This is done partly to ease their sorrow and to soothe their anger at the death. In general Telefolmin do not take such losses lightly, and while those intimate with the deceased wail inconsolably, others are likely to give vent to their anger at the death by chopping down banana trees, hacking at the deceased's house with axes, or voicing angry recriminations that the deceased would still be alive had he or she not been neglected (Scaletta, chapter 11, describes a similar response to death).

Mourning periods range from a few days to a few weeks, or even longer in the case of spouses. During this time all residents must remain in the village, and dancing and drumming are prohibited. It is specifically forbidden to plant new gardens or to make garden fires at this time, and if people go to the bush it may only be for the purpose of harvesting taro to bring back for meals. Sometimes near the end of the mourning period men will stage a collective wild pig hunt, "to get rid of the sorrow."

Mourning officially ceases with the slaying of a domestic pig called the *ataanket kong,* the 'sunshine pig,' after which yellow mourning clay is replaced by festive red ochre. From this point on rejoicing, dancing, drumming, and singing are permitted and the restrictions on villagers' movements are lifted. While others go about their business, spouses may remain in mourning and continue to wear mud. Sometimes widows wear keepsakes such as an arrow point, a shotgun shell, or a chip of wood from a tree felled in garden making; widowers often wear a wife's taro scraper.

THE FATE OF THE DEAD

When a Telefolmin dies, different fates await him depending on who he is, how he led his life, and how he died. When infants die, their bodies are often cast into swamps with no further consequences for them or the living. As infants, their *sinik* 'spirit' is poorly developed. This is evidenced primarily in their whining natures and their inability to hear and understand human language. Water is inimical to spirit and extinguishes or washes it away. In the case of an infant, then, disposal in a swamp or other wet place assures its end. This also means that those who die by drowning or whose bodies are tossed in water (as was sometimes done with enemy corpses) simply cease to exist. For all other deaths, however, there are three alternative modes of existence: *bagel, momoyok,* or *usong.*

Bagel are 'ghosts,' and this mode of existence seems to be the fate of most Telefolmin. As a rule 'ghosts' have nothing to do with the living. They impose no demands, nor can they be of any help: they are simply and irrevocably gone. From time to time Telefolmin encounter them in the bush, but these remain merely strange and inconsequential experiences. When a person dies he or she becomes a 'ghost' almost immediately and remains by the corpse for a little time, frightening anyone nearby. Once the flesh of the corpse has rotted, however, the 'ghost' must depart on its journey. The first stage of the journey is a return to Telefolip. This village contains, in addition to the 'spirit houses,' the first family house built by Afek.[9] Whenever Telefolmin die they return as 'ghosts' to Telefolip and enter the path to the land of the dead (Bagelam) via an entrance under the hearth of this house.

The path of the dead follows the course of the Sepik underground as far as its junction with the Ok Ilam at the bottom of the valley. Here there is a fork: one path heads due west, under the Hindenburg Range and off towards Bultem, the focal hamlet of the Wopkaimin people (see Hyndman 1976); the other follows the Sepik downstream towards

Atbalmin country. At the junction of these two tracks there is a being known as Iltigin Kayaak, whose less well-known name is Bisiilki. Bisiilki is a huge dog whose name means 'The Greedy One.' He is the guardian of the track of the dead, and Telefolmin have good reason to fear him. Bisiilki has two tasks. One is to see to it that the 'ghosts' do not return to the land of the living, but remain in their underground abode. His second task is to see to it that those who contravened Afek's taboos – particularly concerning incest or consuming one's own pigs – are properly dealt with. These people, whose conduct is thought of as greedy, are speedily devoured by Bisiilki and emerge from his anus as feces along the route following the Sepik to the northwest. After this they suffer great pain as they are again devoured by worms and snakes and then proceed to a lake of fire. What happens to them after that, nobody knows. Nor are people very certain about conditions in the land of the dead, for that matter: Bisiilki sees to it that there is no communication back and forth, though some mediums occasionally catch glimpses behind his back. The land of the dead and 'ghosts' are for the most part unknown and hidden from the living; there is little more that one can say about them.

Not all Telefolmin become 'ghosts'. Those who die violently become *momoyok* instead. *Momoyok* do not dwell in the land of the dead but have their own abode in caves high up in mountains to the east of Telefolip. Unlike 'ghosts,' *momoyok* impinge on the world of the living. They are hideous red beings whose heads are severed from their torsos. While at home in the caves of Ifaaltigin they may put on their heads from time to time, but they generally prefer to leave them behind when they venture forth. When they fly through the sky an eery whistling sound is produced by the passage of air over their exposed windpipes. *Momoyok* only go abroad at night, and may sometimes be seen as the fruit bats that raid people's gardens. In general, *momoyok* are not well disposed toward the living, and people explain this by saying that they are angry that their friends and kin allowed them to die in the manner they did.[10]

Usong form the third category of the dead. *Usong,* like *momoyok,* figure in Telefol life and are, in this regard, unlike the ghosts whose contact with the living has ceased. Unlike *momoyok, usong* are men who have died a natural death of old age; they are, on the whole, benevolently disposed toward the living and continue to take part in village life. Indeed, *usong* are more significant than this, for they are in fact essential to villages, whose well-being is in their hands: their relics are the tools necessary for the performance of most rites.

RELATIONS BETWEEN *USONG* AND MEN

Not just anyone can become an *usong*. As with men of flesh and blood, *usong* are divided into two categories: Taro Kind and Arrow Kind.[11] *Usong* are thus old men who were either outstanding gardeners and pig raisers or were notable hunters and warriors. This makes sense because the reason *usong* are brought back among the living is to assist their fellow villagers in these pursuits; a man who was not especially competent in either sphere of activity could not be expected to be very helpful to those who survived him. Becoming an *usong* and rejoining one's village after death, therefore, depend on one's performance in life.[12]

The mortuary rites of a potential *usong* were handled somewhat differently from those of other men. Sometimes his body was taken out from his village secretly under cover of night by the men of the appropriate ritual division (Taro or Arrow). The corpse was placed on an exposure platform that was fenced with special care to prevent rats and other animals from destroying the bones that were to become the *usong's* relics. As the body was placed on the platform one or more of those present addressed the deceased, explaining that they were treating him with suitable preparation and wished him to remain with them instead of going off to the land of the dead. Depending on the particular man's skill, they asked him to help with gardening or hunting, adding that they would look after him well, keep him company, and feed him so that he would be happy among them. After the flesh had rotted his bones would be washed in the juice of a certain banana and painted with red ochre before being placed in a net bag lined with soft, comfortable leaves. Then he would be brought back to his 'spirit house' where a fire would always be kept burning to keep the chill away. *Usong* who are not well taken care of can cause trouble, and if angry or dissatisfied they may leave for the land of the dead on their own so that the net bag containing their bones becomes 'cold' and worthless.

Kun is the word for 'bone' in Telefol, but also means 'hardness', 'strength', and 'endurance'. Thus when Telefolmin retrieved an *usong's* bones they not only maintained a continuity between past and present, but drew upon the strength of the past as well. In this sense, then, the retrieval of *usong* was one of the means available to Telefolmin to combat entropy. Taken collectively, *usong* are the foundation of village strength in the face of the world's generalized tendency towards decay, flux, and chaos. The recovery of *usong* from death is a means of holding the center firm and staking a claim to permanence.

A number of men explained the significance of *usong* in statements about the differences between Europeans and Telefolmin. Europeans have books and writing, while Telefolmin have the 'spirit house,' the *usong*, and all that these stand for. The relics of an *usong* are called *men amem*, and men say that *"men amem* are our books." Telefolmin know that we gain knowledge and some control through writing, as any visitor to the government office would quickly be led to believe.[13] But in addition, the 'spirit house' has much the same significance for Telefolmin as libraries and museums do for us: these houses are the repositories of what is valued from the past and a means of rescuing something human from time.[14]

Yet despite the emphasis on permanence and continuity, relations between men and *usong* are still subject to conditions that characterize Telefol life as a whole. In principle, the relation between men and *usong* is a reciprocal one, each rendering various services contingent upon the other's performance. But, because *usong* are men, they may be irritable and grumpy, as old men occasionally are; when this happens *usong* may bring sickness to village people, particularly women and children. If they feel neglected or left out of consideration when especially tasty foods such as pork and eel are eaten, they may retaliate by attacking those responsible or by departing for the land of the dead. All relations based on reciprocity have a conditional character since the state of the relation is not so much prescribed as it is the outcome of performance. This means that people generally put less stock in assurances than in actions, and this is as true of men's relations with *usong* as with each other. As a consequence, it is not automatically assumed that *usong* will in fact be helpful. For this reason men tested out *usong* before bringing them back to the 'spirit house'.[15] If the indications showed that the *usong* would be helpful, men would look after him well. If not, the bones were merely discarded in the bush without further fuss, since the spirit had already departed for the land of the dead.

It is because the relation between men and *usong* hinges upon reciprocity that it sometimes comes to an end. *Usong* may inflict illness or simply abandon the living. Sometimes disaffected *usong* remain in their 'spirit houses' but slacken their efforts and become half-hearted, so garden yields or hunting successes decline. If men are not attentive to signs of such discontent, *usong* may be amenable to seduction away from them. Visitors who spend the night in the 'spirit house' (also a dormitory for guests) may steal away *usong* with soothing words and promises while the proper caretakers sleep. An *usong* who is unhappy at home will be open to such talk and may sometimes be surreptitiously carried off by such men. The moral, generally speaking, is that if you do not look after your *usong* properly they will not look after you and may run off or be lured away by others. In this they are much like women, children, and pigs, whose affections must also be won and kept secure by hard work.

Like men, *usong* must continually prove themselves. *Usong* sometimes make people sick out of sheer spite or for no other reason than that they yearn for pork. In such cases the *usong* are likely to cost men many pigs, and, if there is no sign of an improvement in the relationship, men may have to take more serious measures, adopting a different tone towards the *usong*. They may deliberately exclude him when bits of cucumber or pork fat are dropped into the net bags of the others in the 'spirit house' and if men speak to him at all they will no longer wheedle or cajole or attempt to reconcile. Instead, they will scold and threaten him. If the *usong* persists in his ways, they will punish him by taking his relics to some wet and cold place in the bush and leave him there until he comes to his senses. Some time later they will return to retrieve him. Men are always a bit fearful at such times, for the *usong* may be vindictive. Nor is it certain that the *usong* has remained with his relics, for he may have gone off for the land of the dead. For such reasons, the *usong* must be tested out once more before being brought back to the village. If, after all this, the *usong* persists in causing trouble, men will finish with him and cast his bones off once and for all in some lonely and miserable spot.[16]

Given all of these considerations, we can see that while *usong* look after their villages and, through the 'spirit house', serve to anchor them in the world, the victory over entropy is neither absolute nor permanent. Instead, it depends on continued effort by both men and *usong*. The continued residence of an *usong* in his village turns upon whether men are successful in pleasing him and whether he is successful at pleasing them. One consequence of this is that only *usong* of demonstrated efficacy and benevolence remain in the 'spirit house' for any length of time. This means, of course, that the oldest *usong* are *ipso facto* the most powerful. If becoming an *usong* seems to offer the prospect of immortality, this can only be had among the living and is, like everything else, contingent on performance.

ENTROPY AND MORTALITY

Far from leading to the sort of cumulative development we term progress, the passage of time is in the direction of entropy and merely
draws Telefolmin and their society nearer to the end of things. Men
thus face a world in which there are no gains and loss is a condition of
existence. Mortality poses the question of loss with the knowledge that
all who live will die and be gone. The dead are, with the exception of
the *usong,* severed irrevocably from the living, and once gone to the
land of the dead may never return: life continually drains away.

The experience of everyday life repeats the lesson over and over
again. Relations between men and their wives hinge upon the men's
ability to keep their wives happy, and disaffected wives are notorious
for abandoning their husbands. So, too, must men look after their children particularly well lest the latter exercise the always available
option of seceding from the parental household. One must find a
husband for daughters at home lest they marry outside the village and
depart. Domestic pigs must assiduously be cared for if they are to be
prevented from running feral. Taro rites must be performed if the taro
is not to run off into the bush. In all of this we can see that nothing
should be taken as secure or given and that everything requires
continual work. This is true even in matters such as land tenure, for
claims to garden land depend upon the continual exercise of such
claims: failure to return to recultivate tracts of land results in the lapse
of land rights.

Men pursue their projects in this context. The retrieval of *usong*
helps to resist the way of the world by underwriting productivity and
continuity. But even here a secure victory cannot be won, for relations
between men and *usong* remain as contingent as relations among the
living. In the end, then, there is no alternative but to carry on. The
place Afek carved out for men began with the tasks of clearing away
the bush and constructing a home for the *usong,* and men's tasks ever
since have consisted in clearing and building in a way that can never
be finally completed: the forest reclaims gardens, houses rot, all that
men possess may leave them. Telefolmin describe entropy as water
running off a taro leaf, and this is man's life.

ANOTHER STORY AND UMOIM'S GIFTS

Aside from the folk tales told for entertainment, there are sacred myths concerning the Ancestress and her younger brother, Umoim. One of these touches upon the issue of mortality and the relations between the living and the dead.

Afek and Umoim lived together in Telefolip. She stayed in the 'spirit house' and he resided in the *unangam,* 'woman house'. Afek would send Umoim off into the bush to find game, but each time he returned he came back empty-handed. Afek, however, greeted him warmly and managed to have some wild pig and cassowary cooking for their dinner. Umoim asked her about this, but she always put him off, saying she had just found the meat 'around.'

One day Umoim tired of searching fruitlessly and decided to find the source of the game Afek cooked for them. He went out into the forest as usual, but doubled back and hid himself so he could spy on his sister. As he watched she called out to the animals and lifted her skirt to expose her vagina. Taro issued forth from her vagina, and she held this out to the animals as they approached. When they came near she would dispatch them easily with a piece of firewood. This time, however, they were nervous, and only skinny animals approached. Then Afek knew what Umoim was up to. She scattered the animals deep into the bush, telling them not to return. When Umoim arrived home she told him that from this time forward men would have to work hard to find game in the bush, for now the animals would avoid villages altogether. Furthermore, taro would no longer come from women's vaginas, and people would now have to work hard clearing forest and planting gardens so that they might eat. All this was because Umoim spied on his sister and shamed her.

Afek remained angry with Umoim and decided to make him pay further. After changing places with him so that he had the 'spirit house' and she had the family house, she decided to kill him. She worked sorcery on some food they had shared, and after a few days Umoim died.

Afek placed Umoim's corpse on an exposure platform. At first it did not rot, but then she managed to bring this about and took his skull, forearm, and collarbones to put in the 'spirit house'. Then she told Umoim to depart and to make an underground path to the west so that people would be able to go to the land of the dead when they died. When he got to the land of the dead, he was to make stone adze blades.

Afek went to visit her brother and see how things were coming along. When she got to his house in the land of the dead he was gone. It was cold, and Afek decided to make a fire. She took one of the adzes Umoim had set against the wall of the house and went out into the bush to chop some firewood. When she was chopping the wood the adze broke. Afraid, she went back to the house and awaited Umoim. When Umoim returned he became angry with her, saying she had spoiled his work with her impatience. The adze blades were not cooked yet, and because of Afek's impatience adzes would continue to break in the future and Afek's descendants would not be able to go to the land of the dead directly in order to obtain them, nor even to visit their relatives. So saying, he told Afek to return to Telefolip and wait for him until he got back.

Afek waited and waited, but Umoim still hadn't come. Finally Afek decided it was time to return to gardening. She left her children behind in Telefolip but she forgot to tell them that their uncle might be returning. Umoim arrived and asked where Afek was. Her children told him she was gardening. He then turned to the children and said, "There is something in my scalp, it itches," and asked the children to de-louse him. He bent his head down, but when they looked they saw maggots, not lice. "Uncle! Maggots are eating you," they said. At this Umoim became upset and ashamed and told them to bow down their heads. When they looked up again he had transformed himself into a *bisan* bird and was calling out to Afek from the gable of her house. Afek ran up to see what was wrong and pleaded with him to come down and visit and talk with them, but Umoim would hear none of this and said that because of her children's insults the dead would depart forever and would no longer be able to visit the living. Then, despite his sister's pleas, he flew off and disappeared into the west.

This myth is associated with the Taro Rite and provides, among other things, the charter for the promotion of taro fertility by planting relics of the dead in consecrated gardens (see McKellin chapter 9).[17] Umoim, through his incestuous spying, is responsible for a chain of events that eventuate in his death and, indeed, in the curse of mortality for all men (cf. Wagner 1967). His transgression is the reason for the male monopoly of 'spirit houses', for he shamed Afek; this is at once the reason that game must be sought far afield and that taro no longer issues from women's vaginas. Chafing at his ineffectuality, he wished to appropriate his sister's secret as his own, but the result was the loss of what he sought. So it is that Telefolmin bear the burden of hard work in a world where plenty is no longer self-generating. Umoim's shaming of Afek is reciprocated by her children's shaming of him, and this double infringement ends with the alienation of the dead from the living.[18]

Umoim pays with his life, but the death yields the three things Telefolmin have that are solid and endure, and which resist entropy by adding to life: the bones that are their cult relics; adzes to clear their forest gardens; the cowrie shells paid out at death and marriage.[19] With the bones, men may retrieve the dead and seek their help in hunting and gardening. With adzes (and now steel axes), productive work becomes possible and taro may be grown in gardens.[20] The maggots that horrified Afek's children – Umoim's atonement and redemption – are in fact the cowries given to bereaved mourners at death and exchanged when brides are given. In this we have the clearest indication that out of death comes life, for the fruit of a corpse enables procreation through marriage (see de Coppet 1981, Errington 1974, Epstein 1979, Strathern 1981). The movement of the myth is one in which the forfeit of innate productivity is replaced by productivity that is contingent on human agency.[21] Umoim's death is not merely the loosing of entropy upon the world, but also the provision of the means whereby men may combat it: ritual, hard work, marriage.

It is in this light that we should appreciate the centrality of ritual in Telefolmin, as well as the cosmological significance of marriage, and it is in this light that we should understand the Telefol passion for productive work: Welagim's pride in his son's size, old Atenok's delight in supplying village youngsters with sugar cane, or Kwiyolim's boast that his hunting provides game for all the children of his village. Telefolmin buck the trend of the cosmos through life-promoting acts joined in the effort to keep the world from slipping away, and this is how Telefol culture makes good the claim that the answer to death is life.

BACK TO THE GARDEN

When I returned to Telefolmin in 1979 I saw Femsep once again. His knees were troubling him, and his eyesight was not what it used to be. Many things had changed, and Telefol life was taking on a new shape. Ever since exposure burial was prohibited it had become impossible to replenish the stocks of 'spirit house' relics which suffered attrition from accident or the active expulsion of difficult *usong;* Telefol religion was in trouble. New-style mediums came on the scene offering novel forms of contact with the dead through spirit possession while others secretly exhumed the bones of recently buried relatives. The whereabouts of friends and kin in the land of the dead became fixed, and sometimes messages for the living got past the huge dog, Bisiilki. Sometime later, in 1978 and 1979, the Holy Spirit talked through women and informed people that Christian Telefolmin went to heaven, not the land of the dead, an announcement that accompanied God's call for the destruction of 'spirit houses' and their relics. Dilemmas were posed, and many had to choose to accept or resist conversion in the light of the fact that one's dead parents and siblings went via Telefolip to the land of the dead, while one's children were likely to go to heaven (see Jorgensen 1981b).[22]

Femsep was concerned about such things too, played an active role in public discussions, and hedged his bets by converting to Christianity while remaining in touch with cult affairs in Telefolip. He still surrounded himself with a flock of children, though this time it was a new mob. He was also, once again, in the middle of clearing his last garden.

NOTES

This chapter is based upon research carried out in Telefolmin in 1974-1975 and in 1979. I would like to take this opportunity to thank the Canada Council, the University of British Columbia, the Social Sciences and Humanities Research Council of Canada, the National Science Foundation, Wenner-Gren, the Smithsonian Institution, and Cultural Survival for financial assistance that enabled this work. I would in addition thank Ken Burridge, David Counts, Dorothy Counts, John Gehman, and Cathy Wylie for many helpful suggestions.

1.   Bidou offers some similar suggestions with regard to our understanding of incest prohibitions (1982:133).
2.   This corresponds in part to an arcane geography that ties the Telefolip 'spirit house' to the surrounding landscape through an umbilicus-like vine promoting taro fertility. This is in an occult way connected to a series of underground streams that link other cult houses in the region to the Telefolip 'spirit house'.
3.   This is not in fact standard Telefol mortuary practice, though it seems to correspond to that of some neighboring peoples.
4.   Twenty-seven is the base of the Telefol counting system and can sometimes be used to signify completion.
5.   I once visited the Wopkaimin hamlet of Bultem in company with some Telefolmin. At the time all the residents were in outlying camps and grass was rank in the centre of the plaza. This disturbed my Telefol companions, and the feeling was akin to the eerieness evoked by ghost towns.
6.   I doubt very much if it is literally true that there are fewer old men now than in previous times; the odds would seem to be against this. Here some demographic facts may be of interest. Figures drawn from Derolengam village in early 1975 show 28 people over the estimated age of 45 out of a population of 223, or 13 percent of the total. This compares with a figure of 107 people under the age of 20, or 48 percent of the total. These proportions are virtually identical to those Rappaport

gives for the Tsembaga, with 13 percent of the population above the age of 45 and 47 percent below 20 (1968:16). On this basis the Telefol figures seem not to be exceptional for populations of highland New Guinea and may even show a relatively higher proportion of older people. Populations in what are apparently less healthy circumstances display a smaller proportion of people in the upper age category and a correspondingly larger proportion in younger brackets. For example, Clarke's figures for the Bomagai-Angoiang show only 5 percent of the population above 45 while 60 percent of the population is under 20 (1971:19). Eyde's figures for the Asmat village of Aman-Namkaj are very similar, with 8 percent over the age of 45 and 57 percent below 20 (1970:150).

7. *Afek* is the feminine form; the corresponding masculine form (most often used with reference to remembered ancestors) is *afaalik*.

8. Exposure burial has been prohibited by the administration since the 1950s. Given the centrality of relics of the dead for Telefol religion, it is not surprising that many Telefolmin suspected administration collusion with missionaries on this score. This prohibition has had far-reaching consequences, some of which are briefly indicated in the conclusion of this chapter; a full treatment demands more time and space than is available here. Contemporary mortuary practices entail burial in village cemeteries rather than exposure in the deceased's garden. *Usong* and their relics remain significant to pagan Telefolmin despite changes in mortuary practices. I use different tenses in the body of the text to take this into account.

9. Stewardship over this house is inherited by the eldest daughter of the eldest daughter of the eldest daughter...of Afek, and this woman is unique among Telefolmin in having an inherited name. She is the caretaker of the entrance to Umoim's track to the land of the dead; see the myth of Afek and Umoim below.

10. While *usong* help the living with life-promoting tasks, *momoyok* are actively hostile to gardens, one of the predominant symbols of life. In this *momoyok* are like wild pigs, who constantly threaten gardens. In Telefol thought wild pigs originate from the spirits of domestic pigs, virtually all of whom are slain by their human fellows. A theme of vengeance seems implicit in all this, as well as the pronounced Telefol dichotomy between life-taking and life-promoting.

11. This comprises a moiety-like dual division within the men's cult that is completely divorced from the realm of kinship (full brothers may belong to different divisions). On an ideological and symbolic plane, the division between Taro and Arrow represents the opposition and interdependence of nurturing and killing.

12. The stipulation that *usong* must have died natural deaths means that all are old men who have successfully escaped early death through violence, misadventure, or illness; hence, they have in one way already demonstrated their power to withstand entropy (see McKellin chapter 9). There are, in addition, some female *usong*, though this is not widely acknowledged. These are almost always called *kong men* 'domestic pig net-bags', and are used to promote domestic pig fertility in the *kong ban*, the only one of the major Telefol rites in which women are active participants. Whereas the relics of male *usong* always include crania, in the case of *kong men* the pelvis is kept instead. Compare details of the myth of Afek and Umoim, below.

13. Telefolmin are also aware of the central role of a book in Christianity, a fact which holds considerable fascination for them.

14. This recalls to me Ong's discussion of the relation between textuality and death, a resonance strengthened by the fact that 'spirit house' relics serve (among other things) as mnemonics for narratives (see Ong 1977:231-271).

15. The procedure, briefly, is this: relics intended to aid in hunting are used in divinations to locate the likely whereabouts of wild pigs, and if the ensuing hunt succeeds

it betokens the *usong's* cooperation; relics intended to aid in gardening are planted with due preparation in a taro garden whose yield is an augury of future help.

16. Compare Fortune's account of the career of a Sir Ghost on Manus (1935).

17. The most significant such relic is Umoim's skull, which always plays a part in the major taro rites performed at Telefolip. The tale is also the charter for mortuary rites and relic retrieval, as well as providing the origin of sorcery and many other practices.

18. The phrase *"ilop kunesib"* 'maggots eat you' is an insult, something like telling someone to drop dead. Though normally even-tempered, Telefolmin say they will kill over this kind of talk. Though Telefol profanity sometimes refers to other matters, swearing *(weng mafak,* 'bad/ugly talk') is preponderantly concerned with references to death. Note that the children here spoke incautiously, and this is one reason why cowries (the 'maggots') must be traded indirectly from the west (i.e., the direction of the land of the dead).

19. The linkage of cowries with both bridewealth and mortuary payments suggests once again that there is a circulation between life and death, for the cowries distributed at death will be used in bridewealth. This reiterates the message that Umoim's death yielded the means to life.

20. Telefolmin say that the old stone adzes possessed a 'heat' or efficacy that promoted garden fecundity. One of the key parts of the Taro Rite consisted of the presentation of adzes to the novices.

21. The analytic distinction between the innate and contingent owes much to the work of Wagner, who has perceptively linked this to gender differences in Melanesia (1975, 1978). One aspect of contingency is the tenet that productivity always comes at a cost. For example, in one phase of the Taro Rite the novices are showered with white ashes, and these are held to impart 'heat' to them while evoking the pervasive Telefol symbolism of whiteness that betokens productivity and nurturing and connotes the flesh of taro and the fat of domestic pigs (taro attributes). Only later will they learn that this ash shower also accelerates aging with its crumbling teeth, dry skin, and white hair. In a like manner, most life-promoting rites connected with curing or with gardening require that domestic pigs (one's figurative children) be slain, even though the spirits of such pigs become the wild pigs that prey upon gardens. See the discussion of 'cuscus', aging and growth above. All this parallels remarks to the effect that reproduction hastens aging. There is no escape from the dilemma, and the Telefol view of the human condition holds that men must realize they will age and die anyway and may as well turn this to good account (similar sentiments are discussed by Counts and Counts in chapter 7, Lepowsky in chapter 8, McKellin in chapter 9, and Scaletta in chapter 11). To live life demands that one come to terms with the reality of death and decay (see Counts and Counts chapter 7, McKellin chapter 9, Scaletta chapter 11).

22. These developments are plainly part of a larger and more complicated picture than the one I have drawn here. This is something I must leave for fuller treatment on another occasion.

11

DEATH BY SORCERY:
THE SOCIAL DYNAMICS OF DYING
IN BARIAI, WEST NEW BRITAIN

Naomi M. Scaletta

INTRODUCTION

We can know nothing of the state of being dead except that it "is the obverse of aliveness and that it involves the dissolution and corruption of the physical body" (Gordon 1978:17). Death is an objective fact. Dealing with the dead can be considered a fairly straightforward procedure. The personal and social trauma experienced by the living is constrained and channeled by the formalization of behaviors, attitudes and activities in funerals, mortuary rites and ceremonies. It is usually assumed that the corpse neither knows nor cares about such goings on. Such a lack of involvement may not be assumed when the prospect of death must be faced in the guise of a living individual who is in the process of dying and who knows it. Although we cannot experience what it is to be dead, we can share in the dying process, as we experience it, or as someone else does.

Despite its uniquely private nature, the process of dying is "far from being a private matter" (Humphreys 1981:265). Dying, like living, is a social process *par excellence,* but it has been treated as non-problematic by anthropologists. Why this is so is a moot point. Perhaps it is because death and dying, like sexuality, have not always been topics "fit for public discussion" (Huntington and Metcalf 1979:xiii). Or, as Jackson has observed (1977:201) North Americans "treat the dying badly, avoid, isolate and generally see them as an embarrassment." More pertinent, perhaps, is the fact that most of us have had little experience with the dying in our own culture. We tend to ignore and deny death and have institutionalized the dying process so that it takes place in hospitals under the management of medical specialists, and outside the mainstream of our lives, individual control, and personal involvement. Whatever the reasons, it would appear that the study of dying is inhibited by the cultural baggage we as anthropologists take with us to the field site. In consequence, "the ethnography of dying is extremely poor" (Humphreys 1981:265; but see Counts and Counts 1983-1984).

The dying process is by definition concerned with change and transformation occurring in a relatively short time span. It is a process that threatens the integrity of interpersonal and social relations. Death is a *fait accompli;* as such it can be objectified, reified, mystified, ritualized. These sorts of categories are disallowed during the dying process, for there is small comfort in philosophical discussions on the meaning of human mortality when faced with its actuality. Herein lies the problematic nature of the dying process.

This chapter is intended to be a contribution to the ethnography of dying. What follows is a single case history documenting the dying process of a particular woman in the village of Kokopo, Bariai Census Division, West New Britain, Papua New Guinea. My aim in presenting the data is not simply to provide a chronology of events, but to show how concepts of life and death became real issues—as opposed to an abstract metaphysic—for all concerned. In their efforts to normalize the situation precipitated by death, as personified by this woman, the villagers had self-consciously to examine their beliefs about life and death in order to accommodate and reduce the threat to personal and social relations posed by the transformational nature of the process. Based on the Kabana premise that human life and death are a consequence of human behavior, two major problems emerged:

1) why is this person dying, who is causing her death, and, what can/should be done about it?

2) when is euthanasia a morally right action, or, what are the criteria by which a person is no longer considered dying, but dead? In order to place these queries in their cultural context, I shall begin with a brief overview of Kabana concepts of life and death.[1]

CONCEPTS OF LIFE AND DEATH

The Bariai Census Division, a political and geographic district on the northwest coast of New Britain, is inhabited by some 750 speakers of Kabana, a Siasi-Austronesian language, and some 100 speakers of Amara, a Lamogai-Austronesian language. The Kabana are linguistically and culturally related to the Kilenge-Lolo to their west, and to the Lusi-speaking Kaliai to their east (see Counts and Counts chapter 7). Rural Bariai is an isolated and economically undeveloped area. The Kabana village of Kokopo, with a population of 190, is the largest of the 10 coastal villages in the division. Subsistence derives from slash and burn horticulture with taro, yams, and sweet potato being the staple foods. As coastal dwellers, the Kabana are also fisherfolk, and supplement their diet with a wide variety of seafoods. Pigs are raised as a source of wealth and are only consumed at the feasts that necessarily accompany ceremonies performed in honor of firstborn children and the dead. Social organization is modeled on a system of cognatic descent. Post-marital residence is ideally virilocal. However, the idiom of cognatic descent offers a great deal of flexibility in the choice of residence and group affiliation. The Kabana are fiercely egalitarian, and there are no formal leaders, political offices, or inherited statuses. Power differentials do exist, and these are based on age, birth order, sex, and the accomplishment of renown. The term *maron,* 'esteemed' or 'rich' person is applied to both men and women who have earned the honorific. Relative to the task at hand, any one of a number of persons in the category *maron* may take on the role of leader. The ideology of egalitarianism is maintained and enforced by the fear of sorcery which operates as a negative social sanction.

The Kabana assert that the necessary conditions for the existence of human life are three: the *tini* 'physical body', the *anunu* and the *tautau*[2] The term *tautau* can be glossed as 'spirit', 'soul', 'vital essence', 'principle'. The *tautau* is contained in, but not by, the body, its locus being the stomach or liver which also serves as the focal point for such emotions as anger, fear, love, hate. The *tautau* permeates the body and, like the notion of aura, extends to an undefinable distance outside and around the body. It is considered impolite to sit or stand too close to another person, for this is an invasion of personal space and an act of shameful familiarity. Similarly, it is forbidden for anyone to step over an individual or his/her belongings, as this encompasses and appropriates aspects of that person's *tautau* and will cause him/her to become ill. In addition to the physical body and its immediate surrounds, aspects of one's *tautau* also pervade one's personal belongings, bodily fluids and wastes; one's partially consumed food and drink, betel spit, tobacco; one's footprints, body heat, breath, voice, glance, hair and nail clippings. Any one of these can be used as a medium to sorcerize the person to whom they belong. The *tautau* has no substance but is contained in substances. It is the intangible and mysterious principle of life that enters the fetus just before birth. Its presence in the fetus causes the unborn infant's eyes to open so it can see the 'road' it must travel as the birthing process begins. The phrase *imata geragera,* 'her eye sees' is used to convey the concept of 'alive'. The physical body, *tini,* or 'skin', 'outer covering', 'husk' incorporates the *tautau.*

The necessary and sufficient condition for human death is the absolute absence of the *tautau*. A corpse is referred to as *ipat sapa*, an 'empty container'. No one knows or really cares from whence the *tautau* originated, and no one knows what becomes of it after death.

The *anunu* is also an animating principle, and the term may be glossed as 'reflection', 'shadow', 'mirror image', or 'persona'. It is associated with that aspect of human life pertaining to thought, speech, rationality, knowledge, and is responsible for the dreaming state. Dreams are out-of-body experiences in which the *anunu* leaves the sleeping body and exists on another plane of reality where it interacts with the *anunu* of other dreamers, spirits, and ghosts. Ghosts are the *anunu* of the dead. People should never be startled out of reverie or sleep as this will sever the connection between *anunu* and body (compare McKellin chapter 9). Unlike the *tautau*, loss of one's *anunu* does not result in the death of the person. One merely becomes temporarily disoriented or permanently deranged. Either condition is recognizable by the individual's asocial, non-rational behavior and/or speech (compare Carucci chapter 6 and the Marshallese concept of *kalok*, flight). The *anunu* is tangible in the sense that it is possible to 'see' a ghost, shadow or reflection. The degree to which the *anunu* is present in the body can be ascertained by objective criteria manifested in speech and behavior patterns. The body, *tautau*, and *anunu* are necessary for human life; the necessary and sufficient conditions for 'humanness' require the addition of a fourth element: socialization.

The *tautau* is a uniquely human attribute. Pigs, dogs, birds, are not human because they do not have a *tautau*. They do have an *anunu*; hence they are animate beings. They cast shadows, have reflections and are capable of limited learning–they can know their owners, the road to the gardens, their homes, their names. Although animals are not human beings, neither are they, as a category, opposed to the category 'human'. There are degrees of humanness. Animals, especially pigs and dogs, are located on the outer limits of what it means to be human and are characteristically the epitome of asocial behavior.

The Kabana do not have a term that can be glossed as embracing the concept 'life'. The term for human being is *eababa*. However, in describing both human beings and animals as 'alive', one says *imata eababa*, 'its eye (is) human', or *itin kemi*, its skin (is) good'. Having a 'good skin' also describes as living such inanimate things as plants and trees. The word *mate*, can mean 'finished' in the sense that a transaction is completed. It may also be glossed as 'mortally wounded', 'terminally ill' 'unconscious', and 'dead'. All of these conditions may or may not be permanent; dead-ness like alive-ness is a matter of degree.

Only animate beings can be referred to as *mate*. Plants and trees that are dead are described as *misi*, 'dry', 'cooked'. This term is also descriptive of human beings, especially the aged and the ill, whose skin becomes dry and lackluster, their bodies shrivelled and bent, their *sulu* 'vital juices' used up. The overlap of terms used to describe the states of being alive and dead in the three categories—human, animal, and vegetal—is reflective of the Kabana cosmology which does not posit an *a priori* separation of elements in the universe. Rather it assumes a universe of systematically interrelated things, persons, and events where boundaries are often hazy, particularly those boundaries that differentiate the living and the dead.

As Rivers cogently observed, the unique character of death in Melanesia originates in a world view where "the facts of the universe have been classified and arranged in categories different from our own" (in Slobodin 1978:213) Additionally, as Humphreys points out (1981:7)

...the concept of 'natural death'—if by this one means a death resulting from the operation of normal processes rather than from their breakdown—has as precarious a status in western medicine as it has in those cultures that ascribe all deaths to witchcraft, but nevertheless show less concern to find the witch in the case of the very old. Medical explanations of death, though couched in a 'natural' idiom still seek to apportion blame (to one organ rather than another); and they can easily be combined with moral judgments.

The Kabana hold that it is both natural and necessary that all things—human, animal, plant—must die. In the best of all possible worlds, human death should occur as a function of extreme old age. In this case death is the result of, and brings closure to, a socially productive and moral lifespan. The aging process is based upon a systemic relationship between the biological and the social. The three elements of human life previously discussed are transformed by the socialization process into 'true' humanness. One's developmental process, from conception to death, is dependent on others (e.g. parents, kin) expending their resources or 'strength' on one's behalf. Production and reproduction require the acquisition and the expenditure of personal and social resources. Kabana cosmology, like that of the Etoro, is founded on the assumption that "accretion at one point in the system entails depletion elsewhere. Life cannot be created *ex nihilo*, and the birth (and growth) of one generation are inextricably linked to the senescence and death of its predecessor" (Kelly 1976:145). As one

Kabana man in his fifties told me, "When I was young I carried my children on my back, now that I am old my children carry me on their backs."

Depletion of one's strength is a condition marked by physical indicators of aging such as loss of teeth, loss of body fat and vital juices, white hair, and deteriorating eyesight. The faded bloom of life is reflected in the eyes and skin–the skin is no longer 'good', the eyes no longer 'see' (compare Carucci chapter 6, McKellin chapter 9). As people age they become more spectators than participants in social life. Their physical debilitation prohibits them from taking part in the demanding activity of finding pigs and shell money. Their spheres of activity become circumscribed, and the elderly do not garden, or go to the bush or the reef; they remain close to the house and are dependent on others for food, firewood, and water. They have given over their knowledge and experience to their children so that their mental strength is also depleted, a condition referred to a *buobuo,* 'having immature or childlike thought processes'. Ideally, all people should achieve extreme old age, with death occurring as a result of their 'bones breaking'. This is a good death (cf. Counts 1976-1977), the culmination of a good life, for persons who survive to extreme old age are, by definition, those individuals who have lived a morally correct life (compare McKellin chapter 9). However, there are very few who die of old age. The most senior adults in the village could remember only one person, a woman, who died of old age and the 'breaking of her bones'. She was a true *maron,* 'esteemed person', a woman of renown, strength and integrity.[3]

With very few exceptions, then, most deaths are bad deaths or deaths occasioned by morally wrong action. Deaths by suicide, accident or illness are bad deaths, not because of the manner in which death occurred, but because of the reasons it was *incurred.* A bad death, like a good death, is not strictly a biological issue: it is a moral issue. A bad death is a morally wrong death because it is incurred by a breach of morality either on the part of the deceased or on the part of others. Even suicide may be a question, not of self-destruction, but of homicide (cf. Counts 1980b; Johnson 1981).

For the Kabana, death by sorcery is a bad death, because the practice of sorcery is in itself a dreadful thing, and because it entails a negative judgment upon the behavior of the victim by relevant others. Sorcery is a social act, its victims are persons who have violated social mores and values. It is a social act also in the sense that the decision to sorcerize and the implementation of that decision are group actions. A sorcerer should never practice his art on his own initiative. His services are solicited and paid for by others who must provide both the means and the opportunity for the sorcerer to fulfill his task.

Sorcery is a male prerogative, and men either inherit or purchase this knowledge from their fathers, male cognates or people in other societies whom they have met. As it is a male activity, the place to learn about sorcery and to seek out a sorcerer is in the *lum*, 'men's house'. There are any number of people involved in the decision to sorcerize. The person instigating the action will have for some time obliquely sounded out the opinions of his kinsmen. If they are not in agreement, the matter is curtailed or deferred. If there is sufficient agreement to warrant action–that is, if others also have complaints against the intended victim– the instigator, accompanied by a close and trusted kinsman, will arrange to meet with the sorcerer in the 'men's house'. When all the details are worked out, the sorcerer is paid in *bula mitsi*, 'white/dry shell money', the most highly valued category of shell money. In turn the sorcerer gives over a length of the same stuff to the men employing him. This exchange is intended to 'buy' the silence of those involved and is also a hedge against false accusation of sorcery. When an accusation is made, the accuser must be able to validate the charges by producing the string of shell money that purchased his silence. The 'men's house' is a semi-public domain, and the meeting and subsequent discussion are likely to have been witnessed by others, so the episode may become a topic for discreet gossip.

Sorcery is, thus, a public secret. The identity of sorcerers and their techniques is common knowledge. Therefore, when a person becomes a victim of sorcery people can, by carefully reconstructing and reinterpreting events, suggest numerous reasons why it happened and who might have instigated it. The above discussion of sorcery provides a conceptual framework for the dying process that is described in the pages to follow. It remains, however, to say something of Jean, the woman whose dying and death is the topic at hand.[4]

THE DEATH OF JEAN

Two days after my arrival in Kokopo in June, 1981, I was visited by a little girl who informed me that her grandmother wanted me to come to her house. I accompanied the child and was introduced to Jean. She apologized for not having come to greet me, explaining that she was in mourning for her sixteen-year-old son who had died ten days before my arrival. She was extravagantly done up in mourning regalia. Her skin was covered in black soot, her hair was also blackened and twisted in tendrils from which dangled globules of soot-blackened pig grease. Because she was newly bereaved, her activities were restricted to the confines of her house, which she shared with her then unmarried daughter. She insisted that I visit her often; she was bored and I was an interesting diversion and source of entertainment, much to my chagrin.

Jean was a great talker and kept up a stream of conversation whether or not there was anyone around to talk to, a trait that everyone found endlessly amusing. She had a reputation as a raconteur, a gossip and a wit. An accomplished diviner with a large repertoire of magical spells, she was in demand as a curer and midwife. When I left the village four months later, Jean's mourning restrictions were still in force, although her sphere of activity had enlarged to include that area of the village where her house stood.

Her situation had changed when I returned to the village in June, 1982. All her mourning regalia had been removed a month or so before and she could now roam the whole village, although she still could not go to the reef, the mangrove swamps, or the gardens. She was fat and apparently healthy, the result, she said, of eating and sleeping too much for lack of anything else to do. She still lived with her daughter and new son-in-law, and spent her time looking after her various grandchildren and visiting other households. She and her immediate family were preoccupied with preparations to attend a ceremonial feast in the Kove area.[5] She seemed robust and healthy when she and twenty-five other villagers departed in August for the Kove feast. She was at the time approximately fifty years of age.

THE DYING PROCESS

It was the first of October when everyone returned from the six-week stay in the Kove village. One of the topics that was repeatedly mentioned as people related their experiences was the news that Jean had become ill shortly after her arrival in the Kove village. Her symptoms included abdominal pain and sporadic bloody discharge in her urine and feces. Those who had been with Jean suggested that she had been sorcerized by a Kove man who had frequently tried to cajole her into putting on her finery and joining in the nightly dancing. She had repeatedly refused, claiming that as a widow and mother in mourning for her son it would be disrespectful to participate in the revelry. According to the witnesses, the man had angrily retorted that if she were observing mourning restrictions, she should not have been at the feast in the first place (compare the social restrictions on the bereaved in Vanatinai in Lepowsky chapter 8).

Jean's illness was discussed often and at length over the next few days. My opinions and assistance were called upon, because I was considered to be a medical 'expert', given my culture of origin. Being anything but expert in such matters, there was little I could do except commiserate and urge that she visit the aid-post or hospital. People debated whether Jean had contracted a European disease or attracted sorcery, hoping it was the former, easily cured by western medication.[6] They feared it was the latter, not so easily cured, and potentially lethal. Even as people speculated and gossiped about her condition and its source, serious attempts to cure her had already begun. While still at the Kove village, a classificatory father (MB) from her natal village had performed a curative spell over her tea. This had seemed to help for a time; but a relapse followed during the voyage home. The hours of sitting in the bottom of a motorized dug-out canoe had shaken up the 'poison' in her system and made her ill again. On her first evening back at home, her husband's brother, Ken, performed a magical spell to cure her. He also performed a spell to magically secure her *tautau*, thus preventing it from leaving her body. He recited a spell over a piece of fragrant wood and then placed the wood and the now secured *tautau* in a piece of pandanus mat, tied it with a cordyline leaf, and then tightly wrapped the whole bundle in a piece of cotton. Usually, when a person is sick the secured *tautau* is worn around the neck, thereby keeping one's 'body and soul together'. In this instance, Jean's *tautau* bundle was taken by her eldest son for safe-keeping because her family was concerned that she would undo the bundle, release her *tautau*, and die. When I asked the family about their concern, they only responded that they were 'worried'. As it turned out, their fears were well-founded, and whether to release the *tautau* later became a contested issue.

The Kabana recognize three categories of illness which are classified according to the way in which the illness responds to treatment. There is no hierarchy implied in listing these three categories; indeed, people usually treat for all three simultaneously. The first category of illness is contracted when a person inadvertently comes into contact with *iriau*, 'bush spirits' (Tok Pisin *masalai)* or with ghosts. 'Bush spirits' snatch up and 'fasten' aspects of a person's *tautau* that have been discarded carelessly in a spot known (or more often, not known, until divined as such) to be a place where a 'bush spirit' resides. Ghosts cause illness by hovering close to, or actually invading a person's body, and the afflicted person manifests symptoms of hysteria, dissociation and asocial behavior. The most feared ghost, and one that figures in many legends and myths, is that of a woman who, with her child, has died in childbirth. Her ghost enters the body of her victim (usually an unfaithful or negligent husband), and kills him by breaking his clavicle.

A skilled diviner, usually but not always a woman, must be called in to effect a cure. She magically prepares a piece of ginger or native tobacco, both considered to be 'hot', and then sleeps with the bespelled item under her head. During sleep she projects her *anunu* out of her body whence it follows the essence of the bespelled item into the spirit domain to locate and identify the offending entity. Having determined the source of the illness, the diviner is able to take appropriate measures to convince the spirit to relinquish its hold on the sick person's *tautau,* thus returning the person to health.

Should these efforts fail, the illness is assumed to be of the category *dibala puda,* 'European disease'. Persons who do not respond to traditional curing techniques will go to the nearest aid-post or hospital for treatment. Should European medicines be unable to effect a cure, or if the person is diagnosed at a hospital as terminally ill, the patient will return home to try traditional techniques again. The ultimate diagnosis in such cases is that the person has been sorcerized and is dying.

Borou, 'sorcery' or 'poison' is the third category of illness and the major cause of death (compare Lepowsky chapter 8, McKellin chapter 9, Counts and Counts chapter 7). People suspect that any illness, no matter how innocuous, may be caused by sorcery. Recovery is dependent on determining why the individual was sorcerized, how, and by whom. The victim and her relatives review their relations with others in order to pinpoint the dispute or wrongful action that may have precipitated the attack. This done, they can negotiate a settlement of the dispute and repair the breach in relations, and the person can be restored to health by paying the sorcerer to rescind his spell. Should these efforts fail, they hire a sorcerer to effect a cure. If the counter sorcery does not work, and if the actual sorcerer cannot be exposed and made to reverse his work, the sick person will surely die (cf. Zelenietz 1981).

For four weeks after her return to the village, diagnosis and treatment of Jean's illness focussed on the first two categories of illness. One forty-year-old man, skilled in the esteemed art of Tolai bush medicine (which he learned while living in Rabaul), began a series of treatments using infusions of tree bark. The first treatment stopped the rectal bleeding, but Jean's abdominal pains, now so intense that she could neither eat nor sleep, continued unabated. Breaking off the treatment, Jean dismissed the man and went to the local aid-post.

There she stayed for several days until the attendant advised her to go to the hospital at Cape Gloucester, fifty kilometers further west. This she did, accompanied by one of her sons, her daughter, and their spouses and children. Regular reports of her condition came back to the village, and the message was always the same: she was getting worse. Some reported that Jean had asked her son to release her *tautau* so that she could die, but he had refused.

There was no question in anyone's mind, including Jean's, that she was dying from sorcery. She wanted to be released from the hospital but was refused by the doctor in charge. Eventually the doctor recommended that she go to the larger and better equipped hospital at Kimbe, the provincial capital some 200 kilometers east of the village. She adamantly refused to do this and insisted on returning to the village.

Later, Jean explained to me that if European medical techniques at the local hospital were ineffective it was because she was not suffering from a European disease but from sorcery. In her view (shared with many), people go to hospital to die, and although she acknowledged that she was dying she and her family still hoped that the process could be reversed by the methods of their ancestral customs. If it could not, she had no desire to die alone, far from her family and her village. Besides, she said, the bodies of those who die in hospital are stored in refrigeration until the family can be advised of the death and transport the body home for burial. Jean expressed horror at this practice, for she feared being cold after she died. Traditionally, all corpses were placed in a shallow pit in the 'men's house' (*lum* also means 'graveyard'), and covered over with a thin layer of earth on which the men built their fires for cooking and warmth. Over a long period of time, the corpse was eventually reduced to ashes and a few bits of bone. This practice was curtailed during the Australian administration which insisted on 'proper graveyards'. I suspect that the negative feelings about being put in cold storage are associated with the symbolism of hot and cold. Coolness is associated with growth and life; hotness is associated with illness and death. The reversal of these symbols is disturbing.

So, against the advice of the hospital and the opinion of some in the village, including myself, Jean returned home on the first of December. At that time she had been ill for about ten weeks and her condition had steadily deteriorated. Her abdominal pain prevented her from sitting or reclining with any comfort and she was unable to sleep. She vomited the little food she ate and continued to pass blood in her urine and feces.

At this point, Jean's identity as a person in the process of dying was formalized terminologically and spatially. The term *idibal,* 'she's sick', is used in reference to those who are 'a little sick'; that is, they have malaria, stomachache, headache or the like, and are expected to recover in a few hours or days. When an illness lingers, the verbal form shifts to become a noun, *dibala,* 'the sick one', and implies a certain loss of identity. It was incorrect, I was told, to say 'I visited Jean'. Instead, I should say *nagera dibala,* 'I visited/saw the sick one'. For months Jean had ceased to participate in daily activities. Her social identity had become unidimensional, for she interacted socially only in her capacity as an invalid. Her relationship with others, however, rather than being simplified, had become more complex.

With her activities restricted, her family and others in the village changed their own daily patterns of activity in order to accommodate her situation. Her family went less often to their gardens and generally stayed within the area of their own hamlet. They concentrated on caring for Jean and on fulfilling their obligations as hosts to a steady stream of visitors. When someone is ill people are expected to visit to show their respect and concern, to offer what assistance they can and, in the case of serious illness where death is expected, to demonstrate that there is no enmity between them and the sick person. The motives of persons who do not visit are suspect; their lack of concern may be construed as evidence of their complicity in the events that caused the illness. Given that illness or death by sorcery is perceived as a negative sanction for the breach of socially expected behavior on the part of the victim and/or her family, Jean's condition heightened people's awareness of a variety of social relations. Relationships between Jean and other individuals, between her family and other family groups, between her hamlet and the other three hamlets in the village, between her village as a unit and other villages, (particularly the two villages where the majority of her cognatic kin resided) were all minutely scrutinized. There was constant re-evaluation and discussion of past events and of Jean's integrity as a formerly active member of society. Her illness focussed the discussants' concern about future relationships among those who were associated with each other through her and led to conjecture about what might transpire in the aftermath of her expected demise.

Her return to the village thus marked a change in her social identity and her social situation. She was installed in a specially built lean-to on the beach, the outer perimeter of the village and peripheral to social life. The lean-to symbolized her liminal status; she was neither 'dead' nor 'alive' but somewhere in between. The lean-to was very small, constructed of split coconut fronds lashed to support poles and covered over with a thatched roof. When three people were inside with Jean, the hut was crowded. Besides her pandanus mat for sleeping, cup and plate, the only personal belongings she kept with her were her basket, one change of clothing, and, hanging on the wall over her head, a framed picture of the Virgin Mary and Child. She was never alone. Her children and their spouses were in constant attendance taking turns caring for her needs and keeping her as comfortable as possible. Jean's kin from other villages came for prolonged visits to show their concern for her, to make known their anger that someone was 'killing' one of their own, and to reproach the people of Kokopo for doing nothing about it. Every afternoon village women and men would congregate to maintain the vigil of the 'living dead', often staying until the small hours of the morning before returning to their homes. For the most part, they sat and talked among themselves, discussing the drought, reviewing past events that might account for Jean being sorcerized, and expressing their concern that the situation could lead to trouble between Kokopo and the two villages where the majority of Jean's kin lived. People came and went from the communal fire outside the lean-to, taking turns going inside the hut to relieve those in attendance there. Jean would sit huddled in a corner or on her mat, dozing or mumbling to herself. When she did interact with those in her company, it was to make charges against three men in the village, accusing them of sorcerizing her.

She accused Ken, her deceased husband's brother, claiming that when he had magically affixed her *tautau* to prevent it from leaving her body, he had in fact taken the opportunity to sorcerize it. His motive, she said, was revenge. Ken and his kin group were avenging the death of their brother by attacking his wife. The second man she accused was Lari, one of the most senior men in the village. She had no specific reason for naming Lari, except that he was a renowned sorcerer and was currently under suspicion by everyone (including the Local Government Council) as the person responsible for the drought. If Lari would cause widespread hardship in his effort to destroy the trees and gardens of the man people 'knew' he was out to ruin, then it was reasonable that he should attack Jean for no motive other than that it was his disposition to do so. The third man she accused was Tomi, her sister's husband. Tomi was extremely jealous of his wife and constantly suspicious that she was having affairs with other men. He rarely let her out of his sight, and accompanied her everywhere including, to everyone's amusement, the area off-limits to males–the women's toilet. Throughout Jean's illness, her sister had spent a good

deal of time caring for Jean. Tomi resented this and berated her for
not being at home with him where he felt she ought to be. On one
occasion, when his wife returned from a night sitting with Jean, Tomi
flew into a rage, beat her, and slashed all her clothing with his bush
knife. He charged that she had not been with her sister, but had
arranged an illicit liaison. It was Tomi's unreasonable jealousy that
Jean saw as his motive for sorcerizing her. By eliminating Jean, Tomi
was eliminating a major competitor for his wife's affections.

In all these accusations, Jean portrayed herself as an innocent
victim. At no time did she name anyone who may have had reason to
do her harm in retaliation for some misdeed on her part. Besides
proclaiming her innocence, she implied that sorcery was being practiced arbitrarily, a notion that was decidedly unsettling and contributed
to the level of anxiety in the village. The suspicion and worry created
by the situation was so great that the most common leisure activity,
visiting the homes of others in the evening, was curtailed. The three
accused men felt angry and shamed by her talk and refused to have
anything to do with her. Perversely, this was interpreted by some as an
indication of their culpability rather than their innocence. The biggest
fear the men harboured was that Jean's relatives would believe her
and, when she died, avenge her death by sorcerizing one of them or a
member of their families.

Jean constantly reiterated that she was 'done for', that she was tired
of 'carrying pain' and wanted to die. She wanted her *tautau* released.
Euthanasia was a frequent topic of discussion, but the issue was not
whether euthanasia itself was morally wrong or right: just as securing
the *tautau* had been a morally right action to take to prevent death, so
releasing it would be a morally right action to take so that death could
come. The issue was when, not if, to release the *tautau,* and the quality
of Jean's life determined the timing.

The final decision to release the *tautau* can be made by the individual to whom it belongs, or by her family. It is not an easy decision
to make. For the Kabana, personal autonomy and dignity are highly
valued attributes. Jean had been withdrawn for weeks. She did not
garden or go to the reef, the bush or the mangrove swamps. She did
not play with or look after her grandchildren. She was a non-
participant in the myriad of conceptual and social minutiae that made
life worth living. In her capacity as an invalid, her interactions were
essentially passive. Her existence was dependent on others who brought
her food, water, firewood, and contact with the living. She suffered the
indignity of having to be fed, bathed and assisted with her bodily
functions. She resented being powerless and saw herself as a victim; a

victim both of a sorcerer's ill-will and of her family's motivations. She complained bitterly because her family disregarded her requests to release her *tautau*, and she berated them for thinking more of themselves and their gardens than of her. The final indignity seemed to be that she was denied the right to take control of her situation and end her own life.

Jean's desire to finish dying was received sympathetically by many in the village who were distressed by her condition and their inability to alleviate it. They argued that she was no longer the happy and vital person that she had been. She did not laugh, tell stories, smoke, or chew betel; she did not participate; she had no freedom to empower her existence, the basic attribute of a 'true' human being. Their argument was based on their notion of the minimum criteria for an acceptable quality of human life. They felt that, for Jean, the quality of life had diminished to the point of non-existence. There was no personal power, only degrading dependency; there was no pleasure, only pain.

Others, however, felt that it was premature to release her *tautau*. They argued that although she was dying, she did not manifest the physical characteristics of a person whose death was a *fait accompli*. Such a person has dry, dusty, lackluster skin (like dead plants); his eyes film over and become opaque (like those of a newborn, unsocialized infant); his nose becomes 'sharp and stands up'; his breath has the decayed odor associated with the putrefaction of dead matter; his body is 'heavy', incapable of independent movement; and he no longer looks at or see those around them. All these characteristics partially described Jean's physical condition, but not to the degree that she could be defined as categorically dead. The deciding factors for those opposed to releasing her *tautau* were that her eyes were still 'clear', that she recognized her family and those around her, and that her speech was rational. In light of the preceding discussion of concepts of life and death it is evident that people were defining 'humanness' according to social criteria and judging Jean's condition accordingly. Her 'eyes were human' *(imata eababa)*, she still recognized social relationships, and she was still sensible. The effects of socialization, which mark the difference between human and other forms of life (e.g. animal and vegetal) were sufficiently in evidence to blur the boundary between dying and dead.

The bundle containing her *tautau* remained in the possession of her eldest son, and the final decision regarding the whole issue rested with him and his siblings—his two married brothers and his married sister—in consultation with their senior cognates, particularly their mother's younger sister and their classificatory fathers. When their mother became ill, the four adult children curtailed their own activities in order to care for her and to fulfill the obligations of hospitality. They had accompanied her to the aid-post and hospital, trekking back and forth to the village to replenish their food supplies from the gardens. Even after they returned to the village, their gardens remained neglected; they could not think of their future hunger and welfare at a time like this, and they did not want to risk the possibility that their mother would die 'alone' while they were out of the village. It was, they said, a bad time to have a death because there was no food. Gardens were normally at a low level of productivity at this point in the annual cycle, but in 1982-1983 there was literally no food at all due to the lengthy drought plaguing the area.[7] There had been no rain for over eight months and the gardens were virtual deserts: there were no yams, sweet potatoes, taro, sugar cane or bananas. Sago flour in a multitude of guises augmented by seafood was the daily fare (neither sago nor sea food are to be considered food *per se,* and they certainly are not ceremonial food). Some food was gleaned from old gardens left fallow, but it did not last long or go very far, given that the rules of hospitality required the provision of food and drink, as well as betel nut and tobacco, to all who came to keep vigil with Jean. It was these factors that prompted Jean's remarks that her family was being selfish, and perhaps they were. They were certainly straightforward about the fact that they could not afford a death; they did not have the where-withal to gift the mourners with food or provide the burial feast. By putting off the actual death they could, perhaps, scrape up the necessary foodstuff and wealth so that they, and their mother, would not be shamed by their penury.

Such pragmatic concerns, although important, were not the major factors in Jean's children's position on the issue of her *tautau.* This family had experienced more than their share of tragedy. In less than five years they had lost their father, a younger brother, a cousin (MBS), the eldest son's first wife, and now their mother. As a family they felt victimized and, understandably, they feared for themselves and their children. The longer their mother remained alive, the more opportunity they had to discover the sorcerer and to curtail his activities, thus saving not only Jean but possibly themselves from death.

A final complication for Jean's family was, of course, the love they felt for her and the loss they would feel when she was no longer a part of their lives. They were willing to carry the burden that her illness imposed on them, and for her to suffer her pain for a while longer. The issue of whether to release Jean's *tautau* was put into abeyance; the family hired a sorcerer to attempt a cure.

The man they called on lived in Gurisi, a small village about five kilometers east of Kokopo. His renown as a curer was such that he was always referred to simply as *dokta* (doctor). He was a man in his sixties, who exuded an aura of competence and controlled energy in his brisk and businesslike demeanor. The work of curing is called *luanga*, 'to heal/help',[8] and the 'doctor's' method of curing was by extraction, *pasunga*. He began by removing the husk from an areca nut, the kernel of which he moved about on Jean's body where she had indicated her pain was localized. The presence of a foreign substance in her body was ascertained when the kernel became 'hot'. He then prepared the kernel with lime and pepper and chewed the mixture in the usual manner. Then he placed a plastic tube (in the past a rolled ginger leaf, a 'hot' substance) over the spot where the foreign object lay inside the body and sucked the object out of Jean's body, up through the tube into his own mouth. His mouth was still full of betol mixture and spittle, and he retched violently and spat the offending object into a receptacle. The treatments were public, the only proviso being that the witnesses and participants in the room be uncontaminated by the smell of sexual intercourse, a condition that will nullify magical spells.

At Jean's first treatment, the 'doctor' extracted a large piece of ginger root. It was the ensorcelled piece of ginger burning inside her that was causing Jean's abdominal pain, making her skin dry and hot, and causing her loss of body fat. Removal of the ginger should, he indicated, alleviate these symptoms. When he finished the treatment, the 'doctor' lingered to visit with Jean and the other people who were gathered around. After eating the obligatory plate of cooked food prepared by Jean's daughter, he departed to return home before sunset. Jean reported that she felt relief from her pain, and indeed, she appeared to us to be much better.

The next day Jean was removed to her son's house in the village, as her lean-to was being inundated by the high seas and strong winds from a tropical storm offshore. She began to feel ill again and by the second day she seemed worse than ever. The 'doctor' was sent for again. The second treatment followed the same procedure as before, but it took a long time before the 'doctor' was able to complete the extraction, and he was obviously exhausted by the time he finished. This time he extracted two bits of broken beer bottle glass and an entire leaf of native tobacco from Jean's abdomen. The bits of glass, he explained, were cutting up her insides and this was why she was in pain and passing blood. The leaf of tobacco was the medium through which she had been sorcerized. This accounted for why Jean, a heavily addicted smoker of native tobacco, had developed an aversion to tobacco. She had quit smoking altogether some weeks before, and could not tolerate others smoking in her presence as it made her nauseated and aggravated her stomach pain. The bits of glass and tobacco leaf were placed in a half coconut shell and passed around so all could get a good look at them. The son who had accompanied Jean to the Kove ceremonial feast pointed out to me that these items constituted proof that his mother had been sorcerized by the Kove man mentioned earlier. The Kove had provided huge quantities of bottled beer to their guests, along with store-bought and home-grown tobacco.

Everyone hoped that these treatments would reverse Jean's condition and restore her to health. They did not, however, and she continued rapidly to decline. No one, including the 'doctor' had further cures to offer. Now, when people came to visit her, they would sit beside her and weep, lamenting her death. Jean began final preparations for her death by disengaging herself from the living. She settled her affairs with her children and gave away her own special knowledge of spells to a classificatory younger sister (compare Lepowsky chapter 8). References to Jean as the 'sick one' *(dibala)* were superceded by reference to her as *budua,* 'the mortally afflicted', or 'dead one'.

Jean's steady decline, the unease generated by the presence of a sorcerer in the community, the intravillage tensions arising from her accusations, and the increasing strain between her cognatic and affinal kin groups had created a situation of uneasy suspense that culminated in the arrival of a delegation of Jean's 'brothers' from her natal village. The men had come to express their anger that someone was 'killing' their sister and to 'break the talk of the dead one': to hold a meeting that would open the conjecture and gossip surrounding Jean's illness to public discussion that, hopefully, would expose the identity of the sorcerer and the person(s) who had hired him. The details of the meeting, which lasted for five hours, are discussed elsewhere (Scaletta 1984, see also Zelenietz 1981). It is sufficient here to note that when the meeting was concluded and all the men had returned home, the consensus was that it had failed. They had not 'broken the talk' and, therefore, the sorcerer was still at large.

DEATH BY SORCERY

A week after the meeting, Jean was moved from the house in the village and installed in a newly constructed lean-to on the beach next to her sister's house. By the first of January she no longer took food or drink, her body was skeletal, and her flesh was cold to the touch. She was semi-comatose and rarely spoke, although on two occasions she roused herself to tell me that she was truly dead now. The two oldest women in the village (both in their late sixties) were in constant attendance and took turns sitting with Jean through the night. People continued to come and maintain the vigil; however, they came less often and primarily visited among themselves, discussing Jean's death and the continuing drought. With the exception of her eldest son, Jean's children had moved back into their own homes and were spending all day away from the village in their gardens

On the second of January, Jean 'died' but she was revived by the old women in attendance. For the next few days she hovered near death. She instructed her sister to bring the new clothes and pandanus mat that she would be buried in, and she kept these items tucked under her pillow. She was having visions of and conversations with her dead son, a sure indication that she was now more involved in the realm of the dead than that of the living. She enquired constantly about the whereabouts of her children and her sister and was annoyed when told that they were at their gardens. She was angry with her family's preoccupation with their gardens and complained that they were more worried about their taro than about her. She threatened that they had better take care or her ghost would come back and ruin their gardens. After this outburst, we were instructed to tell her, if she asked, that her sister or children were occupied with mundane matters like bathing, cooking food, washing dishes, gathering coconuts. Her family was, in fact, preparing to receive the many people who would come to mourn Jean's death.

The issue of whether to release Jean's *tautau* was again a topic of discussion. The consensus was that it should have been released before this time, that her son had waited too long and that if he did not soon release it her ghost would retaliate against him for prolonging her suffering. Still he refused. Her son's refusal to release it reflected his desire not to believe that she was, in fact, already 'dead' and the hope that something might yet be done to make her recover. It also reflected the moral dilemma inherent in euthanasia. To release the *tautau* would be an admission that she was already dead, or, if she was not dead, the release of the *tautau* would sever her tenuous grasp on life and result in her immediate death. This kind of dilemma is also evident in our own culture. The families and doctors of the terminally ill are loath to make the moral decision (or legally prohibited from making that choice) to 'pull the plug' on the life support systems of loved ones who would die without them. Here, too, those involved with the dead or dying person cling to the hope that something, be it God or modern scientific technology, will achieve a breakthrough that will reverse the dying process.

As time went on, Jean's appearance became cadaverous. She was incontinent, she had bed sores, one leg from the knee down was swollen, and she had ulcerated sores covering her lips and inside her mouth. When we came away from a visit with her, we could only weep in despair at her plight and console one another with the observation that she was better off dead.

Several days later, on the ninth of January, Jean's son released her *tautau*. Just before sundown he undid the bundle and flung the materials into the river that wound through the back of the village. That evening the village was silent and dark. There were no visible fires; no babies cried; conversation was subdued and shaded with apprehension. Each family slept together as a group within touching distance of one another, the doors and windows of the houses covered over and secured to prevent the dead woman's ghost from entering and taking with her a companion in death. The next afternoon, less than eighteen hours after the release of her *tautau,* a young man beat a mournful tatoo on the slit-gong at one of the 'men's houses' to announce that Jean was dead.

Immediately the slit-gong sounded, two young men were sent off, one to the east and one to the west, to carry the news of death to the neighboring villages, where other runners would relay the message until the whole district had been advised. In the meantime, Jean's body had been removed from the lean-to and laid out in an old cook-house behind her sister's house. Her body had been washed and dressed in the new burial clothes, and her hair had been trimmed back about ten centimeters all around her head. She was placed in the middle of the large room and covered up to her chin with a length of red cotton. Another piece of material was placed over her mouth and fastened behind her head, to protect the mourners from the odor of death emanating from her mouth. This done, her eldest son came and painted her face with the red and white design of their kin group.

For the rest of that day, the people of Kokopo came to mourn their dead compatriot. As people arrived in the house, they would throw down various items: clothing, utensils, plates, crotons and other plants.

All were snatched up by those mourners already present. These gifts to the dead, and through her to the mourners, expressed the donors' grief and that the loss of this individual had *rabisim* 'beggared' them. Their prestations made, the mourners prostrated themselves across the corpse to weep and decry the loss of their sister, their mother, their companion. As the day wore on, people from other villages began to arrive, and the home villagers gradually removed themselves from the mourning place to allow the newcomers their time to grieve. This also gave the host villagers the opportunity to prepare food, areca nut, tobacco and coconuts for the visitors.

Both women and men participate in the work of mourning. But at midnight of the day of death or, if this is not possible because all of the participants have not arrived, on the third night after death there is a special death dirge sung only by men when, for two or three hours, they sing the songs of *borou*, 'sorcery'. Jean's cognatic and affinal kinsmen sang their privately owned magical spells. When this secret knowledge is made public the spells lose their inherent power, consequently diminishing the power of the men who held them. By making public their private powers, the affinal kin placed themselves in a vulnerable position. Conversely, the cognatic kin showed their lack of intent to attack by diminishing their power to do so.

At first light next morning all the village women went to collect water and food, while the men began to gather and organize shell money and traditional wealth objects for the necessary compensation payments to Jean's kin. By noon all was ready, and the mourners began to depart for their home villages. Delegations from each 'men's house' in every village in the district were given a quantity of shell money to take back and distribute among Jean's female and male kin in that 'men's house'. Each woman who came to mourn was given raw food; sugar cane, cassava and banana stalks to plant; drinking coconuts; and croton plants. They should have received great quantities of taro, taro stalks and sweet potato, but none were available.

It was also necessary at this time to designate one individual as *budua itama,* 'father/owner of the dead one'. This man would be responsible for sponsoring all the necessary mortuary rites for the deceased. The ceremonies are numerous; costly in pigs, traditional wealth objects, money and food; and may take a decade or more to complete. When the immediate family of the deceased chooses the 'owner of the dead', they are both issuing a challenge to him and shaming him. They are challenging his strength and ability, for his failure to do the mortuary work or to do it in a less than opulent manner shows him up as a 'rubbish man', a person of little consequence. Simply to designate him is to shame him, as the person chosen is always one with whom the deceased or her family have been in conflict. In this case the person chosen was Tomi, Jean's sister's husband. He was presented with a huge female pig, two *ulo* 'clay pots', three large *tabla* 'wooden bowls', and sixteen fathoms of shell money—all of which had to be repaid. These were the first of a long string of debts that he incurred as 'owner of the dead one'.[9]

All the business was concluded and all the mourners were gifted and on their way back to their villages by mid-afternoon. It was time to bury Jean. Her daughter had prepared a small coconut shell to put in the grave with Jean. The coconut was whole, about the size of a grapefruit, with an opening cut on one end and the inside scraped clean of meat. It was painted red on one side and white on the other: Jean's family design. The coconut, her daughter explained, was a symbol of the young woman's son, Jean's grandson. Throughout her illness Jean had asked to see and hold the infant. The child's mother was concerned that Jean's ghost would be lonely for the child and hover near it, causing it to sicken and possibly to die. The magically bespelled coconut was a representative of the child which would accompany the body so that Jean's ghost would not be lonely and would leave the baby alone.

Just as the few hours immediately after Jean's death and preceding the arrival of mourners from other villages belonged to Jean's fellow villagers, so too the time of her actual burial belonged to them. In between these times they were kept busy looking after their guests with food and drink and preparing the gifts of food and wealth these people would take away with them. When at last everything was done and all visitors had left, the whole village of Kokopo gathered at the site to bury Jean. A procession of young men, led by Jean's sister, carried the body from the house of mourning to the grave yard. After the catechist had spoken a few prayers and people had taken one last look at her, the crowd dispersed and the grave was filled in. For the next two days the village was quiet and inactive as people slept off their exhaustion and observed the taboos associated with a new death.

On the third day after the death, women from other villages in the district again gathered with the women of Kokopo for the *arilu*, 'the feast to send the ghost away'. The dead woman's sister, who had been in seclusion since the burial, had spent her time composing songs in commemoration of Jean's life. The songs were, in effect, one long epic that traced the events of Jean's life cycle and the circumstances of her death, and highlighted her personality, habits, accomplishments and idiosyncracies. The songs have a particular style and form, and anyone wanting to contribute their special memory of Jean could do so. The songs in her honor, and the expressions of grief by the women, were expected to draw the ghost near, mollify its disposition, and prepare it for its final departure. At dawn the songs of mourning were finished and the ghost had been sent away, banished with the night by the rising sun. All the women present were given gifts of cooked pork and sago flour (in lieu of the drought-starved taro) which they would distribute to their husbands and children when they returned to their homes.

Jean's dying process was finished. The work of mortuary ceremonies had not yet begun and would take years to complete.

CONCLUSIONS

I began this chapter by pointing out that the dying process is a social process *par excellence*. The problematic nature of this process, – the questions about why Jean was dying, who was causing her dying, and what could be done about it – arose as a corollary of the Kabana assumption that human life and death are a consequence of human behavior and are, therefore, within the scope of human understanding and control. The dying person became a focal point for an examination of the values and mores considered to be fundamental to the harmony of social life and human existence. Like a stone disturbing a pond, Jean's dying rippled out to affect her family, her kin group, other kin groups, her entire village, and then several villages. Her dying process made salient Kabana notions of mortality, accountability, and autonomy and provided insights into Kabana attitudes toward social interaction. None of the problems raised by Jean's dying were resolved, nor will they be resolved through the mortuary ceremonies to be performed in the name of the collective dead of which she is now part. As is true of the Lesu of New Ireland, Kabana ceremonies "...have no effect on the dead man...or anything connected with him. They are held to gain prestige for the living ancestors who make them" (Powdermaker 1971:308). The experience will, however, be woven into the fabric of ongoing personal and social interactions where it will affect people's motives and behavior and where it will become a part of the explanatory framework that assigns meaning to human death and life.

NOTES

This discussion is based on sixteen months field research from June through September, 1981 and from June, 1982 through June, 1983. My research in 1981 was conducted as research assistant to Drs. D. and D. Counts, funded by a research grant from the Social Sciences and Humanities Research Council of Canada. In 1982-83 I was funded as a doctoral fellow of the Council. Special thanks go to Rick Goulden and Bil Thurston who provided me with a place to be and a place to work as well as critical commentary throughout the development of this essay. My debt to the Kabana, who taught me more than either they or I realized at the time, is incalculable.

1. The term Bariai not only describes a geographic area and political district but has also been used by Chowning (1978:296) to delimit, on the basis of language groups, three distinct areas in West New Britain Province. These are Arawe, including the Arawe, Lamogai and Whiteman language groups; Bariai, including the Kove, Lusi (Kaliai), Maleu (Kilenge) and Bariai; and finally the Nakanai or Kimbe language group. Within the Bariai political district there are two language groups, the Amara who speak a Lamogai-Austronesian language and Bariai speakers who call their language Kabana. Kabana and Amara speakers consider themselves people of the Bariai district; they do, however, distinguish between themselves on the basis of their linguistic differences although, culturally, there are few discernable differences. My research was conducted in Kabana villages with speakers of Kabana. In the interests of specificity, I refer to the people among whom I worked as Kabanas.

2. Although I have supplied several English words in an effort to translate the concepts in the native terms *anunu* and *tautau,* no one of these English words captures the many shades of meaning implied in the Kabana terms. Furthermore, the glosses are conceptually loaded terms in English so that settling on any one translation e.g. *tautau* = 'soul', bends the reader's mind in the direction of an epistemological framework within which the Kabana terms fit uneasily at best, or not at all. I have, therefore, retained these two native terms throughout my discussion rather than use a specific English gloss.

3. In January, 1983 the village of Kokopo had 45 separate family dwellings and a total population of 190 persons. Based on approximate age, the population can be arranged as follows:

    0-20 years ... 96
    20-30 years ... 42
    30-40 years ... 27
    40-50 years ... 16
    50-60 years ... 6
    60-70 years ... 3

    In the 50-70 age group there are only 2 married couples. Of the five remaining persons, three are widows whose husbands have been dead for many years, and two are widowers whose wives died within weeks of one another in 1981. In the 40-50 age group there are 3 widows whose husbands have been dead for many years. In the 30-40 age group there are 2 widows who show no inclination to remarry and 2 widowers who remarried shortly after the death of their wives. All these persons maintain their spouses were killed by sorcery.

4. Although the persons in this chapter will surely recognize themselves, I have used fictitious names throughout in the event that they may not wish to be recognized by others.

5.   The Kove are also linguistically and culturally related to the Bariai. They inhabit offshore islands in the Kombe Census Division which covers an area east of the Kaliai Division to the western base of the Willaumez Peninsula. The ceremony in question was performed in honor of a Kove firstborn child. In her brief overview of this kind of ceremony among the Kove, Chowning reports (1971:5) that "by their own admission, the Kove took over this and most of their other ceremonies from other groups...." Firstborn ceremonies are specifically Bariai in origin, and the Bariai people who attended the Kove ceremonial did so as participants in the reciprocal obligations between themselves and their Kove affines and trade partners, and because the Kove requested certain knowledgeable Bariai women and men to orchestrate the Kove proceedings to ensure that they were done correctly. When performed by any group other than the Bariai however, the ceremonies are not 'correct' because the Bariai say they never divulge all.

6.   This sentence implies a whole complex of beliefs and judgments the Kabana bring to bear when comparing their technology with western technology. I will not go into these beliefs as they are beyond the scope of this discussion.

7.   The drought during 1982-1983 affected the entire northern coast of the island of New Britain. The drought became so severe in West New Britain that the provincial government spent thousands of *kina* on famine relief, shipping water (especially to the Vitu islands), rice, tinned foods and fresh fruit and vegetables to needy villages throughout the province. People in the Bariai district survived the drought in better shape than others in the province because they had an abundant supply of sago palm ripe for processing. During this 'bad time' there was a constant stream of visitors, 'kin', from the Kove, Kaliai, and Kilenge districts who came to purchase, barter or exchange for sago flour with the people in Kokopo and Gurisi villages. Starvation was never a real possibility in Bariai, although eventually the signs and symptoms of malnutrition became evident, especially among the children. Our constant diet of sago flour was interrupted only when various wild foods, classified as 'famine foods', came into season. These foods were, of course, not plentiful, but for a few days constituted a welcome break from sago flour which, when once again it appeared at our meals, was greated with jokes, grimaces and groans of 'Oh no, not again!'.

8.   *Lua* is also a reflexive verb stem meaning 'to return', 'come back'.

9.   A woman can also be designated *budua itama* 'owner of the dead one', in which case she will appoint her husband, her father, or a brother to act as her proxy at the meetings that take place inside the 'men's house' during the planning stages of the mortuary work.

Part IV: CONCLUSION

12

CONCLUSIONS: AGING AND DYING IN PACIFIC SOCIETIES: IMPLICATIONS FOR THEORY IN SOCIAL GERONTOLOGY

Victor W. Marshall

Introducing one of a number of recently published collections of research papers in the anthropology of aging, Keith and Kertzer allege that "the role of anthropologists in the recent expansion of social-scientific research on age and aging has been primarily altruistic: anthropology has given more than it has received..." (1984:19). Introducing a similar collection, Fry (1981b:11) notes that "the holistic, emic, comparative and evolutionary nature of anthropology makes anthropologists ideally suited to grapple with some of the more difficult and rewarding problems in gerontology." So far, the major contribution made by anthropological studies to social gerontology has been through the anthropologist's ability to reply to over-generalized assertions: "Not in my society they don't." This is what Fry calls the ability to veto universal theories (1981b:1). Holmes calls this power "myth-shattering and misconception-challenging." Putting the negative case, showing the exception, is part of the traditional relativizing function of anthropology and it ought to lead not just to the discrediting of extant theories but to their elaboration and specification (Keith 1981:287). Even when not blatantly contradicting received wisdom of established theories, the fine-grained descriptions of exotica provided by anthropologists extend our sense of variability and potentiality beyond that found in the vast bulk of (largely sociological) studies of aging in modern societies. This can be said while nonetheless holding that the range of variability in the aging experience within modernized societies is still largely unnoticed and undocumented, and while also recognizing the contribution that anthropologists have recently begun to make in studying aging in the modern world (see various papers in Nydegger 1983 and Sokolovsky 1983, and Dominy chapter 3 in this volume). But anthropology need not and surely will not be content to play a secondary or corrective role in social gerontology. If anthropology has given more than it has received to social science research on aging, perhaps it should have taken more. Or perhaps what anthropology has taken from the contribution of other disciplines to social gerontology was not sufficiently selective. Where gerontological theory has nourished the anthropology of aging, the best theory has not always provided the nourishment.

In this concluding chapter, the information provided in the preceding chapters serves as a stimulus to talk about theory in social gerontology. Largely the theory has been developed on a sociological base. Anthropologists have only recently given aging and the aged sustained attention, and their efforts have rarely been primarily theoretical. Rather, they have focused on detailed description of the ways in which age serves as a basis of social organization in specific societies, eschewing the comparative analyses that are requisite for theorizing.[1] By linking some of the material in the preceding chapters to theory, I hope to show the general relevance of the material in a theoretical context, and to point to ways in which the data help us to qualify and critique that theoretical understanding. The relationship between theory and data, in other words, is dialectical.

Following some general comments on the nature of theorizing in social gerontology, I discuss theoretical issues under three general categories: aging and social status, the negotiation of the life course, and the relationship between aging and dying. In each category I will briefly describe the important theoretical issues and relate the findings of earlier chapters to this "perceived wisdom." The chapter concludes with a discussion of some issues of theory and methodology that emerge in the book.

THEORY AND THEORIZING IN SOCIAL GERONTOLOGY

A theory is a set of logically related statements that purports to describe the relationship between variables. Theories need not be stated in formal, deductive language in order to be called theories; nor need they be 'true' or have a close relationship to some putative 'real world'. However, theories should be testable, and that means their language should allow the formulation of statements that are capable, in principle, of being falsified. That is, the propositions which describe the relations between variables must be so stated as to allow for a judgment that an observation, is either in keeping with the proposition, or it is not.[2]

Theory in social gerontology is not highly developed. This reflects both the relatively recent appearance of the field of inquiry on the intellectual scene and an appropriate level of doubt as to the desirability of attempting to construct a theory specific to the area of aging. If "old people are people" (Keith 1982), then why ought we to seek a distinctive theory to understand their behavior?

Attempts to formulate theory in this general area have been largely restricted to efforts to understand the ways in which age becomes an organizing principle in social life, on the one hand, and the ways in which aspects of social and individual life are ordered by time, on the other. Building upon the wreckage of some early failures, the "life course perspective" has arisen in an attempt to link these two areas of inquiry. This is a perspective and not a theory, although theoretical inquiry can proceed within its premises. Twenty years ago, sociologist Leonard Cain, Jr., gave this perspective an early formulation. Drawing extensively on anthropological materials, including Van Gennep, Radcliffe-Brown and Linton, he defined "life-course" as "...those successive statuses individuals are called upon to occupy in various cultures and walks of life as a result of aging," and "age status" as "the system developed by a culture to give order and predictability to the course followed by individuals" (Cain 1964:278). Drawing on earlier work of Anselm Strauss (1969), Cain emphasized that age status systems cannot be viewed as static. Just as life-experiences of individuals change as they pass through the life course, so too the system of age statuses changes in response to other aspects of social change, including social generations and the impact of both youth and age movements (Cain 1964:301-305).

More recently, a group of scholars from several disciplines has begun to articulate this perspective in greater detail. Matilda White Riley, who is at the center of this group, has conveniently summarized four "central premises" of what she called "this emerging perspective":

1. Aging is a life-long process....It starts with birth and ends with death. Thus no single stage of a person's life ... can be understood apart from its antecedents and consequences.
2. Aging consists of three sets of processes – biological, psychological, and social; and these three processes are all systematically interactive with one another over the life course.
3. The life course pattern of any particular person (or cohort of persons all born at the same time) is affected by social and environmental change (or history).
4. New patterns of aging can cause social change. That is, social change not only molds the course of individual lives but, when many persons in the same cohort are affected in similar ways, the change in their collective lives can in turn also produce social

change... (Riley 1979:4-5).

As Glen Elder observes, this perspective attempts to consider three temporal foci simultaneously. The individual is seen as aging in chronological years or developmental age or stage; at the same time he or she passes through a social timetable of the life course defined by social norms and roles tied to age; and all this occurs within a context of social change over historical time (1975:185-186).

The life course perspective is, from a theoretical point of view, quite formal and devoid of content. Those who espouse it vary, for example, in the assumptions they make about human nature and about the relative importance of consensus and conflict as governing forces in society (see Marshall 1981 for a discussion). They also differ along the emic-etic distinction. The guidelines of the perspective are very generally stated and seemingly so commonsensical as to sound like "mom and apple pie." Who could disagree with this perspective?

The perspective nonetheless excludes some styles of theorizing in social gerontology, especially any that are old age centered and that would attempt to understand the nature of old age in isolation from either the entire span of lived experience of an individual or cohort or the entire range of an age stratified system. Of critical importance is the assumption that age-related experiences must be viewed as both caused and causal in relation to historical processes.

Keith and Kertzer have recently suggested that the life course perspective is one congenial to the interests of anthropologists:

> ...many themes of the life-course perspective have long been present in anthropology, and the availability of cross-cultural ethnographic data has encouraged this approach in other disciplines. Both human development processes and the structural significance of age in society have been explored by anthropologists, though such studies have been limited to certain life stages, regions, and domains of activity. We have done the preliminary exercises; it is time to begin full-scale exploration (1984:49).

The life course perspective, and its challenges for anthropology, provide a very general contextual framework through which to assess the contributions of in this volume. On the one hand, many of the chapters characterize the age structure of the society. Here the approach is appropriately emic, and chronological age is shown to be of relatively minor importance in contrast to social age categories. On the other hand, the individual's progress through the age structure is described in many chapters. Here the contribution to the life course perspective is singularly impressive, for these authors take a decidedly voluntaristic stance in characterizing human nature. Most social gerontology, including the life course perspective, emphasizes normative determination of behavior, socialization to age group membership, and the individual as a rule-following creature. In contrast, the dominant theme of the case studies reported here is of active, choosing, struggling people negotiating their careers over the life course. The age stratification system is portrayed as a general cultural resource that permits some measure of prediction of behavior, but the specific nature of an individual's use of this resource in everyday life is something else again.

In summary, the most widely accepted perspective in social gerontology today is the life course perspective, a very general orienting paradigm within the realm of social science. The specifics of its use by social gerontologists varies considerably. The studies in this book suggest the usefulness of an interpretive or hermeneutic perspective. As Geertz notes, interpretive scholars of many disciplines have adopted a wide range of analytical strategies in their shared opposition to positivistic approaches (1983:22). However, "...they all represent attempts to formulate how this people or that, this period or that, this person or that makes sense to itself and, understanding that, what we understand about social order, historical change, or psychic functioning in general."

Anthropology is currently experiencing a great deal of creative tension. Over twenty years ago Leach described British Social Anthropology (which he capitalized!) as functionalist and "concerned with the comparative analysis of social structures" (1961:1). But, Leach said, things were changing rapidly and "most of my colleagues are giving up the attempt to make comparative generalizations; instead they have begun to write impeccably detailed historical ethnographies of particular peoples." That both a logic of cross-cultural comparison and a desire to conduct fine-grained descriptive studies continue as uncomfortable companions in the anthropological endeavor is indicated by Geertz's recent description of the tension as "a sort of cross between a connoisseur's weakness for nuance and an exegete's for comparison" (1983:3). The search is on for a type of comparative anthropology that can serve both poles. As Keith has recently argued, "Understanding old people as people, as human actors in culturally defined settings, requires several perspectives central to anthropological research: cross-cultural comparison, holistic analysis of context, and subjective data" (1982:3).

Cross-cultural comparisons are required in order to test any theories that make claims to universal applicability or, as Keith suggests, "to distinguish universal aspects of aging from the diversity of social responses to it" (Keith 1982:3). Social gerontology has been marked, in its relatively brief history, by this dialectic. At the social psychological level, the disengagement theory of aging was initially formulated as universally applicable, despite its empirical grounding in a nonrandom sample of persons living in just one community, Kansas City, Missouri (Cumming and Henry 1961). But the claim to universality provided a focal point for theory-testing and it was not long before that claim had to be rejected (see Hochschild 1975; Maddox 1965). At the macro-social level of analysis, the theory of aging and modernization, as formulated by Cowgill and Holmes, suggested a relationship between societal modernization and the status of the aged that had cross-cultural universality; but again subsequent research has led to rejection of that claim to universality (see, e.g., Dowd 1980:65-77; Quadagno 1982).

The disengagement theory of aging passes like a ghost through the chapters of this book; and modernization theory provides a major reference point for several authors. The approach to these theoretical perspectives is sometimes critical and qualifying, sometimes supportive. It is worthwhile to consider the significance of the case studies reported here for these two theoretical traditions in social gerontology, especially with respect to claims of universal applicability. A major contribution of this volume is in the description of aging and dying in social contexts that are unfamiliar to most scholars interested in the subject. Studying aging *in situ,* and showing how it is defined and experienced in a variety of other cultures, brings additional information to bear on the diverse ways in which people respond to biological universals. By examining the diversity of the sociocultural life-ways of aging and dying, we better appreciate the ways in which aging is structured in our own form of society. The data presented in these chapters enrich our appreciation of not only the survivability of the human species but the remarkable talent that humans have for not just 'making do' but 'making life rich'.

In a recent 'state of the art' review of cross-cultural research on aging, Palmore points out that cross-cultural research is essential to understand anything that is affected by cultural factors (1983). Aging and dying certainly are such phenomena. While aging and gender are social bases of differentiation in all known societies, and while people everywhere die, the ways in which these biological facts become realized in any society are highly variable. The studies reported here expand the sense of this variability. Palmore notes that most cross-cultural research on aging is primarily descriptive and little informed by theory (1983:46). One objective of this concluding chapter is to consider explicitly the theoretical relevance of the volume's descriptive material. In so doing I will outline some of the major theoretical issues in social gerontology, a heavily sociological enterprise, and in that specialty area within it that refers to the relationship between aging and dying. A second objective will be to highlight some issues of theoretical *perspective* that are well illuminated in this book and that deal with the interpretive or hermeneutic approach to sociocultural studies.

AGING AND SOCIAL STATUS

Keith observes that "the first and major continuing focus in cross-cultural study of old age is status" (1982:3). This focus provides a major meeting place between anthropological and sociological studies of age and aging for in the latter, as well, the status of the aged has been one of the major analytical concerns. One link between sociology and anthropology is found in the theory of aging and modernization, considered below. Before turning to that theory, however, I will look at the nature of status itself, the 'dependent variable' in the theory that modernization affects the status of the aged.

In North American social gerontology, aside from the modernization theory of aging, the "age stratification" approach reigns as the central theoretical paradigm. Not strictly speaking a theory, this perspective distinguishes between cohorts and age strata. Any society is viewed as comprised of an age stratification system in which age groups are arrayed, as on a ladder, with each step differentiated according to expectations or norms for age-appropriate behavior, rewards and sanctions for compliance. Birth cohorts are seen as entering the age stratification system and progressing through it with maturation (Riley 1971, 1976; Riley, Johnson and Foner 1972). Ideally, socialization acts to prepare cohort members to advance to each successive stage and abandon the earlier stage (Riley, Foner, Hess and Toby 1969). Occasionally, when there is a lack of 'fit' between organization properties of the age stratification system and the characteristics of a cohort (such as its size), adjustments occur in the age stratification system itself (Waring 1976). For example, the 'youth' age stratum may be enlarged by expanding the length of education in order to delay the impact of a large 'baby boom' cohort on the labor force.

While the age stratification perspective has gained widespread acceptance, it has been criticized for reliance on functionalist equilibrium mechanisms and for treating cohorts as synthetic rather than concrete, leading to an ahistorical view of social change (Marshal 1983; Tindale and Marshall 1980).   Two scholars within the life course perspective have suggested that the age stratification system of contemporary modern societies is less concretely defined than in many nonmodern societies and that age group conflict is, in consequence, less pronounced (Foner and Kertzer 1978). The age stratification approach nonetheless argues that the age stratification system is important in any society for the allocation of rewards and sanctions for age-appropriate behavior.

When discussing North American society, observers disagree as to the nature of the age stratification system and whether North American society is becoming more or less stratified by age.   On the one hand age stratification theorists assume that the phenomenon is real enough to make a difference in the allocation of expectations, rights and rewards.   Allied with them are Neugarten and colleagues in an early work (Neugarten, Moore and Lowe 1965), and sociologists, such as Rosow, who believe that old age is so distinct a stage of life as to require extensive socialization of persons entering the status (Rosow 1974, 1976).   In addition there are a number of scholars who accept Rose's position that we are moving toward an increasingly articulated "aging subculture" or "aging minority group" (1965).

In earlier writings, Neugarten stressed the social reality of age norms as determinants of regularities of social behavior across the life course.   Her position at that time was congruent with that outlined by the age stratification theorists.   On the other hand, a number of investigators (discussed in Abu-Laban and Abu-Laban 1980) argue that the aged are not, nor are they becoming, a minority group.   On the contrary, age is making less difference than before in such matters as economic status. Subsequently, Neugarten moved to the position that age is becoming less important as a basis of social differentiation as the "young-old," healthy, economically secure older people come to resemble younger cohorts more closely (1970). It is difficult to tell just where North American society is now in terms of age stratification.   It is becoming either more or less age stratified, depending on which theoretical position is taken. The conceptual issues are far from resolved (Bengtson, et al., n.d.; Berger 1984; Marshall 1984).

A major impediment to resolving the issue of the degree to which North American society is age stratified is the lack of an adequate emic base.   It is one thing to find that age or life stage correlates with some form of behavior.   In fact, age is rarely a powerful differentiator unless very rough categories are used. It is quite another to ask how people themselves use age as a basis for organizing social interaction. Reviewing this evidence, Hagestad finds that there are few research efforts to review (these include Neugarten's data) and that while the

> ...findings of these studies indicate an impressive degree of consensus regarding acceptable or unacceptable behavior at different ages...much work remains to be done on the aspects of social control in age systems....there has been no systematic attempt to assess the extent to which individuals experience social constraints and sanctions in connection with timetables....and age norms (Hagestad 1982:469).

In fact, when anthropologist Christine Fry turned to address these issues she found less than impressive evidence that any widespread agreement as to the structure of the age stratification system exists in the United States (1976, 1980b). Asking respondents to distribute 34 cards describing hypothetical career and domestic characteristics into piles based on their judgments of similarity of age brackets, she found that with a mean of 5.7 piles, the standard deviation was 2.7. Some respondents identified as many as 15 different age categories while others identified only 2; and over 100 different terms were used to describe these categories.

How simple, in contrast, do the age stratification systems described in the preceding chapters of this volume appear to be! But is this really so? Neugarten found greater agreement than did Fry because her method (forced choice) directed respondents to express approval or disapproval for a number of items at three differing ages. This structuring produced greater consensus than would have occurred had respondents been free, as in Fry's research, to devise their own age categories or, indeed, to describe age as irrelevant.

The issues here boil down to: (a) methodological adequacy in ascertaining the ethnosemantics of age category labels; (b) the need to measure agreement and stability as to terms and their assignment to targets or stimulus persons, and (c) the relationship of these terms to other aspects of behavior. It is clear from Fry's work that over 100 different age categories are in use in the United States (actually, in Lafayette, Indiana). It would be interesting to employ the same methodology she used with Marshallese, Marquesans or Telefol. The case studies reported here do not claim to have exhaustively catalogued the full range of age categories in any of the study societies. On the other hand, they do represent a methodological approach that is almost totally absent from social gerontological studies in North America.

When attempting to ascertain the importance of age-related phenomena for social status, some closure is gained when it is possible to assign an individual to a social category or a group named by some age-relevant principle. This principle is, in Oceania, rarely chronological age per se. The case studies in this volume reinforce the principle that fine-grained chronological distinctions assume increasing importance with the rise of bureaucratic record keeping as societies modernize or as the state becomes administratively more pervasive (Thomas 1976). Then specific age becomes important for the regulation of such things as military conscription, education, labor force participation and marriage. But in North American society numerous other age-related bases of social organization are found, bases that are identical in principle to those described in the chapters of this volume. These include the dating of persons by historical events, seniority of membership in kinship or other groups, family life course stages, ability to participate in economic and social activities, and health status.

Social gerontologists in North America have adopted a distinction between the "young-old" and the "old-old." Popularized by Neugarten, this dichotomy was intended to distinguish the well-elderly from the ill-elderly. Although certain other characteristics were added to the description of the "young-old," such as economic security, high educational status and leisure orientation, the key to the distinction was health. Unfortunately, because the distinction was suggested to occur roughly around age seventy-five, all too many gerontologists adopted this arbitrary age point to make the distinction. Misuse of the young-old/old-old distinction has perhaps gone so far that one must recommend against the use of the terms. What is needed is a way to distinguish, in the North American context, between the actively functioning, healthy older persons and those who, in some South Pacific societies, might be called "defunct" or "decrepit."

These terms will not be acceptable within the North American context. Leenhardt's term, "defunct," in particular, but also the term "decrepit," has a jarring effect. The documentation provided here demonstrates the difficulty of generalizing about differences in the social valuation of later life, for the chapters reveal variation, not only between these South Pacific societies but sometimes even within them, as Counts and Counts note in their introduction to this volume. It does appear that the social valuation of the old is least positive in the Marquesas (Kirkpatrick chapter 5), one of the most highly modernized of the societies discussed. Carucci (chapter 6) also notes a diminished respect for the elders in the Marshall Islands, and associates this not only with the rise in the proportions and numbers of youth but with the growth of administrative authority. To be called an "old woman" is, Carucci says, an insult.

As is quite generally accepted, age itself is rarely a basis for authority or respect. When age-related differences in authority, respect, or the social value attributed to people are found, these are due to contingencies such as control over knowledge among the people of Pulap (Flinn, chapter 4), the accumulation of descendants or of accomplishments, as among the Marshallese (Carucci, chapter 6), control over economic resources or the ability to maintain and elaborate power bases important in earlier life, as with the Pakeha women described by Dominy (chapter 3). Most of the bases for maintaining a favorable status position in later life, or at least of combating decline in status position, are as mundane as these. Cosmological innovation is the exception rather than the rule in the societies described here. But the Managalase, where survival is taken as a sign of the strength of one's 'soul' (McKellin chapter 9), and the Vanatinai, whose beliefs allow for an older person who is ill-treated to retaliate after death (Lepowsky chapter 8), are notable for the creative use of culture in providing devices to protect the status of old people.

These examples suggest two alternative ways that societies enhance or protect the status of the aged. One possibility is to do away with status distinctions based on age. Another is to elaborate them while developing or emphasizing some power base that is enhanced with increasing age. Both possibilities are found in advanced industrial societies as well as in less modernized societies such as those discussed in this volume. The elimination of mandatory retirement exemplifies the first possibility, as does the argument for generic rather than age-based targeting of services (see Neugarten 1982), while the persistence of seniority and the growth of old age based health and income security systems exemplifies the second strategy (see papers in Guillemard 1983).

The status of old people is not, therefore, just a function of chrono-logical age, nor of relative age. The societies described in the earlier chapters of this book provide examples of diverse bases for the assign-ment of status to people who happen to be at different ages or life stages, and different bases for constructing an age stratification system. But the studies reveal two much more fundamental features of age-related social status. These are that age status is situational rather than fixed and achieved rather than ascribed. This leads to a view of the life course, and of passage through the life course, as negotiated.

THE NEGOTIATION OF THE LIFE COURSE

A major contribution to the study of aging is found in the theme that
unites the chapters of this book: the theme that passage over the life
course is not inexorable but rather is negotiated, being culturally,
socially and situationally contingent. To understand the significance of
this insight it is important to contrast it with the great bulk of social
gerontological theory, that has tended to view aging as something inexorable or fixed, either by timetables of biological maturation or of age
grading.   Two major variants of highly deterministic models of aging
appear in the sociological and social-psychological literature.   In both
cases there has been a decided move away from strict determinism
over the past decade. At the level of the individual, early versions of
developmental psychology were highly deterministic: aging was seen as
a biologically driven progression through a series of qualitatively
different stages. In a separate formulation operative at both the level of
the   individual   and   of   social   structure,   variants   of   structural-
functionalist role theory also posited an inexorable progression through
a series of fixed stages, but the stages in this case were recognized as
social. Here normative, rather than biological, determinism was postulated.
    Baltes has noted that developmental theorists and their kinfolk in
aging, life span theorists, have moved away from the classical or purist
developmental paradigm that sees behavioral change as sequential,
unidirectional, moving toward an end state, irreversible, marked by
qualitative or structural changes, and universal (Baltes 1979:262). As
Ryff observes:

> ...the rigid inflexibility of classical stage theory is not an appro-
> priate characterization of a stage approach within the personality
> domain.   Available theories capitalize on the positive aspects of
> stage theory by formulating optimal development, but they do so
> without the strait-jacket imposed by biological growth models
> (Ryff 1982a:212).

Developmental theorists such as Ryff inquire increasingly about the
sense that individuals themselves give to human development over the
life course. This is an emic approach that asks how people construct
their own sense of human development (Ryff 1982b, n.d.; Ryff and
Heincke 1983). The degree of indeterminism postulated in the recent
life span developmental approaches is variable. For example, some
researchers may focus on the *sense* of development, while others may

focus on the extent to which the individual can personally shape not only the sense of his or her life but the life itself.

Resting on structural-functionalist foundations, the disengagement theory of aging epitomizes a highly deterministic view of aging and human development. Its original formulation saw the individual and the society mutually withdrawing from one another by inexorable logic functional to both. The link between the individual and the society, in keeping with this structural-functionalist approach, is the "role relationship," role being a fundamental building block of social systems. Disengagement, in which the individual withdraws from embeddedness in social roles, is functional for the individual who, with aging, needs time to prepare for death and who no longer has the energy to remain active in role relationships. Paradoxically, 'voluntary' disengagement is inevitably 'determined' by the need to prepare for death and to accommodate reduced energy levels. From the societal point of view (society is reified in this theory), disengagement is functional because mortality can be more smoothly accommodated when individuals slowly withdraw rather than being wrenched unpredictably from those role relationships that contribute to societal functioning.[3]

In social gerontology the term "disengagement" is loaded with deterministic theoretical connotations. It suggests a universal, voluntary and mutual severing of ties between an individual and his or her society, initiated by awareness of finitude. The withdrawal Counts and Counts describe in chapter 7 can be seen as voluntary on the part of the individual, but the initiatory motivation is different and the mutuality of withdrawal between the individual and the society does not occur. Moreover, the withdrawal of the elder Lusi is much more selective than is the disengagement implied by disengagement theorists. Lusi may continue to be socially and sexually active but will avoid behavior that is likely to incur wrath. Other Lusi become impatient, Counts and Counts tell us, with elders who reduce their activity levels on the basis of age alone rather than in adaptation to declining health.

If by disengagement we mean progression toward the final status in an age-status or age stratification system, then the case material presented in this volume certainly leads to a questioning of any notion that this is highly voluntary. The cases presented here hammer another few nails in disengagement theory's coffin by disconfirming its universality postulate. Scaletta (chapter 11) does suggest that among the Kabana of West New Britain, "As people age they become more spectators than participants in social life." She attributes this withdrawal to reduction in both physical vigor and mental strength, a condition that is hardly voluntary. Scaletta notes in her case study that Jean resented the state of exclusion and powerlessness that was a joint function of her illness and the seizure of control over her life by her family.   And Kirkpatrick (chapter 5), who acknowledges that "a process of declining social involvement seems nearly inevitable in old age," in the Marquesas, also says that "people strive to make their old age a prolongation of maturity, not a slow slide into death."   Flinn (chapter 4), who also notes behavioral withdrawal among the Pulap, emphasizes that "only the nature of their contribution changes, as the elderly continue to work and contribute according to their abilities. Old age on Pulap need not entail inactivity or uselessness."

Assessing the disengagement theory in industrialized societies, Shanas and others acknowledged that level of activity does generally decline with age (1968:442).   "Activity theorists" such as Maddox (1965, 1970) and Palmore (1968) would agree.   But Shanas characterized most decreased role engagement as due to widowhood and enforced retirement.   Enforced nonmutual disengagement is in no way supportive of the disengagement theory of aging.

Social structural determinism is advanced in various ways in the literature of social gerontology; prominent among these ways is through structural-functionalist role theory.   Here it is postulated that society can be characterized as a set of status positions to each of which attach clusters of norms, or role-expectations, to guide behavior. Through efficient socialization processes, the individual comes to both learn and internalize such expectations.   As Neugarten and Datan describe this process:

> ...the individual learns to think and to behave in ways that are consonant with the roles he plays, so that performance in a succession of roles leads to predictable personality configurations.... [T]he life cycle can be seen as a succession of roles and changing role constellations, and a certain order and predictability through a given succession of roles (1973:55).

The highly deterministic version of the perspective is evident in the following summary by Neugarten:

> Every society is age-graded, and every society has a system of social expectations regarding age-appropriate behavior.   The individual passes through a socially regulated cycle from birth to death as inexorably as he passes through a biological cycle: a succession of delineated age-statuses, each with its recognized rights, duties, and obligations.... This normative pattern is adhered

to, more or less consistently, by most persons.... For any social group it can be demonstrated that norms and age expectations act as a system of social controls, as prods and brakes upon behavior... (1970:71-87).

Few sociologists of aging today, and indeed few sociologists, take such a highly deterministic view, and Neugarten herself now stresses voluntarism and role negotiation as contrasted with an image of people simply following age-appropriate roles (Neugarten and Hagestad 1976).[4]

A number of theoretical positions in social gerontology, while seemingly diverse, rest on a conceptualization of the individual as a role-player constrained to fulfill age-graded expectations. The diversity of the expectations (as between Neugarten or Riley who see them as quite clear and Rosow who sees them as quite unclear) nonetheless rests on this particular imagery that society is comprised of articulated role expectations and functions adequately when these expectations are met by role incumbents.

This is a view challenged by the chapters of this volume that emphasize a view of people as strategic, as struggling. People are viewed as negotiating or making their way through the "career" of the life course. Within the sociology of aging, a few scholars have advanced this position in recent years (Breytspraak 1975, 1984; Gubrium and Buckholt 1977; Marshall 1978-79, 1980a, 1980b; Matthews 1979; Neugarten and Hagestad 1976; Unruh 1983 are examples). These scholars have stressed that people play active roles in negotiating their careers over the life course and through old age. They accept a dramaturgical metaphor, but see actors in a "free theater," writing their scripts as they go along, rather than merely enacting pre-scripted roles. While the interpretive anthropology of people such as Geertz (1983) and Turner (1969) provide theoretical foundation for some of these social gerontologists, so do phenomenologists and symbolic interactionists such as Berger and Luckmann (Berger 1963; Berger and Luckmann 1966), Goffman (1959) and Schutz (1967). As Geertz has observed, the interpretive perspective relies not on the highly deterministic models of sciences such as physics and chemistry for its imagery, but on models and metaphors from the humanities that see life as analogous to the theater, the game, or the text (1983). The point to emphasize here is that this stance, which informs the chapters of this book, is congruent with exciting recent developments that emanate from sociologists studying aging and age relationships. A new paradigm, or rather the reemergence of a very old paradigm of scholarship, is increasingly gaining acceptance in social gerontology. This paradigm places great importance on the discovery, not only of regularities among events, but of meanings. In social gerontology, this interpretive paradigm has been influential in the subfield of interest in the relationship between aging and dying.

SOCIAL ASPECTS OF AGING AND DYING

The high level of death awareness and concern reported in most of the case studies in this volume is impressive. Although the exceptions are noteworthy, it is generally the case that the people of these societies are highly *aware* of death, which is frequently and vividly present in their societies, and they are highly *concerned* about the process of dying and the fate of the dying or deceased.

North American evidence shows that neither awareness nor concern about death is generally high in individual consciousness; however, social institutions and important societal behavior patterns suggest otherwise. One might say that death is in many ways abstracted from the domain of the individual and handled through more or less impersonal social processes. In the later years, however, awareness and concerns about death are heightened because it is in the later years that death predictably occurs.

Perhaps the greatest contrast between the North American context and the societies described in this book (with the exception of the two in New Zealand) is the location of death in the later years in North America, whereas death typically occurs throughout the years of the life span in Pacific societies. One needs only to compare the age structure of the latter societies as reported by the authors with that of Canada and the United States, both of which have more than ten percent of their population over the age of sixty-five, and in both of which two-thirds of all deaths occur to persons who have attained at least the age of sixty-five. Setting aside difficulties with the ethnosemantics of age categories and the definition of what it means to be old, the timing of death is simply much more predictable in North America than it is in these societies, as measured by standard deviation around the mean. And that mean is much higher in North America than in the South Pacific. This has a number of consequences for awareness and concern about death.

In North America, increasing age is associated with more frequently experiencing the deaths of kin and friends. Older people are more likely to read obituaries and attend funerals than are younger people

(Kalish and Reynolds 1976). These experiences appear to affect both the frequency of thoughts about death and the salience of these thoughts. Riley, who has conducted two national opinion surveys on attitudes toward death, reports an increase, for the general adult population, in the proportion reporting that they thought "often" about "the uncertainty of their own lives or the death of someone close to them," from about one-third in a survey conducted in the 1960s to over four in ten in a survey a decade later (Riley 1970; 1983:195). But thoughts of death were more salient in the old, and the increase in saliency over the decade between the two surveys was also largely among the old.

Although older people appear to think about death more than do the young, they do not fear it more. Attitudinal studies of death and dying are numerous in the North American context but, until recently, they have been hampered by a lack of concern for the multidimensionality of death attitudes and meanings (these studies are critically reviewed in Marshall 1982). Most studies have focused on a single dimension of fear of death. Scores of studies, many with college student samples, have failed to produce convincing evidence that most people live in great fear of death. Surveys that allow for cross-sectional age comparisons show declines in reported fear of death (Bengtson, Cuellar and Ragan 1977; Kalish and Reynolds 1976; Keller, Sherry and Piotrowski 1984; Riley 1970; Sharma and Jain 1969; Templer and Ruff 1971). Other studies, both ethnographic and attitudinal-survey in nature, restricted to older subjects have found little fear of death among the aged (Hochschild 1973; Jeffers, Nichols and Eisdorfer 1961; Marshall 1975; Matthews 1979). Kalish and Johnson attribute this low level of death-fear in part to the fact that death is predictably located in later life (1972:53):

> Apparently, older persons find death and dying more salient, and they discuss it more; but they do not appear to find it more stressful or frightening. Perhaps, having lived their allocated time, death is less of a punishment than it might be for someone who feels that life still owes him additional time.

There are other possible interpretations of the general finding that increased age is associated with decreased fear of death. Diggory and Rothman took a multi-dimensional approach to death fear, but among various reasons why death might be feared they found a concern that plans and projects will come to an end. They relate this to the "utility" of the self: "What one would lament most about his own death is loss of the specific activities in which he is most involved or feels to be most important" Diggory and Rothman 1961:206). In a different sample survey using a version of this indicator, Kalish and Reynolds found less endorsement of that reason with increasing age (1976:208-209).

There are also undoubtedly cohort differences in attitudes toward death and dying in North America. Educational attainment is negatively associated with fear of death, for example, while it increases with each successive cohort to enter the later years. Cohort differences in North American society also reflect profound alterations in culture that shift the meaning of death and of dying. Riley observes that

> As this dramatic postponement of death has come upon us with such rapidity, it is not surprising that social norms and social institutions have lagged behind; that popular interest in death and popular confusion about its meaning have virtually exploded; and that, as many earlier understandings of death have been vitiated, sociologists have only now begun a reassessment (1983:192).

If it is necessary to make sense of death, then the nature of what must be made sense of has changed. Not capricious death, but predictable death; not death at an early age, but death as the culmination of life, calls out for new meaning in the North American context, since older systems of meaning were accommodated to a form of death that is now increasingly rare.

North American meanings of death are in great flux. It has been suggested, however, that one line of polarization is that between the private and public sphere. Klass (1981-82) attributes the widespread popularity of Kubler-Ross' (1969) five-stage theory of the dying process to its symbolic complementarity with American values of the private sphere and to a reaction against public sphere values of rationality and technical control over death. He also points out that few physicians, who represent the technological, rational and bureaucratic handling of dying in North American society, are sympathetic to Kubler-Ross' framework and that the most vigorous critiques launched against her have been directed at her lack of scientific rigor.

In the public sphere, a high level of death concern is reflected in measures that have led to the greater predictability of death and its deflection to the latter stages of the life course. North American and, in general, highly modernized societies spend massively for sanitation and preventive health and medical care in attempts to ward off death. Death is viewed as "the enemy" to be attacked with campaigns or crusades against its causes. If the social institution of high-technology medicine reflects a high degree of concern with the dying and with death (Fox 1981), the funeral industry represents a highly bureaucratic and technical concern for the dead. Sociologist Robert Blauner was among the first to recognize the implications of the "bureaucratization" of death and dying for other aspects of social life" (Blauner 1966:379)

> This separation of the handling of illness and death from the family minimizes the average person's exposure to death and its disruption of the social process. When the dying are segregated among specialists for whom contact with death has become routine and even somewhat impersonal, neither their presence while alive nor as corpses interferes greatly with the mainstream of life.

Talcott Parsons and Victor Lidz have argued that:

> The problem of the *meaning* of death is coming...to be concentrated about death occurring as the completion of a normal life cycle.... This central, irreducible problem is becoming disentangled from the problem of adjusting to deaths that occur earlier in the life cycle, particularly in infancy and early childhood, which was much more general in the premodern period (1967:137).

A number of sociologists working in the area of death and dying agree that the meaning of death is ambiguous in contemporary North American society. Riley summarizes this position and, drawing on Fox (1981), arrives at a conclusion suggestive in terms of the South Pacific societies reported on in this book:

> These twin revolutions, the biomedical and the demographic, challenge some of the most fundamental beliefs in Western culture and give further support to the Fox hypothesis that 'life and death are coming to be viewed less as absolute, hermetic entities, sealed off from one another, and more as different points on a meta-spectrum whose beginning and ending are ambiguous (Riley 1983:121).

I have developed a rudimentary theory of aging and dying based on the assumption that societal attempts will be made to contain the impact of death and that individuals in any society will draw on culturally available meanings in an attempt to render their own impending death sensible or legitimate (Marshall 1980a). Death is therefore problematical both for societies and for individuals, and the resolution of the problematics of death and dying is a dialectical one. Thus, while Malinowski (1948) argued that religious rituals act to alleviate anxieties caused by death, Radcliffe-Brown (1965) suggested that religious ritual creates such anxieties. Homans argues that these positions are complementary:

> Malinowski (1948) is looking at the individual, Radcliffe-Brown at society. Malinowski is saying that the individual tends to feel anxiety on certain occasions; Radcliffe-Brown is saying that society expects the individual to feel anxiety on certain occasions (Homans 1941 in Lessa and Vogt 1965:126).

Although many authors assert that the need to explain death is the basis for the origin of religion, this is not a testable assertion. Whatever its origin, religion plays an important part in the explanation and interpretation of death, describing what death is and why it occurs. The complex and elaborate cosmologies that are typical of Pacific peoples are rich in ability to render death and dying meaningful. As is evident from the various chapters and as noted in the introductory chapter by Counts and Counts, the meanings attributed to death and dying vary considerably from society to society. *But in any one society, to judge from these accounts, the meanings are more or less agreed upon and acted upon.* The possible exceptions to this generalization are found in the modernized and Christianized societies of New Zealand and the Marquesas (Sinclair chapter 2, Dominy chapter 3, Kirkpatrick chapter 5), but note that death is not a focus of these chapters.

As Counts and Counts observe in chapter 1 of this volume, South Pacific systems of meaning provide explanations for the death of the young, for that is where death most frequently occurs. What of a society in which death typically occurs in late life?

Both longer life and a new social form of death as its completion have to be explained. In North America, as in many of the societies described in this volume, very old people are marginalized. In a society that places a high value on active participation in the economic sphere of production, marginalization occurs around the age of sixty-five, and an ethnosemantics of North American age categories would virtually equate the terms "retired" and "old." Old age is, as in any society, a social construction, but it is one in North America in which the reasons for continued living are as problematical as the reasons why death might be seen as appropriate. A new rhetoric of leisure oriented consumption in the "young-old" years, a period in France described as the "third age" (see Guillemard 1980) alleges that this ought to be a time of self-actualization. The extension of this ideology is epitomized in the view that not just the later years but dying itself ought to be viewed as a "growth experience," what Lofland (1978) has called the "happy death movement."

In neither of these areas has the social construction of meanings to make sense of very old age or of dying been so successful as to result in any widespread agreement or cultural consensus (Dumont and Foss 1972; Marshall 1980a). The result is both a freedom and a necessity (if one grants a basic assumption that human beings *are* fundamentally motivated to render their lives more meaningful than meaningless) to engage in meaning-seeking activities in later life.

In an earlier work I summarized these processes as follows (Marshall 1980a:185-186):[5]

1. With aging comes a growing awareness that one's death draws near. This awareness is not a simple function of age but develops through a complex process involving a comparison of one's own age to the age-at-death of significant others, as well as an estimate of health status.
2. The realization that death is drawing closer poses a cognitive problem for the individual, encompassing two related dimensions. The individual will seek a sense of the appropriateness of life as a whole....
3. When people recognize that time is limited, they also seek to make sense of death itself and their own impending death.
4. In addition to the cognitive dilemmas leading to legitimation of the self as dying, people want to exercise some degree of status-passage control....
5. Given the contemporary sociocultural milieu, with its bureaucratization and technological treatment of death and dying, some degree of conflict between the individual and others who have control or jurisdiction over aspects of the terminal status passage is to be expected.

These generalizations were explicitly formulated as relevant in highly modernized societies and not as universally applicable. This restriction in their scope is due to the predictable location of death in later life only in highly modernized societies and to the bureaucratic and technical treatment of death only in such societies. These Pacific case studies make these limitations more vivid but also, it seems to me, suggest some areas where the formulation does have widespread generality.

The content of ideas about death is not so important as the fact that all societies have some ideas. The interpretive perspective can be neutral as to the content of ideas but focuses on the form of sense-making. People do draw on their ideology to make sense of death and dying, and consider that some kinds of death are more appropriate than others (for example, the "good death" in Kaliai). Inappropriate deaths frequently lead to increased ritual response as a sense-making activity. In Kaliai (Counts and Counts chapter 7) and in some of the other societies described in this volume, appropriate deaths at the culmination of life receive little ritual treatment. In North America there is a cultural lag phenomenon from the earlier period when the bulk of deaths were not located in later life. This cultural lag phenomenon has led to elaborate funeral ritual. But the old receive less elaborate ritual upon their deaths than do the young, even in North America (Owen, Fulton and Markusen 1978).

Funeral rituals reaffirm sociocultural meanings of death and dying. Individual meanings, on the other hand, are fashioned by using socio-cultural meanings as a resource. In North American society, but not in the South Pacific, people have little cause to even think about the meaning of death. Death for most people is something located years down the road. And dying in a hospital is not so visible to the community at large as is dying in a special hut constructed on the beach (in Bariai, as described by Scaletta chapter 11), even though both represent liminal states. Dealing with the meaningfulness of death is, therefore, in North America an activity that is either in the hands of experts or is located, for the general population, only in the later years. This would seem to be a major line of contrast between North America and the Pacific societies described in this volume.

I have suggested that concerns for status passage control are partic-ularly important in North American society and at the same time threatened by the technological and bureaucratic modes of dealing with the dying and the dead. In some South Pacific societies, while the cause of conflict differs, a struggle for control over the dying passage is nontheless evident. The case of Jean, described by Scaletta (chapter 11) pits the dying person in a struggle with her family. Jorgensen (chapter 10) describes the search for meaningfulness in death in Telefolmin in relation to a general cosmological struggle against entropy. McKellin (chapter 9) says the Managalase view death as the end of struggle over the powers of sorcery. Lepowsky (chapter 8) describes old people as entering into alliances, so to speak, with pred-ecessors, so as to gain more power in their later years. The struggle for control, then, appears to be universal, although the specifics of exactly what is to be controlled or the techniques used to exert control are socioculturally variable.

The Counts' point in the introduction to this volume is well taken, *contra* Lofland, that dying in pre-modern societies is not always or typically "mean, brutish and short" and that whether or not it is so depends on indigenous definitions. But the context in which dying occurs is affected by the ability to use the tools of high technology medicine to preserve biological life, even when both social and psychological death have occurred, for not months but years (Kalish 1966). Moreover, in North America the application of this technology has its greatest impact precisely in those later years when the value of continued life is most diminished because of the marginalization of the aged.

These caveats aside, the case study material in these chapters is consonant with rather than contradictory to the generalizations that I have suggested apply in the North American context. Counts and Counts say in their introduction to this volume, "The factors that determine how an individual experiences the processes of aging and dying are not necessarily determined by the technological stage of his society." The nuances of *particular* meaning systems and *particular* ways to socially organize aging and dying are what captures the imagination – or my imagination at any rate. Here, then, is a great contribution of the anthropology of aging and dying, and of this volume, in expanding our knowledge of the human capacity to creatively construct and use symbols in dealing with human inevitabilities.

CONCLUSION

The consideration of two theoretical strands of social gerontology has been implicit in many of the case studies reported in this book. These are the modernization thesis and the disengagement theory of aging. I have suggested that none of the case studies provides data highly supportive of either of these theoretical approaches and that some of them provide clearly contrary evidence. Yet, when viewed through a different set of theoretical lenses provided by the emergent life course perspective, the case studies lead toward an interpretation of actors as socially constructing and negotiating the life course. The ethnosemantics of aging and dying in this book testify to the richness and diversity with which human beings creatively use culture. The sense from these studies is of culture as a framework that people use to provide a baseline of stability and predictiveness for the life course. But this cultural map is only a rough guideline that allows considerable choice on the part of the person or group using that map for life course guidance.

The important sense of process and movement of individuals through the social categories of the life course, detailed here, is very much within the life course perspective. This perspective is potent as an organizing framework for this new body of knowledge, which suggests, in turn, that continuing work explicitly formulated on the basis of its still general premises is warranted. So long as that work retains the emic flavor found in the preceding pages, we may still be able to find some compromise between the exegete's desire for comparison and generalization and the connoisseur's quest for nuance. The result, hopefully, will be increased explanatory understanding.

NOTES

My work on this paper has been supported by a National Health Scientist award from Health and Welfare Canada and a grant to myself, Frank Denton and Byron Spencer from the Social Sciences and Humanities Research Council of Canada (no. 492-82-0001) to study the economic and social implications of aging.

1. There are of course notable exceptions to this generalization, including Foner and Kertzer (1978), Maxwell and Silverman (1970), Cowgill and Holmes (1972), Press and McKool (1972), Glascock and Feinman (1981). The pioneering work of Simmons (1945, 1960) is certainly anthropological but he was a sociologist (Holmes 1980:272).

2. This stance toward theory is not accepted by all but is reasonably 'orthodox' in sociology. See Turner (1982, chapter 1) for an elaboration.

3. I present a general critique of disengagement theory in Marshall 1981, and a critique in specific reference to the theory as a theory of aging-and-dying in Marshall 1980a:78-85.

4. Bertaux (19882:148-149) represents a movement beyond social structural determinism in the case of the highly deterministic French structuralism position. Noting that "structuralism focuses upon the way social relations embrace people who are seen as puppets enacted by the strings of sociostructural relationships," he sees structuralism as failing "...whenever some people appear to be literally stepping out of the 'structures' and inventing their praxis, which may eventually end up in creation of new structures." People are, in Bertaux's view, the product of the social structures in which they are embedded, but they are more than that in that, at least potentially, they have their own praxis.

5. This is a condensed summary. The argument in depth is presented in book-length form (Marshall 1980a) and an up-dated version will appear in Marshall (n.d.).

REFERENCES

Abu-Laban, Sharon M., and Baha Abu-Laban
1980 "Women and the aged as minority groups: a critique." In *Aging in Canada: Social Perspectives,* edited by Victor M. Marshall. Toronto: Fitzhenry and Whiteside.

Alexander, William
1978 "Wage labor, urbanization and culture change in the Marshall Islands." Ph.D. dissertation, New School for Social Research, New York.

Alkire, William H.
1965 *Lamotrek Atoll and Inter-Island Socioeconomic Ties.* Illinois Studies in Anthropology No. 5. Urbana: University of Illinois Press.

Anderson, Barbara G.
1972 "The process of deculturation – its dynamics among United States aged." *Anthropological Quarterly* 45:209-216.

Amoss, Pamela T.
1981 "Coast Salish elders." In *Other Ways of Growing Old,* edited by Pamela T. Amoss and Stevan Harrell. Stanford, California: Stanford University Press.

Amoss, Pamela T. and Stevan Harrell
1981a "Introduction: an anthropological perspective on aging." In *Other Ways of Growing Old,* edited by Pamela T. Amoss and Stevan Harrell. Stanford, California: Stanford University Press.

Amoss, Pamela T. and Stevan Harrell (eds.)
1981b *Other Ways of Growing Old: Anthropological Perspectives.* Stanford, California: Stanford University Press.

Arafat, Ibtihaj and Donald E. Allen
  1975   "Attitudes on abortion: legality versus religious and personal
          morality." *Free Inquiry in Creative Sociology* 3:1-15.

Bacdayan, Albert
  1977   "Mechanistic cooperation and sexual equality among the
          Western Bontoc." In *Sexual Stratification: A
          Cross-Cultural View,* edited by Alice Schlegel. New York:
          Columbia University Press.

Baltes, Paul B.
  1979   "Life-span developmental psychology: some converging
          observations on history and theory." In *Life-Span
          Development and Behavior, Volume 2,* edited by P. B.
          Baltes and O. G. Brim, Jr. New York: Academic Press.

Barnett, Rosalind C. and Grace K. Baruch
  1978   "Women in the middle years: a critique of research and
          theory." *Psychology of Women Quarterly* 3:187-197.

Barth, Fredrik
  1975   *Ritual and Knowledge Among the Baktaman of New
          Guinea.* Oslo: Universitestsforlaget. New Haven: Yale
          University Press.

Benedict, Ruth
  1953   "Continuities and discontinuities in cultural conditioning."
          In *Personality in Nature, Society and Culture,* edited by
          Clyde Kluckhohn and Henry A. Murray. Second edition.
          New York: Alfred A. Knopf.

Bengtson, Vern L., Jose B. Cuellar and Pauline K. Ragan
  1977   "Stratum contrasts and similarities in attitudes toward
          death." *Journal of Gerontology* 32:76-88.

Bengtson, V.L., N. Cutler, D. Mangen and V. Marshall
  n.d.   "Generations, cohorts, and relations between age groups." In
          The Handbook of Aging and the Social Sciences, edited by
          Victor W. Marshall. Second Edition. New York: Van
          Nostrand Reinhold. M.S. Forthcoming.

Beresford, H. Richard
　　1978　"Cognitive death: differential problems and legal overtones."
　　　　　In *Brain Death: Interrelated Medical and Social Issues,*
　　　　　edited by Julius Korein. Annals of the New York Academy
　　　　　of Science, Volume 315. New York.

Berezin, Martin A.
　　1978　"The elderly person." In *The Harvard Guide to Modern
　　　　　Psychiatry,* edited by A.M. Nicholi, Jr. Cambridge, Mass.:
　　　　　The Belknap Press of Harvard University.

Berger, Bennett M.
　　1984　"The resonance of the generation concept." In
　　　　　Intergenerational Relationships, edited by V.
　　　　　Garma-Homolova, F.M. Hoerning and D. Schaeffer
　　　　　Lewiston, New York and Toronto, Canada: C. J. Hogrefe,
　　　　　Inc.

Berger, Peter L.
　　1963　*Invitation to Sociology.* Garden City, New York: Doubleday
　　　　　Anchor.

Berger, Peter L. and Thomas Luckmann
　　1966　*The Social Construction of Reality.* Garden City, New
　　　　　York: Doubleday.

Bertaux, Daniel
　　1982　"The life course approach as a challenge to the social
　　　　　sciences." In *Aging and Life Course Transitions: An
　　　　　Interdisciplineary Perspective,* edited by Tamara K.
　　　　　Hareven and Kathleen J. Adams. New York and London:
　　　　　The Guilford Press.

Best, Elsdon
　　1905　"The lore of the Whare Kohanga." *Journal of the
　　　　　Polynesian Society* 14:205-215.

Bidou, P.
　　1982　"On incest and death." In *Between Belief and
　　　　　Transgression,* edited by M. Izard and P. Smith. Chicago:
　　　　　University of Chicago Press.

278

Blank, Arapera
    1980   "The role and status of Maori women." In *Women in New Zealand Society,* edited by P. Bunkle and B. Hughes. Auckland: George Allen and Unwin.

Blauner, Robert
    1966   "Death and Social Structure." *Psychiatry* 29:378-394.

Blythe, Ronald
    1979   *The View in Winter.* New York: Harcourt Brace Jovanovitch.

Borthwick, Mark
    1977   "Aging and social change on Lukunor Atoll, Micronesia." Ph.D. dissertation, University of Iowa, Iowa City.

Boserup, Esther
    1970   *Women's Role in Economic Development.* New York: St. Martin's Press.

Bott, Elizabeth
    1971   *Family and Social Network: Roles, Norms and External Relationships in Ordinary Urban Families.* New York: Free Press. Originally published 1957.

Breytspraak, Linda M.
    1975   "'Self-concept in adulthood': emergent issues and the response of the symbolic interactionist perspective." Paper presented at the 28th Annual Meeting of the Gerontological Society, Louisville, Kentucky. M.S.
    1984   *The Development of Self in Later Life.* Boston and Toronto: Little, Brown and Company.

Brookes, Barbara
    1981   "Housewives' depression: the debate over abortion and birth control in New Zealand in the 1930s." *New Zealand Journal of History 15:115-134.*

Brown, Judith K.
 1982 "Cross-cultural perspectives on middle-aged women." *Current Anthropology* 23:143-156.

Brown, Penelope
 1980 "How and why are women more polite: some evidence from a Mayan community." In *Women and Language in Literature and Society,* edited by Sally McConnell-Ginet, Ruth Borker and Nelly Furman. New York: Praeger.

Bryan, Edwin H., Jr.
 1971 *Guide to Place Names in the Trust Territory of the Pacific Islands.* Honolulu, Hawaii: Pacific Scientific Information Center, Bernice P. Bishop Museum.

Buck, Peter H. (Te Rangi Hiroa)
 1934 *Mangaian Society.* Bernice P. Bishop Museum Bulletin 122. Honolulu: B.P. Bishop Museum.

Bunkle, Phillida
 1980 "The origins of the women's movement in New Zealand: The Women's Christian Temperance Union, 1885-1895." In *Women in New Zealand Society,* edited by Phillida Bunkle and Beryl Hughes. Auckland: George Allen and Unwin.

Burridge, K.O.L.
 1975 "The Melanesian Manager." In *Studies in Social Anthropology,* edited by J. Beatie and G. Lienhardt. Oxford: Clarendon Press.

Burrows, Edwin Grant and Melford E. Spiro
 1953 *An Atoll Culture, Ethnography of Ifaluk in the Central Carolines.* Behavior Science Monographs. New Haven: HRAF Press.

Cain, Leonard D., Jr.
 1964 "Life course and social structure." In *Handbook of Modern Sociology,* edited by Robert E. L. Faris. Chicago: Rand McNally.
 1967 "Age status and generational phenomena: the new old people in contemporary America." *The Gerontologist* 7:83-92.

Calvino, I.
1974   *Invisible Cities.* London: Paladin.

Cannon, Walter B.
1942   "Voodoo death." *American Anthropologist* 44:169-181. (Reprinted in *Reader in Comparative Religion,* edited by W.A. Lessa and Evon Z. Vogt. New York: Harper and Row, 1958.)

Capron, Alexander M.
1978   "Legal definition of death." In *Brain Death: Interrelated Medical and Social Issues,* edited by Julius Korein. Annals of the New York Academy of Science, Volume 315. New York.

Carucci, Laurence Marshall
1980   "The renewal of life: a ritual encounter in the Marshall Islands." Ph.D. dissertation, The University of Chicago, Chicago.

Cassell, Joan
1977   *A Group Called Women: Sisterhood and Symbolism in the Feminist Movement.* New York: David McKay Company.

Caughey, John L.
1977   *Fáánakkar: Cultural Values in a Micronesian Society.* University of Pennsylvania Publications in Anthropology, no. 2. Philadelphia: Department of Anthropology, University of Pennsylvania.

Chowning, Ann
1971   "Ceremonies, shell-money and culture among the Kove." *Expedition* 15:2-8.
1978   "Changes in West New Britain Trading Systems in the twentieth century.: *Mankind* 11:296-307.
1980   "Culture and biology among the Sengseng of New Britain." *The Journal of the Polynesian Society* 89:7-31.
1981   "Family fertility decisions: the Kove." MS.

Chowning, Ann and Jane Goodale
   1971   "The contaminating women." Paper presented at American
          Anthropological Association Meeting, Washington, D.C.
          MS.

Cincotta, Joseph
   1979   "The quality of life: from Roe to Quinlan and beyond."
          Catholic Lawyer 25:13-31.

Clark, Margaret
   1967   "The anthropology of aging: a new area for studies of
          culture and personality." *Gerontologist* 7:55-64.
   1972   "Cultural values and dependency in later life." In *Aging
          and Modernization,* edited by Donald Cowgill and Lowell
          Holmes. New York: Appleton-Century-Crofts.

Clark, Margaret and Barbara Anderson
   1967   *Culture and Aging: An Anthropological Study of Older
          Americans.* Springfield, Illinois: Charles Thomas.

Clarke, William
   1971   *Place and People.* Berkeley: University of California Press.

Cool, Linda and Justine McCabe
   1983   "The 'scheming hag' and the 'dear old thing': the
          anthropology of aging women." In *Growing Old in Different
          Societies. Cross-Cultural Perspectives,* edited by Jay
          Sokolovsky. Belmont, California: Wadsworth Publishing
          Company.

Counts, David
   1976-77 "The good death in Kaliai: preparation for death in western
          New Britain." *Omega* 7:367-372. (Reprinted in *Death and
          Dying: Views from Many Cultures,* edited by R. Kalish.
          Farmingdale, New York: Baywood Publishing Co. 1979.)

Counts, David and Dorothy Ayers Counts
   1974   "The Kaliai *Lupunga:* disputing in the public forum." In
          *Contention and Dispute: Aspects of Social Control in
          Melanesia,* edited by A.L. Epstein. Canberra: Australian
          National University Press.
   1983-84 "Aspects of dying in northwest New Britain." In *Special

Section: Dying in Cross Cultural Perspective, edited by Peter H. Stephenson. *Omega* 14:101-113.

Counts, Dorothy Ayers
1980a "Akro and Gagandewa: A Melanesian myth." *Journal of the Polynesian Society* 89:33-65.
1980b "Fighting back is not the way: suicide and the women of Kaliai." *American Ethnologist* 7:332-351.
1983 "Near-death and out-of-body experiences in a Melanesian society." *Anabiosis 3:115-135.*
1984 "Infant care and feeding in Kaliai, West New Britain." *Ecology of Food and Nutrition* 15:49-59.

Cowgill, Donald O.
1972 "A theory of aging in cross-cultural perspective." In *Aging and Modernization,* edited by Donald Cowgill and Lowell Holmes. New York: Appleton-Century-Crofts.

Cowgill, Donald O. and Lowell D. Holmes (eds.)
1972 *Aging and Modernization* New York: Appleton Century Crofts.

Cumming, Elaine and William E. Henry
1961 *Growing Old: The Process of Disengagement.* New York: Basic Books.

Cutler, R.G.
1975 "Evolution of human longevity...." *Proceedings of the National Academy of Science* 72:4664-4668.

Davis, Dona Lee
1983 *Blood and Nerves. An Ethnographic Focus on Menopause.* Social and Economic Studies No. 28. St. Johns, Newfoundland: Institute of Social and Economic Research, Memorial University.

Deacon, A. Bernard
1934 *Malekula: A Vanishing People of the New Hebrides* London: George Routledge and Sons, Ltd.

De Beauvoir, Simone
1952   *The Second Sex.* New York: Bantam Books

De Coppet, D.
1981   "The life-giving death." In *Mortality and Immortality,* edited by S. Humphreys and H. King. London: Academic Press.

Diggory, J., and D. Rothman
1961   "Values Destroyed by Death." *Journal of Abnormal and Social Psychology* 63:205-210.

Dominy, Michèle D.
1983   "Gender conceptions and political strategies in New Zealand women's networks." Ph.D. dissertation, Cornell University, Ithaca, New York.

Dougherty, Molly C.
1978   "An anthropological perspective on aging and women in the middle years." In *The Anthropology of Health,* edited by Eleanor E. Bauwens. St. Louis: C.V. Mosby Company.

Douglas, Mary
1975   "Pollution." In *Implicit Meanings,* edited by Mary Douglas. London: Routledge and Keegan Paul.

Dowd, James J.
1980   *Stratification Among the Aged.* Monterey, California: Brooks/Cole.

DuBois, Ellen
1977   "The radicalism of the woman suffrage movement: notes toward the reconstruction of nineteenth century feminism." *Feminist Studies* 3:63-71.

Dumont, Richard G. and Dennis C. Foss
1972   *The American View of Death: Acceptance or Denial?* Cambridge, Mass.: Schenkman.

DuToit, Brian M.
1975   *Akuna: A New Guinea Community.* Rotterdam: A A Balkema.

Edgerton, Robert B.
1966   "Conceptions of psychosis in four East African societies." *American Anthropologist* 68:408-425. (Reprinted in *Culture, Disease and Healing: Studies in Medical Anthropology,* edited by David Landy. New York: Macmillan. 1977).

Eisenstadt, Shmuel
1974   "Introduction." In *The Predicament of Homecoming: Cultural and Social Life of North African Immigrants in Israel,* edited by Shlomo Deshen and Moshe Shokeid. Ithaca, New York: Cornell University Press.

Elbert, Samuel H.
1972   *Puluwat Dictionary.* Pacific Linguistics, Series C, no. 24. Canberra: Department of Linguistics, Australian National University.

Elder, Glen H., Jr.
1975   "Age differentiation and the life course." *Annual Review of Sociology* 1:165-190.

Epstein, A.L.
1979   *"Tambu:* the shell-money of the Tolai." In *Fantasy and Symbol,* edited by R. Hook. London: Academic Press.

Errington, Frederick
1974   *Karavar.* Ithaca: Cornell University Press.

Evans-Pritchard, E.E.
1937   *Witchcraft, Oracles and Magic Among the Azande.* Oxford: Oxford University Press.

Eyde, D.B.
1970   "Cultural correlates of warfare among the Asmat of south-west New Guinea." Ph.D. dissertation, Yale University.

Faithorn, E.
    1975   "The concept of pollution among the Kafe of the Papua
            New Guinea Highlands." In *Toward an Anthropology of
            Women,* edited by R.R. Reiter. New York and London:
            Monthly Review Press.

Fallers, Lloyd and Margaret Fallers
    1976   "Sex roles in Edremit." In *Mediterranean Family
            Structures,* edited by J. Peristiany. New York: Cambridge
            University Press.

Fennell, Valeria
    1981   "Friendship and kinship in older women's organizations:
            Curlew Point, 1973." In *Dimensions: Aging, Culture and
            Health,* edited by Christine Fry. New York: J.F. Bergin.

Fischer, John L.
    1949   "Western field trip notes." MS. Archives of the Bernice P.
            Bishop Museum, Honolulu.

Foner, Anne, and David Kertzer
    1978   "Transitions over the life course: lessons from age-set
            societies." *American Journal of Sociology* 83:1081-1104.

Forster, J. and P.D.K. Ramsey
    1970   "Migration, education, and occupation." In *Social Process
            in New Zealand,* edited by J. Forster. Auckland: Longman
            Paul.

Fortes, Meyer
    1958   "Introduction." In *The Developmental Cycle in Domestic
            Groups,* edited by J.R. Goody. Cambridge England:
            Cambridge University Press.

Fortune, Reo
    1935   *Manus Religion.* Lincoln: University of Nebraska Press.
            (Reprinted 1965.)

Foster, George, et al. (eds.)
  1979   *Long-Term Field Research in Social Anthropology.* New York : Academic Press.

Fox, Renee C.
  1981   "The sting of death in American society." *Social Services Review* 55:42-59.

Frake, C.O.
  1961   "The diagnosis of disease among the Subanun of Mindanao." *American Anthropologist* 63:113-132.

Frankel, Stephen
  1980   "'I am dying of man': the pathology of pollution." *Culture, Medicine and Psychiatry* 4:95-117.

Freedman, Estelle
  1979   "Separatism as strategy: female institution building and American feminism, 1870-1930." *Feminist Studies* 5:512-529.

Fries, J.F.
  1980   "Aging, natural death and the compression of morbidity." *The New England Journal of Medicine* 303:130-135.

Fries, J.F. and L. Crapo
  1981   *Vitality and Aging: Implications of the Rectangular Curve.* San Francisco: W.H. Freeman.

Fry, Christine (ed.)
  1976   "The ages of adulthood: a question of numbers." *Journal of Gerontology* 31:170-177.
  1980a *Aging in Culture and Society: Comparative Viewpoints and Strategies.* New York: Praeger
  1980b "Cultural dimensions of age: a multidimensional scaling analysis." In *Aging in Culture and Society,* edited by Christine L. Fry and Contributors. New York: J.F. Bergin.
  1981a *Dimensions: Aging, Culture and Health.* New York: J.F. Bergin.
  1981b "Introduction: anthropology and dimensions of aging." in *Dimensions: Aging, Culture, and Health,* edited by Christine L. Fry and Contributors. New York: Praeger.

Garn, Jake, et. al.
  1981   "Right to life of the unborn." *Congressional Record* (Daily Edition) 127(12):S567-S578.

Geertz, Clifford
  1983   *Local Knowledge: Further Essays in Interpretive Anthropology.* New York: Basic Books.

Gell, Alfred
  1975   *Metamorphosis of the Cassowaries: Umeda Society, Language and Ritual.* New Jersey: Humanities Press.

Glascock, Anthony P., and Susan L. Feinman
  1981   "Social asset or social burden: treatment of the aged in nonindustrialized societies." In *Dimensions: Aging, Culture, and Health,* edited by Christine L. Fry and Contributors. New York: Praeger.

Goffman, Erving
  1959   *The Presentation of Self in Everyday Life.* Garden City, New York: Anchor Books.

Goodale, Jane
  1980   "Gender, sexuality and marriage: a Kaulong model of nature and culture." In *Nature, Culture and Gender,* edited by C. MacCormack and M. Strathern. Cambridge: Cambridge University Press.
  1981   "Siblings as spouse: the reproduction and replacement of Kaulong society." In *Siblingship in Oceania: Studies in the Meaning of Kin Relations,* edited by M. Marshall. ASAO Monograph 8. Ann Arbor: University of Michigan Press.
  1983   "Pig's teeth and skull cycles: both sides of the face of humanity." Paper presented at 12th annual meeting of the ASAO, New Harmony, Indiana, March 12, 1983. MS.

Goodenough, Ward H.
  1951   *Property, Kin, and Community on Truk.* Yale University Publications in Anthropology, no. 46. New Haven: Yale University Press.

Gordon, R.
1978 *Dying and Creating: A Search for Meaning.* The Society of Analytic Psychology Ltd., London.

Gubrium, Jaber F., and D. R. Buckholdt
1977 *Toward Maturity.* San Francisco: Jossey-Bass.

Guillemard, Anne-Marie
1980 *La vieillesse et l'état.* Paris: Presses Universitaires de France.

Guillemard, Anne-Marie (ed.)
1983 *Old Age and the Welfare State.* Beverly Hills and London: Sage.

Gutmann, David
1975 "Parenthood: A key to the comparative psychology of the life cycle." In *Life-Span Development Psychology: Normative Life Crises,* edited by Nancy Datan and L. Ginsberg. New York: Academic Press.

Gutmann, David, J. Grunes, and B. Griffin
1980 "The clinical psychology of later life: developmental paradigms." In *Transitions of Aging,* edited by Nancy Datan and Nancy Lohman. New York: Academic Press.

Hagestad, Gunhild O.
1982 "Life-phase analysis." In *Research Instruments in Social Gerontology, Volume 1, Clinical and Social Psychology,* edited by David J. Mangen and Warren A. Peterson. Minneapolis: University of Minnesota Press.

Hammond, Dorothy and Alta Jablow
1973 *Women: Their Economic Role in Traditional Societies.* Reading, Massachusetts: Addison Wesley Publishing Company.

Hanson, F. Allan
1982 "Female pollution in Polynesia?" *Journal of the Polynesian Society* 91:335-381.

Hauerwas, Stanley
1978 "Religious concepts of brain death and associated problems." In *Brain Death: Interrelated Medical and Social Issues*, edited by Julius Korein. Annals of the New York Academy of Sciences, Volume 315. New York.

Health Care Proposal
1980 "A health care proposal in response to P.L. 96-205 and RFP #14-01-0001-80-R-75." Prepared by Loma Linda University School of Health and submitted to the U.S. Department of the Interior. On file at the new governmental offices of the Republic of the Marshall Islands, Majuro, Marshall Islands.

Heider, Karl
1970 *The Dugum Dani: A Papuan Culture in the Highlands of West New Guinea*. Viking Fund Publications in Anthropology, no. 49. New York: Wenner Gren Foundation for Anthropological Research.

Hendricks, Jon (ed.)
1980 *In the Country of the Old*. Farmingdale, N.Y.: Baywood Publishing Co.

Herdt, Gilbert
1981 *Guardians of the Flutes: Idioms of Masculinity*. New York: McGraw Hill.

Hertz, Robert
1960 *Death and the Right Hand*. Translation of the 1907 essay by Rodney and Claudia Needham. Aberdeen: Cohen and West.

Heuer, Berys
1969 "Maori women in traditional family and tribal life." *Journal of the Polynesian Society* 78:448-494.

Hocart, Arthur Maurice
1952 *The Northern States of Fiji*. Royal Anthropological Institute of Great Britain and Ireland, Occasional Publication no. 11. London: Royal Anthropological Institute.

Hochschild, Arlie R.
1973   *The   Unexpected   Community.*   Englewood   Cliffs:
        Prentice-Hall.
1975   "Disengagement theory: a critique and proposal." *American
        Sociological Review* 40:553-569.

Hoffer, Carol
1974   "Madame Yoko: Ruler of the Kpa Mende confederacy." In
        Woman, Culture and Society, edited by Michelle Rosaldo
        and Louise Lamphere. Stanford: Stanford University Press.

Holmes, Lowell
1980   "Anthropology and age: an assessment." In *Aging in Culture
        and Society: Comparative Viewpoints and Strategies,* edited
        by Christine L. Fry and Contributors. New York: J.F.
        Bergin.

Homans, George C.
1941   "Anxiety and ritual: the theories of Malinowski and
        Radcliffe-Brown." *American Anthropologist* 43:164-172.
        (Reprinted in *Reader in Comparative Religion: An
        Anthropological Approach,* edited by W. Lessa and E. Vogt.
        New York: Harper and Row. 1965.)

Hooper, Antony
1970   "Adoption in the Society Islands." In *Adoption in Eastern
        Oceania,* edited by Vern Carroll. ASAO Monograph no. 1.
        Honolulu: University of Hawaii Press.

Huber, Peter S.
1979   "Death and society among the Anggor of New Guinea." In
        Death and Dying: Views From Many Cultures, edited by
        Richard Kalish. Farmingdale, N.Y.: Baywood Publishing
        Co.

Humphreys, S.C.
1981   "Death and time." In *Mortality and Immortality: The
        Anthropology and Archaeology of Death,* edited by S.C.
        Humphreys and Helen King. Academic Press. London.

Huntington, Richard and Peter Metcalf
  1979   *Celebrations of Death: The Anthropology of Mortuary Ritual.* New York: Cambridge University Press.

Hyndman, David C.
  1976   "Introduction to Wopkaimin subsistence ecology." Paper delivered to Australian and New Zealand Association for the Advancement of Science (ANZAAS), Melbourne.

Jackson, C.O.
  1977   "Death shall have no dominion: the passing of the world of the dead in America." *Omega* 8:195-203.

Japan, Nanyo-cho (South Seas Bureau)
  1931   *Nanyo Gunto Tosei Chosa-sho, Showa 5 nen (A Summary of Conditions in the Japanese Mandated Territories, 1930).* 4 vols. Palau: Nanyo-cho.

Jeffers, F., C. Nichols and C. Eisdorfer
  1961   "Attitudes of older persons toward death: a preliminary study." *Journal of Gerontology* 16:53-56.

Johnson, P.L.
  1981   "When dying is better than living: female suicide among the Gaina of Papua New Guinea." *Ethnology* 20:325-334.

Jorgensen, D.
  1981a   "Taro and arrows." Ph.D. dissertation, University of British Columbia.
  1981b   "Life on the fringe: history and society in Telefolmin." In *The Plight of Peripheral People in Papua New Guinea,* Volume 1, edited by R. Gordon. *Cultural Survival,* Occasional Paper no. 7.

Jury, Mark and Dan Jury
  1976   *Gramp.* New York: Grossman Publishers.

Kalish, Richard A.
  1966   "A continuum of subjectively perceived death." *Gerontologist* 6:73-76.

Kalish, Richard A., and A.I. Johnson
1972 "Value similarities and differences in three generations of women." *Journal of Marriage and the Family* 34:49-54.

Kalish, Richard A., and David K. Reynolds
1976 *Death and Ethnicity: A Psychocultural Study.* Los Angeles: The University of Southern California Press.

Kart, Cary S.
1981 "In the matter of Earle Spring: some thoughts on one court's approach to senility." *Gerontologist* 21:417-423

Keene, Barry
1978 "The Natural Death Act: a well-baby check-up on its first birthday." In *Brain Death: Interrelated Medical and Social Issues,* edited by Julius Korein. Annals of the New York Academy of Science, Volume 315. New York.

Keith, Jennie
1980 "The best is yet to be: toward an anthropology of age." In *Annual Review of Anthropology,* edited by Bernard J. Siegel, Alan R. Beals, and Stephen Tyler, Volume 9. Palo Alto, CA: Annual Reviews Inc.
1981 "The 'Back to Anthropology' movement in gerontology." In *Dimensions: Aging, Culture, and Health,* edited by Christine L. Fry and Contributors. New York: Praeger.
1982 *Old People as People.* Boston: Little, Brown and Company.
1983 "Age and informal interaction." In *Growing Old in Different Societies: Cross Cultural Perspectives,* edited by Jay Sokolovsky. Belmont, CA: Wadsworth.

Keith, Jennie, and David I. Kertzer
1984 "Introduction." In *Age and Anthropological Theory,* edited by David I. Kertzer and Jennie Keith. Ithaca and London: Cornell University Press.

Keller, J.W., D. Sherry and C. Piotrowski
1984 "Perspectives on death: a developmental study." *The Journal of Psychology* 116:137-142.

Kelly, Raymond C.
1976   "Witchcraft and sexual relations: an exploration in the social and semantic implications of the structure of belief." In *Man and Woman in the New Guinea Highlands,* edited by Paula Brown and Georginda Buchbinder. Special publication of the American Anthropological Association, Volume 8.

Kernot, B.J.
1975   "Maori strategies: ethnic politics in New Zealand." In *New Zealand politics: a reader.* edited by S. Levine. Melbourne: Cheshire.
1982   Personal communication to K. Sinclair.

Kerns, Virginia
1980   "Aging and mutual support relations among the Black Carib." In *Aging in Culture and Society,* edited by Christine Fry. New York: Praeger.
1983   *Women and the Ancestors. Black Carib Kinship and Ritual.* Urbana: University of Illinois Press.
1984   "Sexuality and social control among the Garifuna (Belize)." In *In Her Prime: Anthropological Perspectives on Middle-Aged Women,* edited by Judith Brown and Virginia Kerns. South Hadley, MA: J.F. Bergin.

Kessler, Suzanne J. and Wendy McKenna
1978   *Gender: An Ethnomethodological Approach.* New York: Wiley.

King, Michael
1984   *Maori* Auckland: Heinemann.

King, Patricia A.
1979   "The juridical status of the fetus: a proposal for legal protection of the unborn." *Michigan Law Review* 77:1647-1687.

Kirkpatrick, John
1981a   "Appeals for 'unity' in Marquesan local politics." *Journal of the Polynesian Society* 90:439-464.
1981b   "Meanings of siblingship in Marquesan Society." In *Siblingship in Oceania,* edited by Mac Marshall. ASAO Monograph no. 8. Ann Arbor: University of Michigan Press.

1983   *The Marquesan Notion of the Person.* Ann Arbor: UMI Research Press.

n.d.   "Some Marquesan Understandings of Action and Identity." In *Person, Self and Experience: Exploring Pacific Ethno-psychologies,* edited by Geoffrey M. White and John Kirkpatrick. Berkeley: University of California Press. MS. in press.

Kiste, Robert C. and Michael A. Rynkiewich
1976   "Incest and exogamy: a comparative study of two Marshall Islands populations." *Journal of the Polynesian Society* 85:209-225.

Klass, Dennis
1981-82 "Elisabeth Kubler-Ross and the tradition of the private sphere: an analysis of symbols." *Omega* 12:241-267.

Kleemeir, Robert (ed.)
1961   *Aging and Leisure.* New York: Oxford University Press.

Korein, Julius (ed.)
1978a   *Brain Death: Interrelated Medical and Social Issues.* Annual of the New York Academy of Sciences, Volume 315. New York.
1978b   "Preface." In *Brain Death: Interrelated Medical and Social Issues,* edited by Julius Korein. Annals of the New York Academy of Sciences, Volume 315. New York.

Krämer, Augustin
1935   *Inseln um Truk.* Ergebnisse der Südsee Expedition 1908-1910. II.B.6, Subvolume 1. G. Thilenius, ed. Hamburg: Friederichsen, de Gruyter and Co.

Kubler-Ross, Elisabeth
1969   *On Death and Dying.* New York: Macmillan.

La Fontaine, J.S.
1978   "Introduction." In *Sex and Age as Principles of Social Differentiation,* edited by J. S. La Fontaine. London: Academic Press.

Lane, R.B.
1965 "The Melanesians of South Pentecost, New Hebrides." In
Gods, Ghosts and Men in Melanesia, edited by Peter
Lawrence and M.J. Meggitt. Melbourne: Oxford University
Press.

Lavondès, Henri
1972 "Problèmes sociolinguistiques et alphabétisation en Polynésie
Française." *Cahiers O.R.S.T.O.M.* Serie Sciences Humaines
9:49-61.

Lawrence, Peter
1964 *Road Belong Cargo.* Manchester: Manchester University
Press.

Leach, Edmund R.
1961 *Rethinking Anthropology.* London: The Athlone Press.

Leacock, Eleanor
1978 "Women's status in egalitarian society: implications for
social evolution." *Current Anthropology* 19:247-275.

Leenhardt, Maurice
1979 *Do Kamo: Person and Myth in the Melanesian World.*
Translated by Basia Milles Gulati. First published in French
in 1947. Chicago: University of Chicago Press.

Leis, Nancy
1974 "Women in groups: Ijaw women's associations." In *Woman,
Culture and Society,* edited by Michelle Rosaldo and
Louise Lamphere. Stanford: Stanford University Press.

Lepowsky, Maria
1981 "Fruit of the motherland: gender and exchange on
Vanatinai, Papua New Guinea." Ph.D. dissertation,
University of California, Berkeley.
1983 "Sudest Island and the Louisiade Archipelago in Massim
exchange." In *The Kula: New Perspectives on Massim
Exchange,* edited by Jerry Leach and Edmund Leach.
Cambridge: Cambridge University Press.
1984a "Death and exchange: mortuary ritual on Vanatinai (Sudest
Island)." MS.

1984b   "Gender and ideology in an egalitarian society." MS.

Lessa, William A.
1950   *The Ethnography of Ulithi Atoll.* CIMA Report, no. 28. Washington, D.C.: Pacific Science Board.

Lessa, William A. and Evon Vogt (eds.)
1965   *Reader in Comparative Religion: An Anthropological Approach.* New York: Harper and Row.

Le Vine, Robert
1965   "Intergenerational tensions and extended family structures in Africa." In *Social Structure and the Family: Generational Relations,* edited by Ethel Shanas and Gordon Streib. Englewood Cliffs, New Jersey: Prentice Hall

Lewis, Gilbert
1975   *Knowledge of Illness in a Sepik Society: A Study of the Gnau, New Guinea.* London School of Economics Monographs in Social Anthropology no. 52. University of London: The Athlone Press.
1980   *Day of Shining Red.* Cambridge: Cambridge University Press.

Lindenbaum, Shirley
1979   *Kuru Sorcery: Disease and Danger in the New Guinea Highlands.* Palo Alto, CA: Mayfield Publishing Co.

Linton, Ralph
1940   "A neglected aspect of social organization." *American Journal of Sociology* 45:870-886.
1942   "Age and sex categories." *American Sociological Review* 7:589-603.

Lofland, Lyn N.
1978   *The Craft of Dying: The Modern Face of Death.* Beverly Hills, California and London: Sage Publications.

Lowie, Robert
1920   *Primitive Society.* London: George Routledge and Sons. (Reprinted New York: Harper Torchbooks, 1961.)

MacCormack, Carol
1980   "Introduction." In *Nature, Culture and Gender,* edited by Carol MacCormack and Marilyn Strathern. New York: Cambridge University Press.

MacCormack, Carol and Marilyn Strathern
1980   *Nature, Culture and Gender.* New York: Cambridge University Press.

MacPherson, Cluny
1977   "Polynesians in New Zealand: an emerging eth class?" In *Social Class in New Zealand,* edited by D. Pitt. Auckland: Longman Paul.

Maddox, George L.
1965   "Fact and artifact: evidence bearing on disengagement theory." *Human Development* 8:117-130.
1970   "Themes and issues in sociological theories of human aging." *Human Development* 13:17-27.

Malinowski, Bronislaw
1916   "Baloma: the spirits of the dead in the Trobriand Islands." *The Journal of the Royal Anthropological Institute of Great Britain and Ireland* 46:353-430. (Reprinted in B. Malinowski, *Magic, Science and Religion, and Other Essays.* New York: The Free Press, 1948. Garden City, N.J.: Doubleday Anchor Books, 1954.)
1948   *Magic, Science and Religions, and Other Essays.* New York: The Free Press.

Marshall, Mac
1977   "The nature of nurture." *American Ethnologist* 4:643-662.
1981a   "Introduction: approaches to siblingship in Oceania." In *Siblingship in Oceania,* edited by Mac Marshall. ASAO Monograph no. 8. Ann Arbor: University of Michigan Press.
1981b   "Sibling sets as building blocks in Greater Trukese Society." In *Siblingship in Oceania,* edited by Mac Marshall. ASAO Monograph no. 8. Ann Arbor: University of Michigan Press.

Marshall, Victor W.

1975 "Socialization for impending death in a retirement village." *American Journal of Sociology* 80:1124-1144.

1978-79 "No exit: a symbolic interactionist perspective on aging." *International Journal of Aging and Human Development* 9:345-358.

1980a *Last Chapters: A Sociology of Aging and Dying.* Monterey, California: Brooks/Cole.

1980b "No exit: an interpretive perspective on aging." In *Aging in Canada: Social Perspectives,* edited by Victor W. Marshall. Toronto: Fitzhenry and Whiteside.

1981 "State of the art lecture: the sociology of aging." In *Canadian Gerontological Collection III,* edited by John Crawford. Winnipeg: Canadian Association on Gerontology.

1982 "Death and dying." In *Research Instruments in Social Gerontology, Volume 1, Clinical and Social Psychology,* edited by David J. Mangen and Warren A. Peterson. Minneapolis: University of Minnesota Press.

1983 "Generations, age groups and cohorts: conceptual distinctions." *Canadian Journal on Aging* 2:51-62.

1984 "Tendencies in generational research: from the generation to the cohort and back to the generation." In *Intergenerational Relationships,* edited by V. Garms-Homolova, E.M. Hoerning and D. Schaeffer. Lewiston, New York and Toronto, Canada: C.J. Hogrefe, Inc.

n.d. "Individual and societal problematics of aging and dying." In *Later Life: A Microsociology,* edited by V. W. Marshall and A. Harris. Norwood, New Jersey: Ablex. M.S. Forthcoming.

Matthews, Sarah H.

1979 *The Social World of Older Women: Management of Self-Identity.* Beverly Hills and London: Sage.

Maxwell, Robert, and Philip Silverman

1970 "Information and esteem." *Aging and Human Development* 1:361-392.

Mazess, R.B. and S.H. Forman
    1978   "Longevity and age exaggeration in Vilcambamba, Ecuador." *Journal of Gerontology* 34:94-98.

McKellin, William
    1982   "Social stratification and knowledge: the case of rural public employees." In *Elites in Oceania,* edited by M. Howard and P. Lawrence. Special issue of *Oceania* 53:67-81.
    1983   "The transformation of substance: Managalase concepts of reproduction and congenital illness." Paper presented at 12th annual meeting of the ASAO, New Harmony, Indiana, March, 1983.
    1984   "Putting down roots: information in the language of Managalase exchange." In *Dangerous Words: Language and Politics in the Pacific,* edited by D. Brenneis and F. Meyers. New York: New York University Press.

Mead, Margaret
    1928   *Coming of Age in Samoa.* New York: W. Morrow and Company.

Meggitt, M.J.
    1964   "Male-Female Relations in the Highlands of Australian New Guinea." In *New Guinea: The Central Highlands,* edited by James B. Watson. Special publication *American Anthropologist* 66 (pt. 2, no. 4):204-224.

Meigs, Anna S.
    1976   "Male pregnancy and the reduction of sexual opposition in a New Guinea Highlands Society." *Ethnology* 15:393-407.
    1978   "A Papuan perspective on pollution." Man (n.s.) 13:304-318.
    1983   *Food, Sex, and Pollution: A New Guinea Religion.* Baltimore MD.: Rutgers University Press.

Metcalf, Peter
    1982   *A Borneo Journey Into Death: Berawan Eschatology From its Rituals.* Philadelphia: University of Pennsylvania Press.

Metge, A. Joan
   1976   *The Maoris of New Zealand.* London: Routledge and Kegan
           Paul.

Mol, J. J.
   1964   "Race relations with special reference to New Zealand: a
           theoretical discussion." *Journal of the Polynesian Society*
           73:375-381.

Moody, Raymond A.
   1975   *Life after Life.* New York: Bantam Books.

Moore, Sally Falk
   1978   "Old age in a life-term social arena: some Chagga of
           Kilimanjaro in 1974." In *Life's Career – Aging: Cultural
           Variations on Growing Old,* edited by A. Simic and B.
           Myerhoff. Beverly Hills, CA: Sage Publications.

Morison, Robert
   1977   "Death: process or event?" In *Ethical Issues in Death and
           Dying,* edited by R.F. Weir. New York: Columbia
           University Press. Originally published in *Science* 173
           (August 20, 1971):694-698.

Myerhoff, Barbara
   1978   *Number Our Days.* New York: Dutton.

Nason, James D.
   1981   "Respected elder or old person: aging in a Micronesian
           community." In *Other Ways of Growing Old,* edited by
           Pamela T. Amoss and Stevan Harrell. Stanford, CA:
           Stanford University Press.

National Council of Women of New Zealand
   1978   *Handbook.* Wellington: National Council of Women of New
           Zealand.
   1979a   Christchurch Branch Agenda, April 17, 1979.
   1979b   Christchurch Branch Agenda, June 19, 1979.

Nelson, Cynthia
    1974   "Public and private politics: women in the Middle Eastern world." *American Ethnologist* 1:551-563.

Neugarten, Bernice L.
    1968   *Middle Age and Aging.* Chicago: University of Chicago Press.
    1970   "Dynamics of transition of middle age to old age." *Journal of Geriatric Psychiatry* 4:71-87.

Neugarten, Bernice L. (ed.)
    1982   *Age or Need? Public Policies for Older People.* Beverly Hills, London and New Delhi: Sage.

Neugarten, Bernice L, and Nancy Datan
    1973   "Sociological perspectives on the life cycle." In *Life-Span Developmental Psychology: Personality and Socialization,* edited by P.B. Baltes and K.W. Schaie. New York: Academic Press.

Neugarten, Bernice L., and Gunhild O. Hagestad
    1976   "Age and the life course." In *Handbook of Aging and the Social Sciences,* edited by Ethel Shanas and Robert Binstock. New York: Van Nostrand and Reinhold.

Neugarten, Bernice L., J. Moore, and J. Lowe
    1965   "Age norms, age constraints, and adult socialization." *American Journal of Sociology* 70:710-717.

Nydegger, Corinne N. (ed.)
    1983   *Anthropological Approaches to Aging Research: Applications to Modern Societies.* Special issue of *Research on Aging* 5 (no. 4).

Okonjo, Kamene
    1976   "The dual sex political system in operation: Igbo women and community politics in Mid-western Nigeria." In *Women in Africa: Studies in Social and Economic Change,* edited by N. Hafkin and E. Bay. Stanford: Stanford University Press.

Ong, W.J.
1977   *Interfaces of the Word.* Ithaca: Cornell University Press.

Ortner, Sherry B. and Harriet Whitehead
1981   "Introduction: accounting for sexual meanings." In *Sexual Meanings: The Cultural Construction of Gender and Sexuality,* edited by Sherry B. Ortner and Harriet Whitehead. Cambridge, England: Cambridge University Press.

Owen, Greg, Robert Fulton and Eric Markusen
1978   "Death at a distance: a study of family survivors." Paper presented at the 42nd Annual Meeting of the Midwest Sociological Society, Omaha, Nebraska. M.S.

Oxford English Dictionary
1971   *The Compact Edition of the Oxford English Dictionary.* New York: Oxford University Press.

Palmore, Erdman
1968   "The effects of aging on activities and attitudes." *The Gerontologist* 8:259-263.
1983   "Cross-cultural research: state of the art." *Research on Aging* 5:45-57.

Panoff, Michel
1968   "The notion of double-self among the Maenge." *Journal of the Polynesian Society* 77:275-295.

Parsons, Talcott, and Victor Lidz
1967   "Death in American society." In *Essays in Self-Destruction,* edited by E. M. Shneidman. New York: Random House.

Pollock, O.
1980   "Shadow of death over aging: Editorial." *Science* 207:1419.

Poole, Fitz John Porter
1981   "Transforming 'natural' woman: female ritual leaders and gender ideology among Bimin-Kuskusmin." In *Sexual Meanings: The Cultural Construction of Gender,* edited by S. Ortner and H. Whitehead. Cambridge: Cambridge

University Press.

Powdermaker, Hortense
1971   *Life in Lesu: The Study of a Melanesian Society in New Ireland.* W.W. Norton and Company, Inc.

President's Commission for the Study of Ethical Problems
1980   "When is a person dead?" *Science* 209:4457

Press, Irwin, and Michael McKool
1972   "Social structure and status of the aged." *Aging and Human Development* 3:297-302.

Quadango, Jill S.
1982   *Aging in Early Industrial Society: Work, Family, and Social Policy in Nineteenth-Century England.* New York: Academic Press.

Radcliffe-Brown, A. R.
1965   "Taboo." In *Reader in Comparative Religion: An Anthropological Approach,* edited by W. A. Lessa and E. Z. Vogt. Second Edition. New York: Harper and Row. Originally published in 1939.

Rappaport, Roy
1968   *Pigs for the Ancestors.* New Haven: Yale University Press.

Riegelhaupt, Joyce F.
1967   "Salioio women: an analysis of formal and informal politics and economic roles of Portuguese peasant women." *Anthropological Quarterly* 40:109-123.

Riley, John W., Jr.
1970   "What people think about death." In *The Dying Patient,* edited by O.G. Brim, Jr., H.E. Freeman, S. Levine and N.A. Scotch. New York: Russell Sage Foundation.
1983   "Dying and the meanings of death: sociological inquiries." *Annual Review of Sociology* 9:191 216.

Riley, Matilda White
  1971 "Social gerontology and the age stratification of society."
         The Gerontologist 11:79-87.
  1976 "Age strata in social systems." In *Handbook of Aging and
         the Social Sciences,* edited by Robert Binstock and Ethel
         Shanas. New York: Van Nostrand Reinhold.
  1979 "Introduction: life course perspectives." In *Aging from
         Birth to Death: Interdisciplinary Perspectives,* edited by
         Matilda White Riley. Washington, D.C.: American
         Association for the Advancement of Science. (Published by
         Westview Press, Boulder, Colorado.)

Riley, Matilda White, Anne Foner, Beth Hess and Marcia Toby
  1969 "Socialization for the middle and later years." In *Handbook
         of Socialization Theory and Research,* edited by David
         Goslin. Chicago: Rand McNally.

Riley, Matilda White, Marylin Johnson and Anne Foner (Eds.)
  1972 *Aging and Society, Volume Three: A Sociology of Age
         Stratification.* New York: Russell Sage Foundation.

Ritchie, James E., and Jane Ritchie
  1973 "Proper Kiwi mate." In *New Zealand Society:
         Contemporary Perspectives,* edited by S. Webb and J.
         Collette. Sydney: John Wiley and Sons, Australasia, Pty.

Ritchie, Jane, and James Ritchie
  1979 *Growing Up in Polynesia.* Sydney: George Allen and Unwin.

Rivers, W.H.R.
  1926 "The primitive conception of death." In *Psychology and
         Ethnology.* London: Kegan Paul. (Reprinted in Slobodin,
         Richard. *W.H.R. Rivers,* New York: Columbia University
         Press, 1978.)

Rosaldo, Michelle
  1974 "Woman, culture and society: a theoretical overview." In
         Woman, Culture and Society, edited by Michelle Rosaldo
         and Louise Lamphere. Stanford: Stanford University Press.
  1980 "The use and abuse of anthropology: reflections on feminism
         and cross-cultural understanding." *Signs: Journal of
         Woman, Culture and Society* 5:389-418

Rose, Arnold
1965   "The subculture of the aging: a framework in social gerontology." In *Older People and Their Social World*, edited by Arnold Rose and Warren Peterson. Philadelphia: F.A. Davis.

Rosow, Irving
1974   *Socialization to Old Age*. Berkeley: University of California Press.
1976   "Status and role change through the life span." In *Handbook of Aging and the Social Sciences*, edited by Robert H. Binstock and Ethel Shanas. New York: Van Nostrand Reinhold.

Rubinstein, Robert L.
1981   "Siblings in Malo culture." In *Siblingship in Oceania*, edited by Mac Marshall. ASAO Monograph no. 8. Ann Arbor: University of Michigan Press.

Ryan, John
1969   *The Hot Land: Focus on New Guinea*. Melbourne: Macmillan.

Ryan, Mary P.
1979   "The power of women's networks. A case study of female moral reform in antebellum America." *Feminist Studies* 5:66-85.

Ryff, Carol D.
1982a   "Successful aging: a developmental approach." *The Gerontologist* 22:209-214.
1982b   "Self-perceived personality change in adulthood and aging." *Journal of Personality and Social Psychology* 42:108-115.
n.d.   "The subjective construction of self and society: an agenda for life-span research." In *Aging and Later Life: A Microsociology*, edited by V.W. Marshall and A. Harris. Norwood, New Jersey: Ablex. M.S. Forthcoming.

Ryff, Carol D., and Susanne G. Heincke
    1983   "Subjective organization of personality in adulthood and aging." *Journal of Personality and Social Psychology* 44:807-816.

Rynkiewich, Michael A.
    1972   "Land Tenure among Arno Marshallese." Ph.D. dissertation, University of Minnesota.

Sacks, Karen
    1974   Engels revisited: women, the organization of production, and private property. In *Woman, Culture, and Society,* edited by Michelle Rosaldo and Louise Lamphere. Stanford: Stanford University Press.

St. George, Ross
    1972   "Racial intolerance in New Zealand: a review of studies." In *Racial Issues In New Zealand,* edited by Graham Vaughan. Auckland: Akarana Press.

Salmond, Anne
    1975   *Hui.* Wellington: A.H. and A.W. Reed.

Sanday, Peggy
    1973   "Toward a theory of the status of women." *American Anthropologist* 75:1682-1700.
    1974   "Female status in the public domain." In *Woman, Culture, and Society,* edited by Michelle Rosaldo and Louise Lamphere. Stanford: Stanford University Press.

Scaletta, Naomi
    1984   "The question of morality: concepts of deviance among the Kabana of West New Britain and sorcery as a negative social sanction." Paper presented at conference. Deviant Behavior in Cross-Cultural Perspective, Waterloo, Ontario. June 4, 1984. MS.

Schutz, Alfred
    1967   "Common-sense and scientific interpretation of human action." In *Alfred Schutz: Collected Papers I,* edited by M. Natanson. Second Edition. The Hague: Martinus Nijhoff.

Schweitzer, Marjorie
  1983   "The elders: cultural dimensions of aging in two American
         Indian communities." In *Growing Old in Different Societies,*
         edited by Jay Sokolovsky. Belmont, CA: Wadsworth.

Shanas, E.P., D. Wedderburn, H. Friis, P. Miljoh and J. Stehouwer
  1968   *Old People in Three Industrial Societies.* New York:
         Atherton Press.

Sharma, K. L., and U. C. Jain
  1969   "Religiosity and fear of death in young and retired persons."
         Indian Journal of Gerontology 1:110-114.

Sherwin, Susan
  1981   "The concept of a person in the context of abortion."
         Bioethics Quarterly 3:21-34.

Simic, Andrei
  1978a "Winners and losers" aging Yugoslavs in a changing world."
         In *Life's Career – Aging: Cultural Variations on Growing
         Old,* edited by Andrei Simic and Barbara Myerhoff. Beverly
         Hills: Sage Publications.
  1978b "Introduction: aging and the aged in cultural perspective."
         In *Life's Career – Aging: Cultural Variations on Growing
         Old,"* edited by Andrei Simic and Barbara Myerhoff.
         Beverly Hills: Sage Publications.

Simic, A. and B. Myerhoff (eds.)
  1978   *Life's Career – Aging: Cultural Variations in Growing Old.*
         Beverly Hills, CA: Sage Publications.

Simmons, Leo W.
  1945   *The Role of the Aged in Primitive Society.* New Haven,
         Connecticut: Yale University Press. (Reprinted   Archon
         Books 1970.)
  1959   "Aging in modern society." In *Toward A Better
         Understanding of the Aging.* Seminar on Aging, September
         8-13, 1958, Aspen, Colorado. New York: Council on Social
         Work Education.
  1960   "Aging in pre-industrial societies." In *Handbook of Social
         Gerontology,* edited by C. Tibbitts. Chicago: University of
         Chicago Press.

Sinclair, Karen
    1984   "Maori women at midlife." In *In Her Prime: Anthropological Perspectives on Middle-Aged Women,* edited by Judith Brown and Virginia Kerns. South Hadley, MA: Bergin and Garvey.
    1985   "Tangi: Maori funeral rituals and the maintenance of identity." Paper presented at 14th Annual Meeting of the ASAO, Salem, Massachusetts, March, 1985.
    n.d.   "The journey to Waitangi: a Maori pilgrimage." In *Sacred Journeys,* edited by A. Morinis. Cambridge: Cambridge University Press. MS. in press.

Slobodin, Richard
    1978   *W.H.R. Rivers.* New York: Columbia University Press.

Smith, DeVerne Reed
    1981   "Palauan siblingship: A study in structural complementarity." In *Siblingship in Oceania,* edited by Mac Marshall. ASAO Monograph no. 8. Ann Arbor: University of Michigan Press.

Smith, Estellie
    1976   "Networks and migration resettlement: 'Cherchez la femme.'" *Anthropological Quarterly* 49:20-27.

Sokolovsky, J. (ed.)
    1983   *Growing Old in Different Societies: Cross-Cultural Perspectives.* Belmont, CA: Wadsworth Publishing Co.

Stack, Carol
    1974   *All Our Kin: Strategies for Survival in a Black Community.* New York: Harper and Row, Publishers.

Statistics Canada
    1981   Canadian Year Book 1980-1981. A Review of Economic, Social and Political Developments in Canada. Hull, Quebec: Ministry of Supply and Services Canada.

Stinson, Robert and Peggy Stinson
1981 "On the death of a baby." *Journal of Medical Ethics* 7:5-18.

Strathern, A.J.
1981 "Death as exchange: two Melanesian cases." In *Mortality and Immortality,* edited by S. Humphreys and H. King. London: Academic Press.

Strathern, Marilyn
1972 *Women in Between: Female Roles in a Male World: Mount Hagen, New Guinea.* London and New York: Seminar Press.

Strauss, Anselm
1969 *Mirrors and Masks.* Mill Valley, California: Sociology Press. Originally published 1959.

Swain, Cherry
1979 "Images of the good old days: some notes on a gerontological myth." *Mankind* 12:51-60.

Templer, D.I., and C. Ruff
1971 "Death anxiety scale means, standard deviations, and embedding." *Psychological Reports* 29:173-174.

Thomas, John
1980 "The Namonuito solution to the 'matrilineal puzzle'." *American Ethnologist* 7:172-177.

Thomas, Keith
1976 "Age and authority in early modern England." *Proceedings of the British Academy* 42:206-248

Tindale, Joseph A., and Victor W. Marshall
1980 "A generational conflict perspective for gerontology." In *Aging in Canada: Social Perspectives,* edited by V. W. Marshall. Toronto: Fitzhenry and Whiteside.

Tobin, Jack A.
    1967   "The resettlement of the Enewetak people: a study of a displaced community in the Marshall Islands." Ph.D. dissertation, University of California, Berkeley.

Turner, Jonathan H.
    1982   *The Structure of Sociological Theory.* Third Edition. Homewood, Illinois: The Dorsey Press.

Turner, Victor
    1963   *Lundu Medicine and the Treatment of Disease.* Rhodes-Livingstone Paper no. 15.
    1969   *The Ritual Process: Structure and Anti-Structure.* Chicago: Aldine Publishing Company.

Unruh, David R.
    1983   *Invisible Lives: Social Worlds of the Aged.* Beverly Hills, London and New Delhi: Sage.

Van Allen, Judith
    1976   "'Aba riots' or Igbo 'women's war'? Ideology, stratification, and the invisibility of women." In *Women In Africa: Studies in Social and Economic Change,* edited by N. Hafkin and E. Bay. Stanford: Stanford University Press.

Van Arsdale, Peter
    1981   "The elderly Asmat of New Guinea." In *Other Ways of Growing Old: Anthropological Perspectives,* edited by Pamela T. Amoss and Stevan Harrell. Stanford, CA: Stanford University Press.

Van Baal, J.
    1966   *Dema: Description and Analysis of Marind-Anim Culture (South New Guinea).* The Hague: Martinus Nijhoff.

Van Gennep, Arnold
    1960   *The Rites of Passage.* Translation of the 1909 text by Monika B. Vizedom and Gabrielle L. Caffee. Chicago: University of Chicago Press and London: Routledge and Kegan Paul.

Vatuk, Sylvia
  1980   "Withdrawal and disengagement as a cultural response to aging in India." In *Aging in Culture and Society,* edited by Christine Fry. New York: Praeger.

Veach, Robert M.
  1978   "The definition of death: ethical, philosophical, and policy confusion." In *Brain Death: Interrelated Medical and Social Issues,* edited by Julius Korein. Annals of the New York Academy of Science, Volume 315. New York.

Veith, Frank J.
  1978   "Brain death and organ transplant." In *Brain Death: Interrelated Medical and Social Issues,* edited by Julius Korein. Annals of the New York Academy of Science, Volume 315. New York.

Wagner, Roy
  1967   *The Curse of Souw.* Chicago: University of Chicago Press.
  1972   *Habu: The Innovation of Meaning in Daribi Religion.* Chicago: University of Chicago Press.
  1975   *The Invention of Culture.* Englewood Cliffs, N.J.: Prentice-Hall.
  1978   *Lethal Speech.* Ithaca: Cornell University Press.

Walker, Rangi
  1972   "Assimilation or cultural continuity? In *Racial Issues in New Zealand,* edited by Graham Vaughan. Auckland: Akarana Press.

Walsh, A.C.
  1973   *More and More Maoris.* Wellington, New Zealand: Whitcomb and Tombs.

Waring, Joan
  1976   "Social replenishment and social change." In *Age in Society,* edited by Anne Foner. Beverly Hills: Sage.

Watson, Wilbur H., and Robert J. Maxwell (eds.)
   1977   *Human Aging and Dying: A Study in Sociocultural Gerontology.* New York: St. Martin's Press.

Webster
   1967   *Webster's 7th New Collegiate Dictionary.* Springfield, Massachusetts: G. and C. Merriam Company.

Weiner, Annette
   1976   *Women of Value, Men of Renown: New Perspectives on Trobriand Exchange.* Austin: University of Texas Press.
   1979   "Trobriand kinship from another point of view: the reproductive power of women and men." *Man* 14:328-349.
   1980   "Reproduction: a replacement for reciprocity." *American Ethnologist* 7:71-85.

Weiss, K.M.
   1981   "Evolutionary Perspectives on Human Aging." In *Other Ways of Growing Old,* edited by Pamela Amoss and Stevan Harrell. Palo Alto, CA: Stanford University Press.

Werner, Richard
   1979   "Abortion: the ontological and moral status of the unborn." In *Today's Moral Problems,* second edition, edited by Richard A. Wasserstrom. New York: Macmillan.

Winch, P.
   1964   "Understanding a primitive society." *American Philosophical Quarterly* 1:307-324.

Winiata, Maharaia
   1967   *The Changing Role of the Leader in Maori Society.* Auckland: Blackwood and Janet Paul.

Wolf, Margery
   1972   *Women and the Family in Rural Taiwan.* Stanford: Stanford University Press.

Yanagisako, Sylvia
  1977 "Women-centered kin networks in urban bilateral kinship."
        American Ethnologist 4:207-226.

Young, Michael and Peter Willmott
  1957 *Family and Kinship in East London.* Harmondsworth:
        Penguin Books.

Zelenietz, M.
  1981 "One step too far: sorcery and social change in Kilenge,
        West New Britain." *Social Analysis.* No. 8:101-118.

CONTRIBUTORS

LARRY CARUCCI received his anthropology training at Colorado State University (A.B. 1971) and The University of Chicago (M.A. 1973, Ph.D 1980). He has worked with ethnic communities in Chicago, with Hawaiian and Micronesian historical materials, and has conducted thirty-seven months of field research on Enewetak, Ujelang, and Majuro Atolls in the Marshall Islands. Since graduating from Chicago in 1980, Dr. Carucci has been visiting assistant professor at the University of South Carolina, project director of a National Endowment for the Humanities grant on Marshallese social change, and Research associate at the University of Denver. He is currently associate professor at Montana State University.

DAVID COUNTS received a B.A. in anthropology from the University of Texas (1959) and the Ph.D. from Southern Illinois University (1968). Since 1968 he has taught at McMaster University, Hamilton, Ontario, where he is currently professor and chairman of the Department of Anthropology. With Dorothy Counts he has engaged in field research in the Kaliai Census Division, Province of West New Britain, Papua New Guinea in 1966-67, 1971, 1976-76, and 1981. He is author of *A Grammar of Kaliai Kove*, published by the University Press of Hawaii as Special Publication No. 6 in Oceanic Linguistics (1969).

DOROTHY AYERS COUNTS is professor of anthropology at the University of Waterloo, Waterloo, Ontario, where she has taught since 1968. She attended Southwest Texas University (B.S. 1956), the University of Kentucky (M.A. 1963), and Southern Illinois University (Ph.D. 1968). With David Counts she conducted field research in West New Britain Province, Papua New Guinea in 1966-67, 1971, 1975-76, and 1981. She is the author of *The Tales of Laupu: Ol Stori Bilong Laupu* published in 1982 by the Institute of Papua New Guinea Studies, and co-editor of *Middlemen and Brokers in Oceania,* ASAO Monograph No. 9.

MICHELE D. DOMINY is associate professor of anthropology and a faculty member of the Language and Thinking Institute at Bard College, Annandale-on-Hudson, New York where she has taught since 1981. She attended Bryn Mawr College (B.A. Honors 1975), and Cornell University (M.A. 1978 and

Ph.D. 1983). Her field research was conducted in London with New Zealand immigrants in 1977 and in Christchurch, New Zealand with Pakeha women in 1979 and 1980. She has published and spoken on the relationship of gender conceptions to political behavior and ideology.

JULIANA FLINN is currently associate professor of anthropology at the University of Arkansas at Little Rock. She completed her undergraduate work at Barnard College in 1972, received her Ph.D. in anthropology from Stanford University in 1982, and subsequently was a postdoctoral trainee at Columbia University's School of Public Health. Her work in Micronesia includes two years as a teacher in the Peace Corps on Namonuito Atoll from 1974 to 1976 and fieldwork on Pulap Atoll and among Pulap migrants during 1980 and 1981.

JOHN KIRKPATRICK studied anthropology at Princeton and the University of Chicago (Ph.D. 1980). He did fieldwork on Yap before engaging in research with Marquesans. He has taught at the University of Chicago, Brown University and Wesleyan University. He is currently involved in research on Hawaii. He is the author of *The Marquesan Notion of the Person* and editor, with Geoffrey M. White, of *Person, Self and Experience: Exploring Pacific Ethnopsychologies*.

MARIA LEPOWSKY is assistant professor at the University of Wisconsin, Madison. She received her A.B. (1971), M.A. (1973), Ph.D. (1981), and M.P.H. (1984) from the University of California, Berkeley. She was a Public Health Service Fellow in the School of Public Health, University of California, Berkeley, from 1981-1984. She conducted field research on Vanatinai (Sudest Island), Papua New Guinea for fourteen months in 1978-1979 and one month in 1981.

VICTOR W. MARSHALL, a sociologist, is professor of behavioural science in the Faculty of Medicine, University of Toronto and a National Health Scientist. Educated at The University of Calgary and Princeton University, he taught sociology at McMaster University before joining the University of Toronto in 1978. He has published extensively in medical sociology and social gerontology, including a book and numerous articles on social aspects of aging and dying. Currently, he is conducting research on work-stress and well-being in medical students, interns and residents, and on the family relations of older people. He received the Laidlaw Award in 1984 to provide continuing support for applied research in aging and health care. Two books will be published 1985 or 1986. One is an edited collection of advances in social psychological theory of aging, and the other, co-authored with Carolyn Rosenthal, is a textbook in sociological theory of aging. Dr. Marshall is Social Sciences Editor of the *Canadian Journal on Aging*.

WILLIAM McKELLIN is assistant professor of anthropology at the University of British Columbia. He attended Wheaton College (B.A. 1972) and the University of Toronto (M.A. 1973, Ph.D. 1980). He conducted fieldwork with the Managalase of Oro Province, Papua New Guinea in 1976-1977 and again in 1984.

DAN JORGENSEN (Ph.D. 1981 University of British Columbia) has spent a total of two and a half years in Telefolmin working on traditional religion and its relation to everyday life. His most recent research was on the impact of the OK Tedi mining project on rural villagers in Telefolmin in 1983-84. He is associate professor in the Department of Anthropology at the University of Western Ontario.

NAOMI M. SCALETTA received her B.A. in sociology and anthropology from Simon Fraser University (1979) and her Ph.D. from McMaster University, Hamilton, Ontario. Her hosts during sixteen months field research (1981, 1982-83), were the people of the Bariai Census Division, West New Britain Province, Papua New Guinea. She is currently assistant professor of anthropology, Okanagon College, Kelowna, B.C.

KAREN SINCLAIR is professor of anthropology and coordinator of women's studies at Eastern Michigan University. She received her Ph.D. from Brown University. She has published articles on Maori religion and Maori women and is a contributor to *In Her Prime: A New View of Middle-Aged Women*, edited by Judith Brown and Virginia Kerns.

INDEX